KV-197-825

Contemporary Education Policy

Edited by John Ahier and Michael Flude

CROOM HELM London & Canberra

© 1983 John Ahier and Michael Flude
Croom Helm Ltd, Provident House, Burrell Row
Beckenham, Kent BR3 1AT

British Library Cataloguing in Publication Data

Contemporary education policy.
  1. Education and State — Great Britain
  I. Ahier, John   II. Flude, Michael
  379.41   LA 632
  I SBN 0-7099-0512-2 Pbk

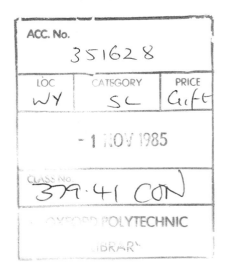

ACC. No.		
	351628	
LOC	CATEGORY	PRICE
WY	SC	Gift

- 1 NOV 1985

CLASS No.
379.41 CON

OXFORD POLYTECHNIC
LIBRARY

Printed and bound in Great Britain by
Biddles Ltd, Guildford and King's Lynn

CONTENTS

EDITORS' INTRODUCTION

It has been eight years since we published
Educability, Schools and Ideology. At that time
the sociology of education was engaged in discussions about the merits and demerits of social
phenomenology, symbolic interactionism and ethno-
methodology. Whilst those concerns have not completely disappeared the orientation of the sociology
of education has shifted to a more macro-level
political and economic dimension. This has not
necessarily been the result of any resolution of
those earlier conflicts but more an effect of
certain changes in the conditions within which
teachers and lecturers now interact with their
pupils and students. The more recent developments
have included, for example, neo-Marxism and its
internal and external criticisms, the histories of
state schooling, and the rapid growth of research
and debate on questions of gender and ethnicity.
In a certain sense this new volume represents
an attempt to move both forwards and backwards:
forwards to a more policy-oriented and politically
aware sociology of education, and backwards to the
brief period where a sociological approach to
education informed educational priorities.
We believe that the papers in this book raise
important problems not only for the discipline of
sociology of education itself but also for the
understanding of education in economic and political
terms. The first two papers consider theoretical
approaches to educational policy and their political
implications. Subsequent papers by A.D. Edwards,
Colin Hunter, Gwen Wallace, Henry Miller and Mark
Ginsburg examine changes in the context of the cuts
in educational expenditure, dramatically high levels
of unemployment and demographic changes. The

effects of the political, economic and social contexts of schooling are further explored in a comparative way by Bill Williamson's study of youth
programmes in the Federal Republic of Germany and
Britain. Direct central governmental intervention
in the British education system is an implicit issue
in a number of papers, including Geoff Whitty's
analysis of new examination proposals. At a time
when resources for education are limited then the
control of schools and their curricula and the participation of interest groups in the educational
policy-making process are of crucial importance.
The papers by Professor Halsey and John Beck refer
to some pertinent problems in these fields.

We think that it is a progressive step also to
discuss the positions of political parties on these
matters rather than treating educational change as
simply a reflection of the social state of Britain
or of the stage of capitalist development which
this society has reached. The last two papers in
the book attempt to locate the educational policies
of the Conservative and Social Democratic Parties
in relation to their wider political programmes.

1. HISTORY AND SOCIOLOGY OF EDUCATIONAL POLICY

John Ahier

Ever since sociology of education, as a taught subject, became accepted as a sub-discipline in the
study of education within colleges and departments
of education its relation to questions of social and
educational policy have become more distant. Initially it may have been thought that it was precocious
for young, intending teachers to be interested in
school policy. An interest in educational policy in
general must have seemed quite beyond their legitimate concern. An introduction to the functions of
the family and school and some social explanations
of why working class children fail was often regarded as quite sufficient for the development of socially sensitive teachers. Certainly a group of
sociologists had some influence on government policy
during the fifties and sixties, but an explicit concern for educational or social policy rarely became
part of the taught discipline. Even the so-called
'new sociology of education', with its more critical
stance, provided little basis for the consideration
of educational and social policy in institutions of
teacher education. Some of its criticisms of
Positivism led to difficulties in taking quantitive
expressions of social conditions seriously, and to
the extent that much previous work on educational
and social policy relied on such data then the relations with policy matters were strained. Alternative, favoured methodologies could have been used to
study decision-making in the field of policy, but
this has only recently been developed (Batley &
Edwards, 1978). Hitherto effort has been concentrated on schools and classrooms. Further, many
aspects of critical and radical sociology, which
seemed to find a resting place in this sociology of
education, were set against the possibility of a

generative relationship between policy and sociology on the grounds that such a union would necessarily involve sociologists in immoral programmes and irrational calculations on behalf of either repressive states or self-seeking professions.

In these harder times it is all too easy to look back and moralistically condemn such self-indulgence and failure to take politics and policies seriously and, on such a basis, perhaps, declare yet another 'new direction'. This is certainly not the intention here. Indeed, in support for a re-alignment of the socio-historical study of education in the direction of policy it is important to avoid another incommensurability (Kuhn, 1968), but rather to reinterpret and use the findings on such things as educability, the distribution of facilities, home-school relations and historical work on state policy. Richard Johnson has written critically about what he called 'a kind of intellectual lumber-jacking' on the grounds that such a mode is rarely accumulative (1979, p.69). The point is rather that the practices associated with policy formulation can use and transform data which may have been presented by those different paradigms or problematics. Instead of building any new sociologistic models of socio-educational systems, the argument here is that the focus be changed onto social and educational policy. As policy analysis and development must concern the possible and probable, the failure to use such data is unrealistic. For example, even if we have misgivings about much of what passes for political sociology we should not disregard findings on such matters as the location and forms of support for Labour and Conservative Parties. (Butler and Stokes, 1974; Eatwell, 1979).

Why should the orientation of such sub-disciplines as the sociology of education towards policy be considered important? At least in part it is because deciding on policy corresponds, in many respects, with a necessary form of democratic decision-making at the levels of institutions, enterprises or states under most circumstances, except, perhaps, in the unlikely event of absolute equality and plenty. Within any given form of representation, the spheres of priority, control and the means of articulating production and distribution are central, as are the means of calculation within these spheres. Any kind of democratic decision-making where there is not an identity of needs, interests and resources must proceed on this terrain in the sense that the formation and presentation of policies is a central part of winning consent. There is no easy escape from these aspects of policy.

Because so much Marxist sociology and history continues to comprehend the social totality as an expressive unity (Althusser, 1969) the winning of consent in this tradition is more often presented as the winning support for socialism or egalitarian values rather than for a set of policies in which socialist and egalitarian advances can be made. Such an error does not correspond to the commonly held beliefs in many parts of the Left that the power of the Civil Service, especially the Treasury, on incoming Labour administrations is too great, and that the working class has developed no love for capitalism or its enterprises, but only an instrumental attachment. It is more likely that a coherent body of policies, which included priorities and methods of funding, explicitly constructed by and submitted to Party and then to voters, would both help protect any party in government and appeal to a calculating electorate.

Some recent work on education and on social policy does acknowledge politics but is not fully compatible with policy discourse, because there are significant differences between serious consideration of policy and either the declaration of commitments or just leaving space within one's theory for political action. If there have been few attempts to reassert the relation between sociology and educational policy there has not been a lack of overt declarations of political and ideological commitment in recent texts on the socio-historical development of schooling. In a sociological account of comprehensive schooling the author declares himself a Marxist within the second paragraph! (Bellaby, 1977, p.9). Similarly the authors of the text which will be examined in the second half of this paper declare that, 'As individuals we are also involved in political struggles, and we offer here an account which is informed by a socialist perspective. We therefore hope that our work will contribute to the furtherance of socialist and feminist struggles, not only in education but also more widely.' (Baron, Finn, Grant, Green, Johnson, 1981, p.8). Rachel Sharp, after similar explicit statements of commitment, proceeds to mount a number of criticisms of the 'old' and the 'new' sociologies of education for their failure to grasp the functions of ideology in the maintenance of class dominance (Sharp, 1980).

5

In fact, the much maligned 'new' sociology of education was never short of commitment, (Young, 1977) but such declarations, whilst they may resolve the consciences of sociologists and historians who dismiss the possibility of value freedom and neutrality, cannot enter the forms in which public policy debate can develop. Quite apart from the irrational tendencies implicit in any inflation in the use of concepts of commitment (Trigg, 1973) it is difficult to see how such declarations can be fed into what is necessarily a public debate about what ought to be done, in particular circumstances, and how. Taking the case of Rachel Sharp's commitments to Marxism as an example, an examination of the last chapter of her book will show that the generality of such a commitment begets an equally unspecific conception of political action and practice. Whether she is writing about the spheres of schools or 'a broader political arena' (p.162) her conclusions reveal that what acts is individuals and what struggles is classes. The only form these actions or struggles can take is counter-hegemonic. For the individual educator this amounts to making the pupils aware of class domination via a programme of limited school democracy, in spite of the acknowledged dangers of incorporation. For the politicised beyond the school even less possibilities exist, for trade unions and political parties have already been incorporated and fail to foster the vital counter-hegemonic vision (p.168). The only hope here is that new organisational forms will emerge. A central problem with such uses of Gramsci's concept of counter-hegemony is that it offers a message without a medium, a faith without a church. The language of commitment and the ways it is related to action in general takes the shape of traditional individual moral persuasion to lead the good political and ideological life, but with no acknowledgement of the forms in which it could be sustained.

It may be thought that the substitution of commitment and action by the more down to earth language of socialist strategy and tactics might make it more possible to re-orientate social and historical studies to policy. The concept of strategy has been used quite widely in recent Marxist and radical literature on education and welfare (Bowles and Gintis 1976, pp.282-288; Corrigan and Leonard 1978, pp.141-157). The recently launched journal, Critical Social Policy, for example, is devoted to 'develop and debate about political strategies for welfare' and an article in the first

edition criticises the failure of Marxists to present any alternative socialist social policy (Deacon,
1981). In that article Bob Deacon's list of questions for socialist policy correctly includes those
of priority, resources, and agency, and it may be
thought an advance on such texts as George and
Wilding's Ideology and Social Welfare (George and
Wilding, 1976), and Corrigan and Leonard's Social
Work Practice Under Capitalism (Corrigan and Leonard,
1978), but it is clear that the questions are for a
future socialist society. He admits that his article, 'does not concern itself, except in passing,
with the problems of the transition stage, enormous
though these are' (p.47). By transposing policy
questions to a future vision of a socialist society,
however, the basic problems facing socialist policy
are resolved in a utopia. Questions of resources
and needs, for example, and the constitution of
representation and decision-making which surrounds
them just collapse into a belief that, because of
the nature of socialism, every individual in such a
society expresses the needs of all the others (p.51).
What with the state having withered away, everyone's
essential social nature realised, and the realm of
plenty established, then it is difficult to imagine
any issues of policy ever having to arise. In this
approach it is Fabians who have policies and socialists who have dreams.

If policy can only be contemplated in a future
in which there is hardly a need for it, then present
political considerations are expressed in terms of
'strategy' and 'tactics'. Unless insurrection is
being considered then the exclusive consideration of
current political practice under such military analogies is unlikely to be productive because of the
inbuilt assumptions. First it is assumed that there
is a body or agency (the working class, the Left, or
even the people) whose actions can be planned and
led; second that there is a unitary opposition (the
state or capital) whose actions are of a similar
kind but essentially in opposition; third, that
there is a future point in which the hostile forces
will be brought into contact. Much has already been
written on the problems in seeing classes or the
Labour Movement as unified agencies (Hindness, 1977;
1980) and on the assumed unity of the state and
social policy (Potter, 1981; Hirst, 1980). Military
analogies may rally the faithful in certain contexts,
but at present seem to inhibit the public development of national and international policy and instead sustain localised, conspiratorial politics

within union branches and constituency parties. It is not that strategic considerations are unnecessary in the development and presentation of policy but rather that they should not be a substitute.

CULTURAL STUDIES AND A HISTORY OF LABOUR'S EDUCATIONAL POLICY

There are some signs that questions of educational policy are now coming to be treated more seriously by those writing in the area of what has hitherto been called the sociology of education. Jack Demaine, although keeping his attention on the standard material in the field has indicated that a reorientation to policy is required (Demaine, 1981). The new Open University courst 'Society, Education and the State' could potentially open up to its students a consideration of policy matters, albeit within a formalistic presentation of theories of the state and various radical critiques of welfare and state provision. Perhaps most interesting is some recent work from the University of Birmingham Centre for Contemporary Cultural Studies which I shall consider in more detail now, concentrating on the recent study entitled Unpopular Education (Baron et al., 1981), although reference will also be made to other work by those associated with the Centre.

In Unpopular Education we are given an extended historical treatment of Labour Party policies on schooling from the inter-war years. The approach is similar to that pursued in an earlier paper by some of the same authors (Finn, Grant and Johnson, 1978). It is to make explicit, by quotation and critique, 'the fundamental assumptions underlying those policies' (Johnson, 1979). This methodology proceeds by a careful consideration of some statements of educational and social policy and philosophy which are considered illustrative of the repertoire of social democratic ideas during the period, and of their critics. There is a diversity of historical sources for these statements, varying from a pamphlet written by G.C.T. Giles, President of the National Union of Teachers, in 1946, which is taken as an expression of 'post-war radical populism' (p.66) to statements by editors of the Black Papers, which are seen as heralding a new populism of the Right (p.200-205).

The narrative is one of crises and settlements at the levels of politics and ideology, underpinned by the unfolding of British capitalism and its crises. In much of the text the relations between these levels is an implicit one. Political ideas

and political practices had certain economic conditions of existence, and when the latter changed, or
were perceived to have changed, then the repertoire
breaks up. In the centre of the book, however,
there is a clear expression of the belief that the
political reformism of the type represented by the
Labour Party hitherto, 'depends on the ability to
grant reforms to the working class without endanger-
ing capital's reproduction' (p.174). The somewhat
mechanical relation implied here between the working
class and economy leads the authors to believe reforms could not be extended to that ever-demanding
class because of the crisis in profitability (and
hence lack of funds for the social wage) and that
the working class could come to feel the past state
provision as unpopular and inefficient imposition.
Such reactions come to be played upon by populist
Conservatism, and also orchestrated by James
Callaghan and the Labour Government in the Great
Debate. The Arbitration and Conciliation Service,
National Enterprise Board and the Manpower Services
Commission are all seen as attempts to reach a new,
suspect harmonisation of interests. At the end of
the book the political message is made clear. There
is a demand for 'a fundamental remaking of the main
patterns of post-war social-democratic politics';
'a popular socialist strategy will have to be defined' (p.243). There is support for a Labour Party
which is a more localised agitational agency, as
opposed to a centralised Party trying to harmonise
diverse, conflicting interests by the pursuit of
central state policies of distribution. The aim is
for a popularly supported education in general, not
a set of centrally provided, handed down policies.
The role of researchers and intellectuals, unlike
that of the Fabian experts of the past, must be to
take seriously forms of popular knowledge and local
struggle so that new links can be made between Party
and people. The remainder of this paper is devoted
to analysing why and how this delineation of Labour,
socialist political action and theory is inadequate
in contemporary conditions.

The first question which arises is how can such
'sociological' histories be given a political significance? Richard Johnson, a member of the Centre's
Education Group put this problem in terms of how one
could write 'with a historical form and a political
purpose' (Johnson, 1979). At least two possibilities
emerge in the work of the Centre. One way is by the
choice of subject matter; to write histories of soc-

ialist traditions and origins, and of the trials and tribulations of the working class. The effect of this is to put present day socialists into connection with their origins, thus developing depth of commitment and identity, not unlike the functions of genetic myths in non-industrial societies (Malinowski, 1974). In particular such work can point to the possibilities of a popular, immanent education by providing a history of an earlier, non-state working class schooling. Thus Richard Johnson has written on the radical tradition of the Nineteenth Century (Johnson, 1981a) and reference is made in Unpopular Education to 'an inherited popular radical tradition' (p.44).

The second possibility is to use history in a certain way to break the determinist mould of some Marxist theory, whilst at the same time taking seriously some of the concepts and insights generated within that theory. Those associated with the Centre have developed a midway stand on these matters between the theoreticians and the 'experiential' position of E.P. Thompson (Johnson, 1981b and Johnson, McLennan and Schwarz, 1978). In Unpopular Education the point is clearly made that, in comparison with a historical, functionalist Marxism the use of historical material provides a sense of movement and possibility (p.246-247).

Together, the hoped-for effect is to reaffirm the possibilities of life, action and struggle in the working class and other oppressed social groups. But as far as socialist politics is concerned, at least, such life is problematic in two ways. It has very tentative connections with important forms of political practice in the present conjuncture, and it helps construct and maintain in theory political agencies which do not really exist in any unified form in the Left and the working class. In particular it is difficult to see how it can inform what is, for quite good reasons, a centralised Party, about national policy, because the constraints from which an empirical and theoretical escape has been made by Richard Johnson and others of the Centre are not the most noticeable constraints on the policies of any Labour government in Britain.

These sociologists and historians, critical in the ways they are of some aspects of structuralist theory and economic determinism, are not so equipped to deal with the forms of national and international constraints within which any government has to work, whether committed to the privatisation or socialisation of economic relations. If political

space is created by history then the relationship
offered in Unpopular Education between the concept-
ualising of the economy on the one hand, and the
agencies of struggle on the other, demands some
scrutiny.
     For a judgemental history of the Labour Party's
educational policies there is a sad lack of serious
consideration of certain economic conditions under
which such policy developed. When the book deals
with the crisis in policies associated with the so-
called social democratic educational settlement,
based on investment in human capital and attendant
technological advance, its characterisation of the
economic background is in terms of standard economic
indicators. If its general Marxist diagnosis is of
a crisis in capital accumulation this is taken as
being exemplified by unemployment rates, investment
rates, profits, growth rates, shares of the world
market, price levels and balance of payments. It is
considered that these all show, 'the steady, and
later severe, decline in British capitalism over the
period' (p.170). In fact some of these indicators
could be taken as indicators of the relative position of any national economy, even one with a large
non-capitalist sector. So, to the extent that they
tell us about the economic conditions for the pursuit of social and educational policy, then they
would apply regardless of the particular 'repertoire'
of ideas held by those in government. Of course
other political and economic ideas and practices may
help produce and protect institutions which change
the relations between production and distribution,
but the relative economic position of the United
Kingdom would remain a condition of any 'social'
policy-making. Certainly Crosland, taken in Unpopular Education as one of the key contributors to
mistaken social democratic thinking, took some time
to appreciate such matters. Writing in 1956 he considered that, 'the level of material welfare will
soon be such that marginal changes in the allocation
of resources will make little difference to anyone's
contentment' (Crosland, 1964, p.357). By the middle
1960's, however, he, at least, could see the problems, and in the Gaitskill Memorial Lecture advocated a policy very much like the Alternative
Economic Strategy (Crosland, 1965 and 1974). Such a
rediscovery of scarcity, like the rediscovery of
poverty, does not necessarily produce progressive
policy. A recent book which makes much of the inevitability of scarcity and is sub-titled 'Crosland's

11

Legacy' is evidence of that (Lipsey and Leonard, 1981). But at least it warns us that prioritisation is an unavoidable part of what has been argued to be the central political practice of policy construction.

It is not that the economic is absent in the text under consideration, or, indeed, in other work associated with the Centre, but that the understanding of it is restricted by virtue of the function it performs for Marxist sociology. Richard Johnson, not wishing to write a history concerned exclusively with the quality of human relationships, argues for a consideration of an economic structure, but only in terms of its social, class-forming effects (Johnson, 1979, p.223). In the case of the arguments in Unpopular Education against social democratic views of class in terms of degree (p.73) and against its educational rhetoric about skills and technology, then the functions which economic concepts have to perform are to reaffirm class categories and to undermine the view of a capitalist economy requiring more skills of the workforce. Braverman's thesis on labour is referred to (Braverman, 1974), not only to dismiss the latter social democratic belief, but also to give life to the working class and its struggle, because the basis of Braverman's position is that labour, by its very nature, resists insertion into de-skilling capitalist production. The anthropological and other assumptions in this are considerable, and have been dealt with elsewhere (Cutler, 1978). At issue is the form of the economic references within this text; they acknowledge the economy, but tend to reduce it to the labour process. This may guarantee a particular existence for the working class and its resistance, but it leads to a problematic view of past and future politics and policies in certain respects.

Such a view of economy and class encourages a judgement of the Labour Party as a failure in representing its class, and an interpretation of all recent actions as incorporative, in which the ideas and philosophy of professionals have predominated. Thus the Party failed to articulate the resistance which the class expresses in the indirect and convoluted forms studied by the Centre, as in the resistance of 'the lads' in Paul Willis's Learning to Labour (Willis, 1977). Politics is thereby understood as the expression of economic interests, and suggestions for future policy are built on the supposition that there is a neglected class waiting to support socialism, because its members have an affinity with it by virtue of their experience in labour. The clearest expression of the implications of a reassertion of the reality of classes and its effects on policy considerations are to be found in a passage in an earlier text from the Centre on social democracy and education (Finn, Grant and Johnson, 1978). Criticising Crosland's view of the residual nature of class the authors argue as follows:

> ......what if class in capitalist society is neither residual, not passive, nor removable but an ever present source of transformations? What if they are systematically and daily reproduced as part of the organic workings of the society along with their concomitant inequalities? What, in short, if class is rooted in social relations of production, a category which is quite invisible in social democratic ideology? From the standpoint of such a conception of the social formation the futility of social policy can be fully grasped. It can deal with no more than occasional symptoms which must constantly re-appear and must serve to hide what lies beneath them (p.189).

The difficulty is not that an already unified working class is postulated instead. There is no suggestion of this. The problem is that the economy has to be understood, in its very essence and entirety, as a class producing one. This ensures that any attempts to deal with some aspects of that economy, via policies of control of prices and incomes for example, or even the Alternative Economic Strategy, can only be seen as attempts to raise the rate of exploitation, because the crisis in the economy is _itself_ seen as arising only from internal social and political struggle. Unpopular Education suggests that the economic problems of the United Kingdom must be seen as 'a sustained crisis of capital accumulation arising from social and political relations of struggle' (p.170).

In a history which, as I have suggested, seeks to identify with one side of these struggles, then the political options and calculations for any socialist party informed by such ideas is unnecessarily limited by its reactions to an over optimistic social democracy. Such ideas hardly permit a socialist party to seek national government in the

present circumstances because any national government must attempt to tackle the variety of economic
problems, and this would be seen as a socialist
party working against its roots. Agreement on a coordinated set of social and economic policies, necessary to secure the conditions for a stable, effective and hopefully more democratic health and education service, for example, would seem impossible.

What is offered to the Labour Party, almost in
exchange for what has been seen here as the central
aspects of political action and calculation, is an
essentially educative and localised role. In
Unpopular Education, for example, it is claimed that,
'if the party is to perform an educative role, the
emphasis must move away from the concern with state
and parliamentary politics towards the grass roots
work of branches, away from the shifting around of
already constituted blocks of influence (the card
vote) towards a local agitational politics which
discovers as it acts' (p.261). There can be no
objection to a more educative party. The Labour
Party's record in this respect since 1945 has been a
poor one, especially at local level. Here the informed consideration of policy has been sadly lacking, no doubt partly because of the distance of the
Parliamentary Labour Party from the grass roots.
Recent changes could alter this. But the very idea
of 'agitational politics which discovers as it acts'
- a kind of progressive infant teacher's view of
politics in terms of learning by doing - is hope-
lessly anti-intellectual and degenerative. It is
the localising of both politics and education which
is problematic here, especially in the conditional
way it is offered in the quote above. We can either
be educative or involved with the state.

THE LOCALISING OF POLITICS AND EDUCATION

Finally it is necessary to bring together again
political and educational concerns to understand
what is at stake in both spheres. The tendency, in
Unpopular Education and elsewhere, to resolve certain 'dualities' and 'contradictions' in social
democratic thought by this localising of politics
and education has numerous problems. It over-
simplifies issues of representation and control,
undermines the necessity of rational co-ordination
of national educational provision and it could
restrict educational and political possibilities.
But it would be unfair to over-simplify the position
represented in this text. There is a genuine inter-

nal debate, especially in Part One. In distinguishing between statist and substitutional strategies
the authors acknowledge that statist forms need not
necessarily be reformist or corporate. On the other
hand they do seem to agree that strategies using the
state have been 'exceedingly contradictory from the
viewpoint of a socialist conception of popular
interests' (p.36). They do not deny the possibility
of popular forms of statist agitation (p.39), but
reject the loss of popular concern with the content
and control of education and its containment in
labourism. Their complaint is that the Labour Party
has been 'the educational provider _for_ popular
groups and classes, not an education agency of and
within them' (p.46). In their conclusion, however,
the acknowledgement of the problems of popular spon-
taneity, for example, has become more gestural (p.
256) and the preferred strategies are clearly localised.

It is in the use of the concept of popular that
the difficulties are to be found. In political and
educational discourse there are at least three uses
which must be distinguished.
1. First there is the use which refers to empiri-
    cally detectable likings and preferences held
    by a large number of people, but not necessar-
    ily a majority. In this sense state education
    and the National Health Service, although they
    may be bureaucratic, centralised and profess-
    ionalist, may still be regarded as popular.
    There is evidence that many people want to see
    them preserved and given further support even
    in their present form. (Mayo, 1982, p.15)
2. Second there is the use which refers to the
    openness of institutions. Popular, here, would
    mean open to all people, and without in-built
    exclusions of, or disadvantages for any parti-
    cular groups. Currently programmes of 'open
    access' and community-oriented schooling
    attempt to pursue this end. But, again, it
    should be noted that the hitherto excluded or
    disadvantaged groups do not necessarily give
    their 'popular' support to such programmes.
    In the case of community-oriented education,
    for example, some minority groups may quite
    reasonably prefer a professionally led and
    centrally state-administered system because of
    its comparative freedom from localised politi-
    cal insecurity, and because of the more
    general legitimacy of its curriculum. Even
    West Indian Saturday schools, whilst existing

outside formal state provision, emphasise standards within the traditional curriculum (Stone, 1981).

3. The third use of the concept is that which usually refers to political entities (parties, alliances, etc.) where it is claimed that they are 'of the people'. Popular fronts, for example, may claim to be the expression of the essential unity, interests and consciousness of the people against their exploiters and oppressers.

In Unpopular Education all these uses of popular and unpopular are to be found in uneasy and inexplicit relations. The only attempt to establish the unpopularity of schooling in the first, empirical sense is by reference to such research as Learning to Labour by Paul Willis (Willis, 1977). Here it is thought that the anti-school culture of many working class boys exemplifies the overall ambivalence of the working class to schooling (p. 157). Popular knowledge is said to have a more realistic view of education than the economists and sociologists.

The second use of 'popular' is more developed in the book, and essentially sociological arguments are made against any beliefs in the homogeneity of 'the public' (p.256). Elsewhere Richard Johnson has criticised 'simple populism' because it fails to analyse the constituents of the popular, the different positions and needs of sections of the people (Johnson, 1981b). Education may be seen as unpopular in this sense because it is offered to the people by politicians, professionals and the central state, in an undifferentiated alien form, which continues to disadvantage large groupings of people; women, blacks, the working class.

But 'the people' are put together again within the text in its use of the third meaning. It is clear, in its reference to 'popular groups and classes' (p.46) and the duality of popular interests versus capital (p.263), that the Labour Party is being attacked for not being a party of the people, but of the 'professional managerial classes', who do not qualify for membership. What is problematic about this combination of uses is its political and educational naivety. Taking the political first, Labour politicians can hardly be criticised for using 'populist' language if they wish to seek general support for parliamentary election. Indeed it could be argued that it is only by seeking broad popular support in the first, empirical sense of the

word, and maintaining it within the present parliamentary system, that laws can be passed which can
advance the second meaning of popular. What sociological discourse may be good at is analysing the
significant divisions in life chances, ideologies,
interests, and so on within such apparent unities as
'the public' or even 'the working class'. Political
discourse and calculation must take account of these,
but has also, in its polemical expression, to rec-
ruit and build support. The problem for the Labour
Party in the present form of representation is
whether it can gain significant electoral support by
courting the separately identified and disadvantaged
groups or whether it has to continue to use the
broadest conceptions of 'the people'. The Education
Group of the Centre for Contemporary Cultural
Studies would seem to favour the first. The problem
with that position is that it so easily lends itself
to essentialist views of the working class and almost Lukacsian beliefs about the universal 'true'
consciousness of the exploited. The 'realism' and
'partial penetrations' of the working class boys in
Willis's study (Willis, 1977) and the belief that
'popular knowledge' (p.157) has a realistic view of
education goes some way in this suspect direction.
Along with this the tendency in Unpopular Education
to criticise statism and to advocate local participatory forms encourages an unnecessary contradiction
between national social planning and local democratic control (Rose, 1980, pp.130-131). There are
good arguments for more participatory and localised
forms of education, political practice and research,
but such decentralization can only proceed within
centrally established priorities and by legally
supported and defined agencies. In the case of educational administration not only must the problems
of co-ordination between the different age levels be
dealt with, but the popular, local and direct control of primary and secondary levels of education
does nothing for the accountability and control of
the higher bodies. In education, as in other spheres of social provision, there can be no substitute
for the legal constitution of agencies which is both
enabling and limiting. There must exist legal
limits on both the central state and the local popular organisations, to protect minorities and oppose
maladministration (Hirst, 1980). It could be argued
that whilst post-war social democratic educational
administration was certainly lacking in real local,
community participation, its outcomes were in some
respects, _too_ determined at the Local Education

Authority level. This was especially noticeable over comprehensivisation, where the definitions of catchment areas could be seen as having been left too much in the hands of the local politicians, administrators and pressure groups (Marsden, 1971). Some social educational aims of comprehensivisation were thus ignored in the more local administration of schooling.

This questioning of localism is not intended to be part of a desire to perpetuate the liberal, social democratic state forms, which have necessarily co-existed with a predominantly privatised, home-centred, consumed-oriented life over the last forty years (Hadley and Hatch, 1981, p.106). The ideological task of prising large numbers of the working class and middle class out of this combination is considerable. Among other things it must deal with popular, idealised, conceptions of community and locality which are still very much based on English ruralist images. It must also support feminist critiques of domesticity. On the other hand it should not try to perpetuate or re-create combinations of urban proletarian self-help and isolated agitation from an earlier period of socialist struggle. The scale of the problems, and the accumulated mental and material capital, are now too great.

To return to the beginning of this paper one could argue that at least part of this ideological task must be pursued within the institutions of professional education, including those concerned with teacher education. During the recent period of radical, Marxist sociology, however, this has been difficult because of an implicit and explicit anti-professionalism. Certainly some of this criticism has been justified. What has not been appreciated, however, is that whilst some aspects of the knowledge which the lower professions claim to possess is mere bureaucratic opinion and attitude, other aspects are vital for the success of the services in which they work. Some of this knowledge could be re-distributed but some, when combined within skills, probably could not. If this is accepted, then what is necessary is the progressive enrolment of this expertise, because it includes an ability to discover human needs which may not be known to the public at large. This means a re-thinking of the position of these professions, not so much in terms of their ultimate class position (Ginsburg, Meyenn and Miller, 1980), from which little can follow, but in terms of their constitutional location. It is the system of representation

18

which has located them as servants of the representative assembly. They currently act within institutions, whose forms are legally sanctioned by that
assembly, and where they make available a given set
of services to mostly unrepresented clients. It is
this which needs consideration. There is nothing
necessarily self-seeking about professions or necessarily repressive about agents of the state.

That having been said, the present economic and
political education of these state employed professionals remains greatly underdeveloped. If more
democratic and participatory forms of state provision of education, health and welfare are envisaged
in the future, then there must be changes in the
economic and political innocence of workers in these
fields. Critiques of the inhumanity of capitalist
industry, a reverence for popular knowledge and an
unnerving anti-professionalism are no substitutes
for a sophisticated education in economic and social
policies.

BIBLIOGRAPHY

Althusser, L. (1969) For Marx, Penguin, Harmonds-
    worth, pp. 200-218.
Baron, S., Finn, D., Grant, N., Green, M., Johnson,
    R. (1981) Unpopular Education, Hutchinson,
    London.
Batley, R. & Edwards, J. (1978) Politics of
    Positive Discrimination, Tavistock, London.
Bellaby, P. (1977) The Sociology of Comprehensive
    Schooling, Methuen, London.
Bowles, S. & Gintis, H. (1976) Schooling in Capital-
    ist America, Routledge & Kegan Paul, London.
Braverman, H. (1974) Labov and Monopoly Capital,
    Monthly Review Press, New York.
Butler, D. & Stokes, D. (1974) Political Change in
    Britain, Macmillan, London.
Corrigan, P. & Leonard, P. (1978) Social Work
    Practice Under Capitalism, Macmillan, London.
Crosland, C.A.R. (1964) The Future of Socialism,
    Jonathan Cape, London.
Crosland, C.A.R. (1965) The British Economy in 1965,
    University of Nottingham.
Crosland, C.A.R. (1974) Socialism Now and Other
    Essays, Jonathan Cape, London.
Cutler, A. (1978) 'The Romance of Labour', Economy
    and Society 7, pp. 74-95.

Deacon, B. (1981) 'Social Administration, Social Policy and Socialism', Critical Social Policy, 1, pp.43-46.

Demaine, J. (1981) Contemporary Theories in the Sociology of Education, Macmillan, London.

Eatwell, R. (1979) The 1945-1951 Labour Governments, Batsford, London.

Finn, D., Grant, N. & Johnson, R. (1978) 'Social Democracy, Education and the Crisis' in The Centre for Contemporary Cultural Studies, On Ideology, Hutchinson, London.

Ginsbury, M., Meyenn, R. & Miller, H. (1980) 'Teachers, Professionalism and Trades Unionism, an Ideological Analysis in P. Woods (ed.) Teachers' Strategies: Explorations in the Sociology of the School, Croom Helm, London.

George, V. & Wilding, P. (1976) Ideology and Social Welfare, Routledge & Kegan Paul, London.

Hadley, R. & Hatch, S. (1981) Social Welfare and the Failure of the State, George Allen & Unwin, London.

Hindness, B. (1977) 'The Concept of Class in Marxist Theory and Marxist Politics' in J. Bloomfield (ed.) Class, Hegemony and Party, Lawrence & Wishart, London, pp.95-107.

Hindness, B. (1980) 'A "Left" Labour Government?' in Politics and Power 2, pp.37-61.

Hirst, P. (1980) 'Law, Socialism and Rights' in P. Carlen & M. Collison (eds.) Radical Issues in Criminology, Martin Robertson, Oxford, pp. 58-105.

Johnson, R. (1979) 'Culture and the Historians' in J. Clarke, C. Critcher and R. Johnson (eds.) Working Class Culture, Hutchinson, London.

Johnson, R. (1981a) 'Really Useful Knowledge: Radical Education and Working Class Culture, 1790-1848' in R. Dale, G. Esland, R. Fergusson and M. MacDonald (eds.) Education and the State, Vol. II, Falmer Press, Lewes, pp.3-9.

Johnson R. (1981b) 'Against Absolutism' in R. Samuel (ed.) People's History and Socialist Theory, Routledge & Kegan Paul, London, pp.386-396.

Kuhn, T.S. (1968) The Structure of Scientific Revolutions, Chicago University Press, Chicago.

Lipsey, D. & Leonard, D. (1981) The Socialist Agenda, Crosland's Legacy, Jonathan Cape, London.

Malinowski, B. (1974) Magic, Science, and Religion, Souvenir Press, London, pp.111-126.

Marsden, D. (1971) Politicians, Equality and Comprehensives, Fabian Tract No. 411.

Mayo, M. (1982) 'Community Action Programmes in the Early Eighties - What Future?' Critical Social Policy, 1, pp.5-18.

Potter, M. (1981) 'The State as Welfare', Economy and Society, 10, No. 1.

Rose, N. (1980) 'Socialism and Social Policy: the Problems of Inequality' in Politics and Power 2, Routledge & Kegan Paul, London, pp.111-137.

Young, M.F.D. (1977) 'Taking Sides Against the Probable' in C. Jenks (ed.) Rationality, Education, and the Social Organisation of Knowledge, Routledge & Kegan Paul, London, pp.86-96.

Sharp, R. (1980) Knowledge, Ideology and the Politics of Schooling, Routledge & Kegan Paul, London.

Stone, M. (1981) The Education of the Black Child in Britain, Fontana, London.

Trigg, R. (1973) Reason and Commitment, Cambridge University Press, London.

Willis, P. (1977) Learning to Labour, Saxon House, Farnborough.

2. THE POLITICS OF ADMINISTRATIVE CONVENIENCE – the case of middle schools

Andy Hargreaves

Broadly speaking, there are two contrasting traditions in the study of educational policy: pluralism
and Marxism. These differ greatly in the theoretical and methodological approaches they adopt, to the
extent that they are professionally embedded in
distinctive kinds of discourse and in separate,
relatively insulated communities of academic exchange. As is usual in such circumstances, each
tradition tends either to neglect the work of the
other, or to construe it in terms of a limited
number of unflattering stereotypical features which
do little justice to the complex positions and
nuances of argument that would be uncovered by a
more thorough examination. This is a pity, for such
neglect, hostility and mistrust serves only to inhibit the traditions from appreciating and building
upon their very real complementary strengths in the
service of improved understanding of the educational
policy-making process, its determinants and effects.
     In this paper, I want to sketch out a provision-
al framework which might allow these two approaches
to be brought more closely together. This will not
simply be an occasion for 'free-floating' theoretical speculation, but will also provide an opportunity
to ground the framework in a detailed empirical
analysis of one particularly illuminating case of
post-war educational policy - the origin of English
middle schools.

EXPLANATIONS OF EDUCATION AND THE STATE

Pluralism

Until very recently, the study of educational policy
was virtually monopolized by a tradition of 'admini-

23

stration and management' studies not especially
renowned for their theoretical sophistication. These
studies document the nuts and bolts of the educational decision-making process in rich detail; pointing
to the relative influences exerted by a plurality of
interest groups in the control and administration of
education; to the complex interactions, negotiations
and mutual influences between political, administrative, professional and lay groups in the educational
decision-making process at local and national levels
(e.g. Peschek & Brand, 1966; Batley, O'Brien &
Parris, 1970; Saran, 1973; James, 1980). But while
writers in this tradition have been admirable
sticklers for empirical detail, and while to their
credit, they have sifted through the apparent messiness of educational politics and administration with
great precision, it would also be fair to say that
on occasion they have been less meticulous with
theory, leaping to rash and premature conclusions
that such messiness effectively discredits the false
prophets of Marxism and their crude doctrines of
economic determinism (Bell, 1981).[1]

To pluralists, then, the superficial appearance
of immense political and administrative variety in
educational decision-making has a strong ideological
appeal. As a result, their accounts are usually
permeated by a sense of there being an almost limit-
less diversity of influences within and upon the
decision-making process; a diversity which is matched only by the apparent elusiveness of the whole
process, its seeming capacity to confound systematic
analysis within an overall theoretical framework.
The consequence is that while the study of educational policy abounds in elaborate taxonomies of different kinds of pressure groups and different modes of
exerting political influence, it is weak on any kind
of integrating theory. In Glennester and Hoyle's
words (1976, p.196), 'these studies are often useful at the level of description but lack explanatory
power'.

On occasion, the underlying pluralistic assumptions emerge with more clarity and explicitness
though. Kogan (1978), for instance, states that
educational decision-making is characterised by
diversity, conflict and reconciliation. The whole
process, he argues is underpinned by the pursuit of
a plurality of both sectional and promotional interests which leads to widespread political conflict
about education. But this conflict is not damaging:
indeed it is viewed as absolutely vital to the workings of a democratic society, for through it compro-

mises are forged and agreement is reached. As Kogan
himself puts it -

> education is political. It is volatile. It
> strongly reflects the often conflicting and
> wide-ranging preferences of a society which
> it also helps to sustain, improve and
> embellish and from which it draws resources.
> If politics are the way in which individuals
> assert their claims and have them reconciled
> with the claims of others, education reflects
> and clarifies and expresses these claims in
> the society, though it cannot of itself,
> reconcile them.
>   (Kogan 1978, p.20, my emphasis)

Contrary to the accusations of a number of Marxist
critics (e.g. Dale, 1981; Esland, 1981) it is not
assumed that these interests and influences are dispersed evenly throughout society; or that the State
merely acts as neutral arbiter in the process of
educational conflict and negotiation. Indeed, Kogan
argues elsewhere that the DES in particular has
altogether too strong a say in the running of the
educational system, sometimes not playing neutral
arbiter at all, but acting as a powerful and decisive interest group of its own (Kogan, 1975, p.238;
also Lawton, 1980; Salter and Tapper, 1981).
    Notwithstanding these important qualifications,
though, pluralists still assume that power and influence is widely dispersed, albeit unevenly and it
is this assumption which provides their base-line
for discussion and analysis of educational policy.
The system might be a less-than-perfect example of
democratic pluralism, but it is pluralistic nonetheless and for those who doubt the point, they need
only look at the complexity of educational change as
revealed in numerous empirical studies to allay their
anxieties.

Marxism

The weakness or absence of theory in the administration and management tradition has been more than
compensated for in recent Marxist writings on education, the state and capitalism. This interest of
Marxists in the state and its educational system
marks their brave and ambitious progression beyond
earlier rather simplistic explanations of the relationship between schooling and capitalism (Bowles
and Gintis, 1976)[2] in an effort to understand the

complex political processes of modern capitalist
societies and the dynamics of educational policy-
making as part of those processes.

The aim of dealing with current political and
educational complexities while still retaining allegiance to the concepts and framework of Marxist
analysis has not been achieved without cost, however
- mainly to intelligibility and coherence. This is
apparent in the frequent juxtaposition of different,
apparently contradictory assertions about the relationship between education, the state and capitalism.
These include the following:

- that the state maintains the conditions for
  capital accumulation and thereby protects the long
  term interests of capital by reproducing a skilled,
  adaptable and compliant workforce; by averting
  social unrest either through policies of law and
  order or ones of social and educational amelioration; and by direct intervention in the management
  of the economy (Jessop, 1977, 1980; Scase, 1980).

- that the actions of the state are not, however,
  directly determined by the needs or demands of the
  capitalist economy: the state, that is to say, has
  its own relative autonomy or political specificity
  (Poulantzas, 1973).

- that while the state is an instrument of class
  domination, it is also a site of class struggle
  and resistance (Corrigan, 1979).

- that the state is a site of contestation among a
  number of groups (political and professional as
  well as class ones) and that state policies are a
  product of 'the balance of political forces' in
  any instance rather than a direct consequence of
  economic influences (CCCS, 1981).

While individually, perhaps, few of these statements would arouse vigorous objections, the inclusion of many or all of them often within a single
account of educational policy (e.g. CCCS, 1981;
Dale, 1982) makes it extremely difficult to assess
their relative importance in any particular case, or
indeed to deduce whether or not economic factors are
the major determinents of educational policies in
those cases, and if so, to what extent. In other
words, while, in the name of theoretical openness,
an important role for political, professional and
other influences as well as class and economic ones
is allowed, the additional insistence that economic
factors rooted in the nature of the capitalist mode

of production are nonetheless somehow ultimately
determinant in the last instance, seems to owe less
to measured scholarly judgement and analysis than to
unexamined belief and political commitment
(Hargreaves, 1982; Hargreaves and Hammersley, 1982).
    Because they are pitched at such a high level
of generality, current Marxist analyses of educational policy really tell us only that schooling and the
state are somehow and to varying degrees both dependent on and independent from the capitalist economy.
This is not an especially profound insight; more a
testimony to our ignorance than a tribute to our
knowledge about the relationship between schooling
and capitalism or, indeed, any other mode of production (Edwards, 1980). In the case of the rather
nebulous concept of 'relative autonomy', for instance, it is not made clear just when such autonomy
will be functional for the capitalist system and
when it will not. Nor is it possible to ascertain
when the implications of the relative autonomy
thesis will (in socialist terms) be optimistic,
arousing expectations that schools might be sources
of resistance and struggle against the capitalist
system (Whitty and Young, 1976; Giroux, 1981), and
when they will be pessimistic, underlining the
school's power to reproduce the capitalist system
smoothly and unobtrusively beneath a deceptive
appearance of detachment from direct capitalist
influence (Bourdieu and Passeron, 1977).
    In the light of these criticisms, it is easy to
succumb to the temptation to write off Marxist analysis altogether for wanting to have its cake and
eat it; for insisting that politics and schooling
are both determined by the capitalist economy, and
that they are not. I want to resist this temptation,
though, and instead take up Hindess' more constructive if somewhat tongue-in-cheek suggestion that "the
onus is on advocates (of Marxist theories of the
state) to establish the mechanisms of the ultimately
determining role of the economy, to show how they
are effective rather than merely assert that they
are" (Hindess, 1980, p.41).
    These comments of Hindess' have two implications
for the future study of educational policy. First,
relationships between education, the state and
capitalism cannot be explained at the level of
theory alone but must be demonstrated through detailed treatment of empirical evidence. At some point
or other, then, it is important that the specula-
tions of theoreticians are squared with the 'real
world'. However, if this seems to grant premature

victory to the pluralists with their meticulous eye
for detail, I should like to add an important if
rather obvious qualification - that evidence does not
and cannot speak for itself in isolation from a set
of theoretical propositions. It would be a mistake,
then, to insist that Marxists should construct
theories and pluralists test them out, for even if
such a crude division of labour were possible or
desirable, we would still be left with the problem
that much contemporary Marxist theory and its associated concepts of relative autonomy and the like
are not in their present form sufficiently clear or
precise to be open to any test at all.

This brings me to the second implication of
Hindess' remarks. If evidence is to be employed in
any meaningful way, concepts such as relative autonomy will need to be carefully unpacked in order to
identify different possible propositions of a more
testable nature that are contained within them. In
this sense, it is incumbent upon Marxists to be open
not only to the empirical contributions of other
traditions, but to the theoretical implications of
non-Marxist work as well. My sympathies here are
with Silver when he argues that:

> If a greater concern with the theoretical
> implications of historical analysis is of major
> importance in Britain, the concern needs to be
> pursued with two reservations: theoretical
> questions, not ritualistic gestures need to
> be built into the historical search for
> explanations, and theoretical tantrums which
> do not attempt to engage with historical
> commonalities and diversities are of little
> use in that approach to the social condition
> which requires understandings and action.
> (Silver, 1980, p.84)

Accordingly, my purpose in the rest of the
paper is to explore two very different yet broadly
compatible interpretations of the determination of
educational policy in order to identify different
possible relations and strengths of connection between education, the state and capitalism. This
will be done with reference to an empirical analysis
of the emergence of English middle schools. This
evidence is deliberately selected in order to high-
light complexities and variations in the politics
of educational change. By pursuing such a course,
I hope to contribute to the understanding of the
establishment of middle schools, to sketch out

possible relations between political and administrative complexities of educational decision making and the broad structural context in which such processes are located, and to illustrate areas of possible compatibility between Marxist and pluralist analyses of educational policy.

THE CASE OF MIDDLE SCHOOLS

In legal terms, middle schools were made possible by the Education Act of 1964. This allowed, for the first time, transfer between primary and secondary education at ages other than 11. But it was an act of more mature vintage - Butler's Education Act of 1944 - which created the problem to which middle schools would eventually provide an answer. From the point of view of post-war educational reoganisation, this Act left two important legacies: a tripartite system of educational provision which included a sizeable collection of relatively small but architecturally sound secondary modern schools;[3] and a firm legal distinction between primary and secondary education fixed at 11. When several local authorities began to push hard for comprehensive schooling during the late 1950s, these legacies jarred awkwardly with one another.

The reason for this was the Ministry of Education's insistence that unless new school building was warranted by population expansion or urban renewal, local authorities who wished to reorganise their secondary education systems should do so within the existing stock of school buildings. Why the Ministry should adopt this stance is taken up later. Its effect, though, was to prevent the establishment of inevitably large 11-18 comprehensive schools in many areas since they would far outstrip the accommodation then available.[4] Those LEAs who retained a strong commitment to comprehensive schooling would therefore have to divide up the secondary school sector in some way or other. But one of the most manageable ways of doing this - a three tier system of 5-9, 9-13, 13-18 schools - was then illegal and was therefore either ruled out by most LEAs after the briefest of enquiries (Marsh, 1980), or not really seriously considered by them all.

The following account explores some of the detailed negotiations that took place within just one LEA - the West Riding of Yorkshire - which attempted in some of its 28 regional divisions to grapple with this difficult issue.[5] When those particular divisions elected to go comprehensive, the West

Riding's Chief Education Officer (now Sir) Alec Clegg, mindful of the limited money that the Ministry was prepared to make available for school building purposes, drew up plans for effecting the various reorganisations within existing premises. In very many cases, this entailed a system of junior (11-14) and senior (11-18) high schools. The fortunes of this proposal in three separate divisions or part-divisions, will be analysed in order to illustrate the range of outcomes that can follow from a single policy initiative such as this.

In two of those divisions, the junior high school proposal was rejected - leading in one instance to the eventual establishment of all-through 11-18 provision (Ecclesfield - part of the Wharncliffe division), and in the other to one of the country's first sixth-form colleges (Mexborough). In the third division (Hemsworth), the junior high school proposal was accepted but only to meet with subsequent resistance from the Ministry of Education. It was as a result of this impasse that Clegg came up with the middle school formula, Hemsworth eventually being one of the first two areas to receive ministerial approval for the middle school experiment, and to host the opening of the first such schools in 1968.

In empirical terms then, this paper seeks to explain the conditions which led to the framing of that middle school proposal, while also sketching out a provisional theoretical framework of two different kinds of determination through which the genesis of those conditions might be more completely understood.

STRUCTURAL LIMITATION - THE ROLE OF ADMINISTRATIVE CONVENIENCE

When we think of how one thing is determined by another, we usually have in mind some kind of direct pressure, or immediately observable process of cause and effect. In this respect, educational changes might be seen as the outcome of such things as political sponsorship as with the Labour Party and comprehensive schooling (Parkinson, 1970), or pressing economic demands as with the rise of the Manpower Services Commission (CCCS, 1981). However, the idea of exertion of pressure provides only one sense (albeit an extremely important one) of the meaning of 'determination'. As Williams (1976) points out, the original meaning of the term was very different from this, referring, in fact, to the

setting of bounds or limits to possible actions.
Wright (1979) calls this boundary-setting process,
<u>structural limitation</u>. This, he argues,

> constitutes a pattern of determination in which
> some social structure establishes limits within
> which some other structure or process can vary,
> and establishes probabilities for the specific
> structures or processes that are possible
> within those limits. That is, structural
> limitation implies that certain forms of the
> determined structure have been excluded
> entirely and some possible forms are more
> likely than others. This pattern of deter-
> mination is especially important for under-
> standing the sense in which economic structures
> "ultimately" determine political and ideolo-
> gical structures: economic structures set
> limits on possible forms of political and
> ideological structures, and make some of
> these possible forms more likely than others,
> but they do not rigidly determine in a mech-
> anistic manner any given form of political
> and ideological relations.
>
> (Wright, 1979, pp.15-16)

What Wright is saying here is that while one cannot
predict exactly what kind of political system or
ideology will follow from any given economic mode
of production such as capitalism - that mode of
production nonetheless <u>sets limits</u> to the range of
political and ideological forms that are possible
and probable. Structural limitation, therefore, is
what makes the autonomy of education and politics
<u>relative</u> rather than <u>complete</u>.

For writers such as Dale (1982), it makes no
fundamental difference which particular educational
policy options are considered within the capitalist
state. The important thing is that all viable
options <u>must not and cannot be inimical to</u> the
capital accumulation process. What is interesting
for Dale and other contemporary Marxist writers,
that is, is not so much whether this or that particular change occurs in educational policy-making;
why middle schools are established in one LEA,
sixth form colleges in another and 11-18 schools
in another, for instance. Rather, they are much
more fascinated by the negative case; by what
<u>doesn't</u> happen, the educational changes that <u>don't</u>
take place, the radical social transformations that
<u>fail</u> to come to fruition. The reason for these

absences, they argue, is to be located in the limits
to change set by the capitalist mode of production;
in particular its need for the reproduction of a
skilled and flexible labour force and an acquiescent
citizenry.

Action, change and conflict in educational
policy-making, then, is a remarkably diverse and,
in many respects, an unpredictable process. However
the extent of unpredictability in educational change
is not infinite; the range of policy options not
without limit. As Raymond Williams puts it, citing
Engels in support, 'We make history ourselves, but,
in the first place, under very definite assumptions
and conditions' (Engels). What this recognizes,
Williams continues, 'is the idea of direct agency:
we make history ourselves. The 'definite' or
'objective' assumptions and conditions are then the
qualifying terms of this agency: in fact, 'determination' as 'the setting of limits'' (Williams,
1978, p.85). Conflicts and struggles about education may very well be based on or organised around
all kinds of non-economic considerations - those of
race, gender, religion and professional status,
for instance. But at the end of the day, the scope
of these multifaceted conflicts is significantly
limited by factors rooted in the capitalist mode of
production and the logic of its development.

Assumptions

There are, to recall Williams' statement, two aspects to such structural limitation: assumptions and
conditions. Assumptions about the naturalness and
legitimacy of the existing order are deeply influential upon the educational policy process. Alec
Clegg, for instance, though an eminent proposer of
many educational innovations, was no great critic
of the capitalist economic order, being a keen
public supporter of the expansion of such a system
and of the preparation and deployment of labour to
this end. Thus, commenting in 1958 on the problems
of educational underachievement in the South
Yorkshire coalfield he remarked that,

> in the last 40 years vast new industries have
> arisen dealing with plastics, non-ferrous
> metals, aeronautics, radio, radar, tele-
> vision; not to mention the nationalised
> industries and the welfare state all of
> which have to be manned and serviced by people
> who are much more highly trained than those

> who manned the 19th century economy. In
> these circumstances, it appears to be the
> height of national folly to waste ability as
> we are wasting it in South Yorkshire.[6]

These remarks were not unusual for the time,
being duplicated in a string of education reports
such as those of Newsom, Robbins, Plowden and
Crowther (to which Clegg made a contribution). Together these displayed a taken-for-granted support
of the existing economic order, urging not large-
scale change, but certain adjustments to improve its
efficiency. To have argued otherwise would have
given an impression of being altogether bereft of
reason, being <u>against</u> growth and prosperity, rather
than opposed to the specific economic system in
which such growth occurred (Tapper & Salter, 1978).
Whatever particular educational changes they favoured and sponsored, therefore, educational policy-
makers such as Clegg invariably assumed that schooling would contribute to or at least, in Dale's words,
<u>not be inimical</u> to capital accumulation, and the
schemes and proposals that were presented by them
reflected those limiting assumptions.

Within British society such assumptions have
been given a particular inflection through a dominant style of educational and political reform by
piecemeal and pragmatic means. As Antonio Gramsci
(1971, p.372) put it, such "pragmatism cannot be
criticised without taking account of the Anglo-
Saxon historical context in which it was born and
developed." The origins of that tradition lie deep
rooted in the intellectual and social fabric of
eighteenth and nineteenth century Britain, but the
approach is best epitomised in the longstanding political orientation of the British Labour Party,
especially in its Fabian branch. Even when the
Labour Representation Committee (the Labour party's
predecessor) was founded in 1900, Keir Hardie termed this 'Labourism' a

> body of working-class political theory and
> practice which accepted the possibility of
> social change within the existing framework
> of society; which rejected the revolutionary
> violence and action implicit in Chartist ideas
> of physical force; and which increasingly
> recognised the working or political democracy
> of the Parliamentary variety as the practical
> means of achieving its own aims and object-
> ives. (quoted in Coates, 1975, p.6)

33

This orientation persisted through to the First (Barker 1972, p.24) and Second World Wars when, even in its most apparently radical phase of post-war reconstruction

> Labour sought to improve the existing social order, not to change it. However much the party might remain symbolically committed to the achievement of a socialist commonwealth, its behaviour in the coalition of World War II was suggestive of a commitment to amelioration, not to radical transformation.
> (Howell, 1976, p.118)

There was no abatement of this approach in the 1950s and 60s; indeed the Conservative Governments of that period were themselves increasingly drawn into the broad educational and social concerns of economic expansion and amelioration through educational and social reform which characterised the era of social democracy (Finn, Grant and Johnson, 1977; CCCS, 1981). In other words educational change has for a long time taken place according to a principle of gradualistic reform and amelioration within the parameters of existing institutional arrangements. Innovation has therefore moved slowly, building incrementally on past changes, adapting to local circumstances, and utilising limited resources (see Robinson, 1977).

Conditions

Educational and social assumptions of this kind, however, are not simply indicative of the unenlightened outlook of educational administrators, but are themselves rooted in a set of deeply constraining economic conditions in which educational policy has been developed and implemented. This can be seen most clearly in the phenomenon of administrative convenience. Administrative convenience had a powerful effect on patterns of educational reorganization in the West Riding and elsewhere. In Ecclesfield, for instance, the West Riding Education Committee noted that school buildings were generally of high quality. The one existing grammar school contained some excellent post-war extensions, three of the secondary modern schools had been built since the 1944 Act, and of the remaining three one was an attractive pre-war school, another required some improvements which had already been incorporated into the school building programme, and only one re-

quired much larger scale alterations. In these circumstances, the Committee felt it most unlikely that
any proposed scheme for 11-18 schools would be
accepted by the Ministry, given the amount of re-
building involved.

> The Committee must...realise that the accom-
> modation does completely limit what can be
> done. It is inconceivable that when children
> are so excellently accommodated, this or any
> future Ministry would allow any bids for
> Comprehensive adaptations until the more
> squalid old buildings elsewhere have been
> replaced or improved.[7]

The story was the same in Mexborough where
'the amount of building involved would be so considerable that it would be unlikely that the scheme
would be brought into operation for a very long
time indeed'.[8] Suggesting a similar solution as
that proposed for Ecclesfield, Clegg continued, 'It
seems to me, therefore, that if the Division wishes
to avoid this, it will be necessary to think in
terms of some sort of a Junior and Senior High
School organisation.'[9]

In the third division, Hemsworth, the conditions arising from administrative convenience were
more restrictive still, 'The difficulty about the
Hemsworth division', Clegg wrote, 'is the existence
in it of a large number of small secondary schools,
which means that there is no easy or obvious solution to the problem'.[10] He later stressed that
given the buildings available a programme based
upon 11-18 comprehensive schools would be utterly
impractical.[11] His solution yet again, was a
junior high school system where all pupils would
be transferred at ages 11 and 14.

But the proposal, practical though it seemed,
became caught between two competing forces. While
the existence of many small secondary modern schools
meant that any new scheme would have to make use of
at least some of the buildings in which those
schools were housed, at the same time, a considerable proportion of those schools were regarded as
inadequate and as needing replacement. Indeed,
Hemsworth's Divisional Education Officer, in a
letter to the West Riding Education Committee complained that, 'the facilities in the Division are
appalling when compared with other Divisions'.[12]
And Clegg himself commented that 'Quite apart from

the question of the organisation of secondary
education...new building is urgently required in
this Division.'[13]
   In view of the 'very considerable capital expenditure' which would be involved in any scheme,
the Committee decided to press in the first instance
for reorganisation in the southern part of the division only, proposals for Hemsworth being shelved
until later.[14] Even this plan was not sufficiently
persuasive, though, and the Ministry withheld their
approval and, despite repeated pressure from the
West Riding, had still not granted it by late 1963.
As Clegg explained to Hemsworth's increasingly
irate Education Officer:

> The recent delay in the development of
> secondary education in the Hemsworth Division
> is due to one thing and one thing alone and
> that is the failure of the Ministry of
> Education, despite all the efforts of the
> County Education Committee, to sanction the
> building of the necessary new schools...
> The Authority is only too anxious to build
> these schools but...despite the most
> vigorous protests by the Education Committee
> the Ministry has simply not sanctioned the
> schools which are so badly needed.[15]

The difficulties were becoming almost insuperable.
Clegg was being pressured by his Divisional
Executive to force through a scheme of comprehensive schooling, yet the building limitations restricted the feasible proposals to a Junior High
School scheme only. Furthermore, while the scattered provision of small secondary schools
certainly prevented 11-18 schools being established,
the poor physical condition of many school buildings meant that virtually any scheme including one
involving junior high schools would entail considerable expenditure on new premises which the Ministry
would not be prepared to sanction.
   In large part it was this highly restrictive
set of conditions which pushed Clegg to 'float' the
middle school idea with the Ministry in May 1963,
naming Hemsworth as one of two possible areas where
such a plan might be implemented. For as Clegg
later confided to Councillor Palmer in March 1964,
'It is more likely that we shall be able to use and
adapt existing premises if we can have 9-13 schools
than if we have to make the transfer at 14'.[16]
Certainly, figures for the new middle school scheme

presented to the Ministry in October 1964 did not
appear to exceed those already agreed for its Junior
High School predecessor.[17] Moreover, the middle
school alternative would allow reorganisation
throughout a larger area of Hemsworth than would
have been the case had the Junior High School scheme
been adopted.[18] Though Clegg would later question
the fact, it appears then that in this area at
least, middle schools offered an even more expedient
solution to going comprehensive than did junior
highs.[19] Indeed, their relative cost-effectiveness
greatly impressed the Schools Branch at the Ministry
of Education, Hemsworth eventually being the first
area to be granted ministerial approval for a
middle school scheme.[20]

Middle schools, then, offered an administrat-
ively expedient way of going comprehensive, and
because of that fact were eventually legalized
through the 1964 Education Act which gave cautious
approval to middle schools as an interesting though
limited educational experiment. Indeed, Edwards
(1972, pp.64-65) suggests that the middle school was
surreptitiously sponsored by the Department of
Education around 1964.

> since it was seen as a useful experiment
> which would be an economic method of going
> comprehensive and which would also relieve
> considerably the pressures on secondary
> school accommodation which would follow the
> projected raising of the school leaving age.

Many LEAs in addition to the West Riding were quick
to appreciate the economic attractions of middle
schools and with the announcement in 1966 of the
raising of the school leaving age to 16 and the
obvious pressures this would place on building
accommodation in the secondary sector, together with
the DES's insistence that no new money would be made
available for this purpose, the middle school option
became more attractive still (Hargreaves & Tickle,
1980) and was even selected by a number of LEAs who
had previously committed themselves to very different modes of comprehensive reorganisation(Hargreaves,
forthcoming).

It is tempting,in the light of these findings,
simply to agree with Doe's (1976, p.22) rather
cynical observation that middle schools 'were created for the best of all educational reasons -
because they were cheap' - to dismiss them in
effect, as a mere administrative convenience and

end the analysis there, noting only perhaps that
middle schools are not unusual in this respect,
being just one of many such conveniences in British
educational history. In fact, most accounts of the
emergence of middle schools which explain them primarily in terms of expediency do just this (e.g.
Marsh 1973, Bryan and Hardcastle 1977, 1978). They
view administrative convenience either as an irrita-
ting preoccupation of educational politicians and
administrators which fouls up the process of school
reform (as in Edwards, 1972), or they imply that
economic expediency is an irremovable feature of the
policy making process; an unavoidable, though somewhat irksome constraint which all those who work in
the education system have to confront (as in Stone,
1978). As they stand, however, such interpretations
are insufficient for three reasons:
- they treat 'administrative convenience' as
  an adequate explanation in itself without
  locating it in the economic and political
  conditions of modern British society;
- they fail to account for the diversity of
  supposedly convenient arrangements between
  and within LEAs;
- they overestimate the importance of administrative convenience, at times even implying
  it is the only causal factor of any significance. Other equally important determinants of the middle school thereby tend to
  get neglected.
I shall deal with the latter two points a little
later. My present concern is with the first; with
the ways in which the issue of administrative convenience points to deeper questions concerning
problems of management and control in advanced capitalist societies.

To some degree, of course, a certain amount of
administrative convenience is unavoidable. It is
part of the global problem of scarcity. Only in
imaginary utopias are there enough resources to
satisfy all human needs, be they ones of health,
education or whatever. In other words, all societies, whatever their economic base or political
orientation, provide social and educational services
at levels less than they would ideally prefer.
Administrative convenience, in this sense, is simply
a fact of life; a natural inevitability. While this
is true enough, the problem takes on an additional
dimension in capitalist societies, for here the
economic system is not primarily geared to the satisfaction of human need at all, but in order to

guarantee its own survival, to the maximisation of profits. In such circumstances, continuous efforts are made, if not always successfully, to tailor human fortunes and ambitions to the needs of capital. The effect of this upon education in the 1960s was to encourage growing state involvement in and expansion of educational provision in order to produce a technically equipped, socially compliant labour force; and to 'buy' broad social and political consent by accommodating educational demands (Adams, 1979; Dale, 1981). Much of the official support for comprehensive schooling can be explained in terms such as these (Bellaby, 1977).

But herein lies a crucial dilemma. For while comprehensive schooling was in part introduced to maintain and enhance the process of capital accumulation by providing a suitably adapatable and acquiescent labour force, and while it was to some extent also the price paid for securing broad social consent; the investment could not be too costly, the price not too high. If it was; if state expenditure on education reached an apparently exhorbitant level, investment in the business of social reproduction would seriously threaten to exhaust the fruits, the surplus value realised from production. It would become a drain on society's resources rather than a crucial investment in its seeming well being. Educational expenditure, therefore, was limited; and the sums channelled into the programme of comprehensive school reform were, as a result, remarkably meagre.

Viewed in this light, 'administrative convenience' as it has been experienced in modern British society takes on a broader significance than that which has conventionally been accorded it. It highlights, in fact, a central and endemic tension within modern capitalism between the actual and perceived requirements of industrial production and the direct accumulation of wealth on the one hand, and those of reproducing the conditions in which such wealth creation can continue on the other. This tension places firm limits on the policy options for social and educational change within such a society. Administrative convenience in educational policy making is therefore part of a broader set of tensions and contradictions generated by the capital accumulation process and is thus a vivid example of what Habermas (1976, p.46) calls the <u>rationality crisis</u> in modern capitalism 'in which the administrative system does not succeed in reconciling and fulfilling the imperatives received from the economic system'.

To sum up, there are certain tendencies inherent in capitalism as an economic mode of production which place important though exceptionally broad limits on the options for educational and social reform, both through the logic of resource allocation to social and educational ends in a profit orientated system, and through the boundary reaffirming assumptions of what changes are desirable, possible and even thinkable within such a system. As we have seen by examining the fate of junior high school proposals in the West Riding, these limits have played their part in determining (in the widest sense) the patterns of comprehensive reorganisation in different LEAs; by ruling out the most radical alternatives and severely restricting the more politically acceptable ones to what is feasible given existing resources. It is here, in the explanation of how educational policy options are structurally and hegemonically contained, that Marxist thought has a crucial role to play which must not be underestimated. In this respect, Marxism deals exceptionally well with important aspects of educational policy making that have been sadly neglected in other traditions such as political pluralism.

For all that, though, it cannot explain the whole story. Many things are possible within the limits: policies vary greatly from one LEA to the next; the same policy is often adopted for widely varying reasons, even in the same LEA; and nationally generated initiatives are frequently resisted at the local level and vice versa. When it comes to explaining these kind of complexities, Marxist theory with its rather loose talk of the impact of 'balances of political forces' and the like, within 'relatively autonomous trajectories' of educational change (CCCS, 1981, p.176) is much less helpful. It is at this point that we must turn elsewhere for firmer theoretical support and more precise empirical assistance.

WITHIN THE LIMITS: VARIATIONS IN EDUCATIONAL POLICY

Multicausality

In examining the determination of educational policy and practice, most non-Marxists, particularly those drawn to pluralism and to the writings of Max Weber, are rightly anxious not to reduce all aspects of educational conflict and negotiation to forces implicated in the capitalist mode of production and the means of its preservation. Education, as other social processes, rather, is viewed as a diversely determined process and detailed empirical study is advocated and undertaken in order to establish who is most influential in the control of education in any particular instance and to ascertain which goals have been realised through the exercise of that control (Archer, 1979).

The struggle for and implementation of comprehensive schooling provides a good example of such many-sided conflicts and oddly composed alliances in the process of educational change; for invested in that single educational reform were many of the different hopes and aspirations of a wide range of social groups (Marsden, 1971). For certain sections of the working class and the Labour Party, for instance, comprehensive schooling stood for radical and egalitarian social reform (Parkinson, 1970); elsewhere, it was seen to hold out the prospect of greater all-round educational opportunities within a truly meritocratic educational system; and at the highest levels in particular, among politicians and their advisors, comprehensive schooling promised the realisation of economic growth and prosperity. Moreover, these varying and differently grounded justifications were often skilfully run together by policy makers in their pronouncements on the comprehensive issue. Such convergences of disparate interests and justifications and their diverse consequences for educational policy can be seen in the case of the West Riding at the time when junior high schools were being discussed.

In some cases, in some of the more solidly working class mining districts of South Yorkshire, the interpretation of and commitment to comprehensive schooling was unambiguously egalitarian. Thus, Labour councillors in Mexborough rejected Clegg's suggested junior high school scheme with transfer at 14, because for them it had too many selective connotations. In particular, it called to mind the Leicestershire Plan - a scheme where children were only allowed to transfer to the senior high school at 14 if their parents agreed to them staying on beyond the minimum leaving age (Mason, 1964). Given such elitist associations, the junior high school scheme was not, as the councillors themselves saw it, 'full-blooded comprehension' (sic).[21]

Meritocratic arguments were also broadly influential on the attempts to reorganise secondary education; perhaps even more so. The Ecclesfield sub-division provides a good example of this. Here,

while junior high schools offered definite administrative advantages in going comprehensive, Clegg was
worried that such schemes did not allow pupils to
be prepared sufficiently for external examinations
at 16 plus.[22] Moreover, in a letter to the
Divisional Education Officer, Clegg argued that the
junior high school proposals for Ecclesfield ignored
what he rather misleadingly called 'the purely educational problem'.[23]

By this, Clegg meant access to Oxbridge. In
the 1950s and 1960s, this was dependent upon an
examination qualification in Latin. Continued
access to Oxbridge therefore required that 'it will
have to be possible for every child of appropriate
ability in...the Junior High Schools to take Latin,
and for that matter a modern foreign language, and
science and mathematics from the first year'.[24]
To get around this problem, a solution was tenta-
tively advanced for itinerant teachers based in the
senior high schools to devote four or five periods
a week to teaching in the junior highs. Although
Clegg was less happy about this, he felt constrained
into putting it forward because 'We have to face
that fact that Oxford and Cambridge demand it
(Latin) for all students, and almost every Arts
Faculty in every red-brick University also demands
it'.[25]

In the event, this arrangement proved too difficult and the junior high school proposal was
dropped. Nevertheless, the very reason the scheme
was rejected and comprehensivisation in Ecclesfield
subsequently delayed was because the divisional
education committee along with Alec Clegg himself
only wanted a system of comprehensive schooling if
it was compatible with efficient grooming of the
tiniest proportion of pupils for a privileged
Oxbridge education. In Clegg's own words,

> the able child in the South of the Riding
> is obviously at the present time labouring
> under a severe handicap. It is important
> that this handicap should be reduced and
> not increased by the introduction of a
> Comprehensive scheme.[26]

Meritocratic concerns defined in an exceedingly
rigid way were therefore highly influential in
determining the fate of comprehensive school proposals in the Ecclesfield division.

The interesting thing about the junior high
school proposal, therefore, is that while it suffer-

ed rejection in both Ecclesfield and Mexborough; it
was, in fact, turned down for very different reasons
- in Mexborough, by egalitarian-minded Labour
councillors, and in Ecclesfield by a meritocratic-
orientated divisional education committee, following
the advice of their Chief Education Officer, Sir
Alec Clegg. This interesting contrast is indicative
of the fact that the very same educational change
may be supported or rejected by very different
groups and for strikingly different reasons. It
rather depends who is pursuing what goals and with
what effect in each case.

In this sense, educational change is undoubtedly a 'multicausal' process in the way claimed by
many contemporary Weberians (e.g. Collins, 1977,
1979; King, 1980, 1982); education being an important cultural resource through which different groups
pursue their own ends, be they ones of an economic,
political or status-related kind. It is not un-
common for the ends these different groups pursue to
be opposed to one another, this leading to situations of intense and protracted political conflict.
But equally, they may at times be rendered compatible within a single educational proposal such as
comprehensive schooling. Within the broad limits
to educational change, then, policy-makers like Alec
Clegg virtually <u>have</u> to exercise strategic dexterity
in order to devise proposals for change which are
acceptable to the various groups who voice their
competing educational demands in any particular
locality.

But we must also not forget, of course, that
they do so in such a way as to realise social and
educational goals which are distinctively their own.
Though there is not the space to document such goals
in detail here, in Clegg's case these mainly concerned the maintenance of manageable school communities. These concerns were expressed in his
opposition to 11-13 schools where all pupils were
entrants or leavers; to split-site schools which
divided the school community; to conventional
Leicestershire Plan 11-14 Schools whose tone would
be set by the 'truncated group' of less able 15
year olds who had elected not to move on to the
senior high; and to 11-18 schools where young boys
and girls would be mixed with men eligible for the
services and women 'of marriageable age' (sic). To
these concerns Clegg later added the extension of
innovative primary school regimes to older pupils
in the middle school. And later still, he suggested that middle schools were institutions with

their own distinctive ethos and identity (Hargreaves, 1980).

Greatness as a highly innovative and influential educational administrator therefore, is as much thrust upon the individual as it is his or her own unique accomplishment. Here I would concur with Carr (1964, p.55) when he asks us 'to recognize in the great man an outstanding individual who is at once a product and an agent of the historical process'; someone, we might add, who in this case is burdened with the educational dilemmas and constraints of his time, assailed by a multiplicity of educational demands emanating from numerous political and social groups and yet who, from all this, manages not just to cobble together an unsatisfactory administrative compromise, but actually succeeds in forging a major new educational initiative that secures broad social support.

Administrative complexity

The multifaceted nature of educational change is complicated still further by the fact that variations in outlook, interpretation and social support occur not only between different localities, but also at different levels of the educational decision making process, each level having the capacity to generate proposals of its own and to frustrate or obstruct the implementation of proposals framed at other levels. In other words, when the state acts as a determinant of schooling, it does not do so as a unitary force. There are important divisions between national and local state (Cockburn, 1977) - in education, between the DES and LEAs for instance - which often make themselves felt in marked differences over policy.[27]

In the case of Hemsworth, for example, where both local and county council were agreed upon the necessity for a junior high school scheme as the only apparently feasible way of going comprehensive, the Ministry of Education would not sanction the necessary building changes. Partly, this was for reasons of economic expediency of the kind discussed earlier, but also because of a set of unspecified objections to the idea of junior high schools hinted at in correspondence between Clegg and the Ministry, though never fully revealed by them.[28] Indeed, it was because of this resistance at the highest level to secondary school reorganisation in Hemsworth, that Clegg's hand was effectively forced into the craftsmanlike shaping and skilled marketing

44

of the middle school idea; a proposal which appeared to be cheaper still than its junior high school predecessor and therefore better suited to the economic constraints of the Hemsworth division. In addition, of course, middle schools, unlike their junior high school counterparts with their later age of transfer at 14, would not undermine the preparation of pupils for external examinations. They would, that is to say, be very much compatible with the meritocratic, examination-dominated interpretation of comprehensive schooling which Harold Wilson once saw as offering 'grammar schools for all'.

The involvement of the State in the determination of schooling is therefore a multilayered one: there are important degrees of autonomy within the State, as well as between it and the mode of production. To speak of 'relative autonomy' in this sense is therefore not to talk of properties of educational systems or the State in general but of much more precise relations between specific sets of institutions within society.

One effect of such degrees of autonomy between different parts of the State can be seen in the remarkable diversity of educational provision that came about under the auspices of comprehensive reorganisation - middle schools and junior high schools being just two of a multitude of options. As Seaborne and Lowe (1977, p.157) point out, by 1970 the range of such provision was extensive and complex. These variations, they argue, 'arose partly out of theoretical but mainly out of practical considerations. The most significant of the latter were the limitations imposed by existing buildings.'

The point being made here is that what is convenient in one area may not, because of the condition of local buildings, the extent of population expansion or contraction and so on, be convenient in another. For instance, while middle schools were cheaper than junior highs in the early yet crucial case of Hemsworth, the position was completely reversed in Gateshead which, on the grounds of sheer expediency, threw out a middle school scheme for one based on junior and senior high schools. As the authors of a study of educational policy-making in that borough remark, 'ultimately, the age of transfer was settled on the grounds that only 14 plus was possible, given the existing school buildings' (Batley, O'Brien and Parris, 1970, p.68). In some cases at least, then, though not in others,

the claim made by Clegg and others (WRYECR 1965, p.4;
Halsall, 1971, p.193) that 14 plus was a more convenient age of transfer than 13 plus can be upheld.

The really important issue, however, is that in
an internally differentiated or decentralised state
system, the restrictions of expediency lead not to
uniformity but to diversity of educational provision;
a state of affairs which is further compounded by
the many-sided nature of the conflicts and negotiations concerning education that are played out, with
different results, in each locality.

So far, then, I have drawn attention to two
aspects of educational decision-making that take
place within the boundaries set by the capital accumulation process: I have outlined the multicausal
nature of group conflict over educational provision;
and I have pointed to internal differentiations
within the state apparatus, to the ways in which
national initiatives are complexly filtered down
through numerous levels in the hierarchy of state
control, and to converse processes by which reforms
sometimes percolate upwards through the system,
being blocked at the higher levels in some cases and
allowed to pass in others. I now wish to discuss a
third complicating factor - the effect of various
historical lags on the process of educational change.

Historical lags

In a 'perfect' capitalist world, the state, its
policies and ideologies would respond swiftly and
appropriately to the shifting demands and pressures of the labour market, technological change and
social unrest. It would equip the future workforce
with new skills and shape its most basic wants so
that its members would wish to become scientists instead of technologists, mothers and housewives rather than competitors in a contracting male job market, and so on. In the normal course of events,
though, the response is, for a number of reasons,
sluggish rather than swift, and if it comes at all,
from the point of view of capital, it often comes
too late. Why should this be so?

In part, in the sphere of schooling, these lags
take the form of persisting ideas and beliefs about
education which are inappropriate to a changed economic and political context. An example here is
those middle-aged, career-blocked secondary modern
school teachers who tenaciously clung to the aims
and ethos of the secondary modern school even when
they had been redeployed to work within a merito-

cratically-oriented, academically pressured comprehensive system (Riseborough, 1981). But the failure
to undo the old tripartite system is not only a
result of entrenched beliefs and conventions among
those for whom educational reform offers no obvious
advantages. It is also a product of past policy
commitments making themselves felt in harsh and intractable material realities; in the very bricks and
mortar of schooling (Williamson, 1974).

To that extent, the failure of the post-war
Labour government to establish comprehensive schooling, choosing instead under the Education Minister,
Ellen Wilkinson, to endorse the tripartite system as
outlined in the Spens and Norwood reports which preceded the 1944 Act, must be seen not just as what
Marsden (1971) calls "an opportunity lost", in post-
poning large scale comprehensive reorganisation for
two decades; but also it must be viewed as effectively restructuring the future possible ways in
which any reorganisation of secondary education
might be managed. Commitment to tripartism was not
just commitment to an educational principle but also
to the construction of many new, rather small secondary modern schools. And when, in the late 1950s
and early 1960s, the imperatives of economic expansion and the concerns for social justice charged the
educational system with the task of selecting talent
more efficiently than hitherto, and with rescuing
its human potential from atrophy in the secondary
modern schools, this stock of small secondary modern
schools designed for a fading educational tradition
severely restricted the possibilities for bringing
about comprehensive school reform. As we have seen,
it was this very dilemma, fraught with administrative difficulties, which led to the production in
turn of proposals for junior high schools then
middle schools in the West Riding, and to the large
scale adoption of similar compromise solutions nationally.

To sum up, much of the inefficiency of state
responses to economic change is a result of historically induced restrictions, of commitments to past
policies and beliefs not well suited to the demands
of the present. Partly, of course, these lags are
reinforced in de-centralized educational systems
such as that in Britain where the negotiation of
educational change is often a long, involved and
broadly-based process. But equally, once a restrict-
ion has been recognized and confronted, as with the
tripartite legacy of buildings unsuited for the
purposes of comprehensive schooling, de-centralized

systems may actually <u>accelerate</u> the devising of
practical solutions since they make it possible for
the circumstances of each locality in which change
is to take place to be appreciated and responded to:
hence the variety of institutional structures - middle schools, 6th form, colleges, etc. - in which
comprehensive schooling came to be established.

CONCLUSION

In this paper, I have focused on one small episode
in the recent history of educational change - the
consideration of proposals to establish junior and
senior high schools in certain areas of the West
Riding in the late 1950s and early 1960s; proposals
which immediately preceded Alec Clegg's vigorously
conducted campaign to secure the establishment of
English middle schools. Thus, we have seen that an
important condition of the middle school's success
was the junior high school's failure. That failure
was documented in the case of three divisions of the
West Riding; divisions which were selected quite
deliberately not to provide convenient illustrations
of an already existing theory, but to point to the
diverse nature of policy outcomes even under economic and political conditions which appear very similar. In that sense, they offered a fruitful opportunity for contributing to theoretical development
through careful empirical analysis.

The differential fate of the junior high school
proposal in the three divisions or part divisions
of Ecclesfield, Mexborough and Hemsworth respectively
was put down to the immediate intersection of three
broad factors. First, there was the existence of
multiple conflicts in the educational policy-making
process, played out in the pursuit of different
social and educational ends. In the case of the
junior high school discussions these were most evident in the competing arguments presented by those
who held to egalitarian and meritocratic definitions
of comprehensive schooling respectively. The Chief
Education Officer was credited with an important
role here in devising solutions which were not only
ostensibly compatible with these competing claims,
but which also went some way towards realising his
own educational ambitions.[29] Second, policy proposals were selectively filtered through the system,
going on to successful implementation in some cases
and early rejection in others. A good indication
of the latter was the way that the Hemsworth proposal for junior high schools was rejected at mini-

sterial level. This was taken as evidence of the
differentiated nature of the state; of the fact that
it acts not as a unitary body but is characterised
by a certain 'structural looseness' which leads at
times to problems of co-ordination (Bidwell, 1968).
Lastly, educational policies in the West Riding were
as much shaped by the material and ideological
legacies of the past as by the economic or political
demands of the present - hence the need to develop
a comprehensive system within a material infrastruc-
ture more suited to the purposes of explicitly selective, tripartite schooling.

Multicausal, pluralistic conflict, administrative complexity and historical inertia can therefore
tell us a great deal about the dynamics of educational policy-making, its determinants and its outcomes. And careful documentation of these processes
can tell us more about the complex nature of educational decision-making and state policy than
mysterious invocations of concepts like 'relative
autonomy' which simply tend to gloss over these
differences and subtleties. But saying this does
not amount to a refutation of the Marxist thesis.
For all these administrative and political complexities, immensely important as they are, are nonetheless still confined within broad limits to educational change which are set down by factors rooted in
the nature of capitalism as a mode of production and
the logic of its development. We have seen this not
only in the enduring and pervasive assumptions of
policy-makers which tacitly endorse the existing
economic order, but also in the phenomenon of administrative convenience - an example in the educational
sphere of much more extensive and deep-seated
irrationalities in the administration of the
capitalist order as a whole.[30]

It is difficult and perhaps futile to argue
that one half of this two-sided problem is more
important or more politically and educationally
'fundamental' than the other: to propose that the
limits to change are more significant than the different possibilities contained within them, or vice
versa. This is the trap, however, in which Marxists
and their enemies have been caught; one in which a
dialogue of the deaf prevails; each side falsely
assuming that the one who wins the argument will be
the one who shouts longest and loudest.

Studying the limits or what goes on within them
are therefore complementary, not competing ventures.
Choosing between the two options is a matter of
value choice, not one of theoretical correctness.

The more complete explanation however, will attempt
(with unavoidable difficulty) to combine them in a
theoretically open and empirically grounded way.
This is as true for the analysis of current educational issues where, arguably, the limits to change
have been drawn in by the strengthening of central
government control over curriculum and examinations
in the context of deepening economic recession
(Salter & Tapper, 1981) as it is for the social-
democratic era of educational policy-making with
which this paper has been concerned. Indeed, the
more crucial that education and political issues
become for the lives of ourselves and our children,
the more we must try to ensure that we get the
analysis of them right. In this sense, theoretical
openness and empirical rigour are not the nit-picking
enemies of a policy-relevant sociology of education,
but its closest allies.

This paper has been offered as an attempt to
illustrate how such a sociologically sensitive,
policy-relevant but politically uncertain venture
might be undertaken.

NOTES

1.   This claim is not entirely without foundation; but it is one which applies only to certain
rather vulgar kinds of Marxist analysis which
attempt to reduce all aspects of the dynamic of
educational change to factors implicated in the
capitalist mode of production. (e.g. Bowles &
Gintis 1976)

2.   These explanations suggested the existence
of straightforward correspondences between the
social relations of schooling and those of capitalist production. Their very existence, it was
proposed, was a result of the 'needs' of the capitalist economy. The role played by the State in
mediating, interpreting and on occasion frustrating
the fulfilment of these needs was never really
addressed in studies of this kind.

3.   Strictly speaking, of course, no stipula-
tions about a tripartite system of secondary
education were set down in the Act at all, but in
the absence of firm guidance most LEAs went on to
follow the recommendations of the Spens and Norwood
Reports in adopting such a pattern of organisation.

4.   The inevitability of size was based on
then current assumptions that curriculum choice at
'A' level required large sixth forms of academically

able youngsters, and an accordingly massive pool of
pupils aged 11-16 from which this highly selected
body of students could be recruited.

5. The data on which this account is based
consists of the correspondence and memoranda of the
West Riding Authority at the time prior to and
during that Authority's consideration and implementation of the middle school system. I am grateful to
Paul Sharp of Leeds University School of Education
for drawing the existence of these records to my
attention in the late 1970s. A fuller account of
the whole history of the West Riding LEA is provided
in Gosden and Sharp (1978). Sharp (1980) has also
subsequently written a short account of the development of middle schools in that authority.

6. 'The Education of the Gifted Child in the
Comprehensive School of the Yorkshire Coalfield',
presented to Policy and Finance Sub-Committee,
9.12.58.

7. "The Request for Comprehensive Schools or
a Comprehensive Scheme of Education - Ecclesfield
Area", Policy and Finance Sub-Committee, 9.12.58.

8. Letter from Alec Clegg to Mr. Stockdale,
Divisional Education Officer for Mexborough, 21.9.59.

9. Ibid.

10. Letter to Mr. Cockell, Divisional
Education Officer for Hemsworth, 19.6.59.

11. Further letter to Mr. Cockell, 22.9.59.

12. Letter from Mr. Thorpe, Divisional
Education Officer for Hemsworth to Mr. Petty, West
Riding Education Committee, 10.4.63.

13. 'Hemsworth Division - organisation of
Secondary Education', memorandum to Policy and
Finance Sub-Committee, 8.3.60.

14. Ibid.

15. Letter to Mr. Thorpe, 16.9.63.

16. Letter to Councillor Palmer, 4.3.64.

17. As Clegg recorded in a memorandum to the
Policy and Finance Sub-Committee (13.10.64).

> 'The future organisation of the Hemsworth
> Division was under discussion at the time
> the Department of Education and Science
> was compiling the 1966/67 (Building)
> Programme and for this reason a specific
> project could not be included for Hemsworth.
> 'Some new secondary provision for Hemsworth
> was however included on the understanding
> that whatever projects the Authority did
> put forward (e.g. for middle schools)...
> would be financially comparable to the
> proposals (for junior high schools) already

made'.'

18. Ibid.

19. As in the second West Riding document presenting the case for middle schools (WRYECR, 1965).

20. Such a demonstration was offered in relation to the establishment of middle schools in the Castleford Division where Clegg was asked by Miss Small at the Schools Branch of the Ministry to document the relative costs of junior high and middle school schemes respectively for that division. Clegg seized this opportunity to stress the economic advantages of the middle school scheme. Replying to Miss Small (26.11.63), he wrote:

'May I emphasise that if approval were to be given to our present suggestion (for middle schools), all these developments could take place without the provision of major new building, whereas the situation described in the Public Notices (in terms of a junior high school proposal) referred to the future and depended on new buildings being provided.'

21. A reported extract from a conversation held between one of Clegg's colleagues and the Mexborough Divisional Education Officer, Mr. Stockdale. Stockdale was reporting the comments of the Labour Group on Clegg's junior high school proposal. (Memo dated 9.11.59)

22. 'The Request for Comprehensive Schools or a Comprehensive Scheme of Education, Ecclesfield Area', op. cit., 9.12.58.

23. Letter to S. Wright, Wharncliffe Divisional Education Officer, 20.8.58.

24. Ibid.

25. Ibid.

26. 'The Request for Comprehensive Schools...' op. cit.

27. Of course, these are not the only important differences. The DES itself is by no means in uniform agreement about educational policy, HMI often presenting an important source of polite but firm dissent in this respect (Salter & Tapper 1981).

28. Letter from Clegg to L.R. Fletcher, Schools Branch, Ministry of Education, 15.5.63.

29. In this sense, Clegg is clearly what David (1978) calls an 'educator' rather than a 'conciliator'.

30. An important question worth pursuing however is that these limits while having a powerful economic component, may not be entirely constituted by factors to be located within the mode of product-

ion. Feminist writers, for instance, have pointed to the limits to educational change set by patriarchal relations (e.g. McDonald, 1980) and it would be difficult to conduct a research project in Northern Ireland without being aware, possibly on pain of death or serious injury, of the limits to change set down by religious factors (e.g. Jenkins, 1981). These problems are currently unresolved in the sociology of education, but a serious treatment of them must lead us not only to reassess our understandings of educational change, but also to place in honest doubt the superior explanatory power of Marxist analysis even at this level. On this matter, my own position is not yet resolved.

BIBLIOGRAPHY

Adams, P. (1978) 'Social Control or Social Wage: on the political economy of the 'welfare state'.' Journal of Sociology & Social Welfare Vol. 5.
Archer, M. (1979) Social Origins of Educational Systems, Sage, London.
Barker, P. (1972) Educational Politics, 1900-51: a study of the Labour Party, Oxford University Press, Oxford.
Batley, R., O'Brien, O. and Parris, H. (1970) Going Comprehensive, Routledge & Kegan Paul, London.
Bell, R. (1981) 'Institutions of Educational Government', Unit 8, E200 Contemporary Issues in Education, Open University, Milton Keynes.
Bellaby, P. (1977) The Sociology of Comprehensive Schooling, Methuen, London.
Bidwell, C. (1968) 'The School as a Formal Organization' in March, J.G. Handbook of Organizations, Rand-McNally, Chicago.
Bourdieu, P. and Passeron, J-C (1977) Reproduction: in Education, Society & Culture, Sage, London.
Bowles, S. & Gintis, H. (1976) Schooling in Capitalist America, Routledge & Kegan Paul, London.
Bryan, K. and Hardcastle, K. (1977) 'The Growth of Middle Schools: educational rhetoric & economic reality'. British Journal of Educational Administration & History, January.
Bryan, K. and Hardcastle, K. (1978) 'Middle Years & Middle Schools: an analysis of national policy', Education 3-13, Vol. 6, No. 1.

Carr, E.H. (1964) What is History?. Penguin, Harmondsworth.

Centre for Contemporary Cultural Studies (CCCS) (1981) Unpopular Education, Hutchinson, London.

Coates, D. (1975) The Labour Party & the Struggle for Socialism, Cambridge University Press, Cambridge.

Cockburn, C. (1977) The Local State, Pluto Press, London.

Collins, R. (1977) 'Some Comparative Principles of Educational Stratification'. Harvard Educational Review, Vol. 47, No. 1.

Collins, R. (1979) The Credential Society, Academic Press, New York.

Corrigan, P. (1979) Capitalism, State Formation & Marxist Theory, Quartet Books, London.

Dale, R. (1981) 'The State & Education: some theoretical approaches', Unit 3, E353, Society, Education & the State, Open University, Milton Keynes.

Dale, R. (1982) 'Education and the Capitalist State: contributions and contradictions' in Apple, M. (ed.) Cultural & Economic Reproduction in Education, Routledge & Kegan Paul, London.

David, M. (1977) Reform, Reaction & Resources, NFER, Windsor.

Doe, B. (1976) 'The End of the Middle', The Times Educational Supplement, 28 September.

Edwards, A.D. (1980) 'Schooling for Change: function correspondence & cause' in Barton, L.; Meighan R. & Walker, S. Schooling, Ideology & the Curriculum, Falmer Press, Lewes.

Edwards, R. (1972) The Middle School Experiment, Routledge & Kegan Paul, London.

Esland, G. (1981) 'Education & the Corporate Economy', Unit 2, E353, Society, Education & the State, Open University, Milton Keynes.

Finn, D; Grant, N. and Johnson, R. (1977) 'Social Democracy, Education & the Crisis' in Centre for Contemporary Cultural Studies. On Ideology Working Paper 10.

Giroux, H. (1981) Ideology, Culture & the Process of Schooling, Falmer Press, Lewes.

Glennester, H. and Hoyle, E. (1976) 'Educational Research and Education Policy', Journal of Social Policy, Vol. 1, No. 3.

Gosden, P.H.J.H. and Sharp, P.R. (1978) The Development of an Education Service: the West Riding 1889-1974, Martin Robertson, Oxford.

Gramsci, A. (1971) Selections from the Prison Notebooks, Lawrence & Wishart, London.

Habermas, J. (1976) <u>Legitimation Crisis</u>, Heinemann,
    London.
Halsall, E. (1971) <u>Becoming Comprehensive</u>, Pergamon,
    London.
Hargreaves, A. (1980) 'The Ideology of the Middle
    School' in Hargreaves & Tickel. op. cit.
Hargreaves, A. (1982) 'Resistance & Relative Auto-
    nomy Theories: some problems in Marxist
    sociology of education', <u>British Journal of</u>
    <u>Sociology of Education</u>, Vol. 3, No. 2.
Hargreaves, A. (forthcoming) 'Marxism Revisited:
    Resistance & Relative Autonomy Theories', Unit
    23, E205, <u>Conflict & Change in Education</u>,
    Open University, Milton Keynes.
Hargreaves, A. and Hammersley, M. (1982) 'CCCS Gas:
    politics & science in the work of the Centre
    for Contemporary Cultural Studies', <u>Oxford</u>
    <u>Review of Education</u>.
Hargreaves, A. and Tickle, L. (1980) <u>Middle Schools:</u>
    <u>origins, ideology & practice</u>, Harper & Row,
    London.
Hindess, B. (1980) 'Marxism & Parliamentary Demo-
    cracy' in Hunt, A. (ed.) <u>Marxism & Democracy</u>,
    Lawrence & Wishart, London.
Howell, D. (1976) <u>British Social Democracy</u>, Croom
    Helm, London.
James, P.H. (1980) <u>The Reorganisation of Secondary</u>
    <u>Education</u>, NFER, Windsor.
Jenkins, D. et. al. (1981) <u>Chocolate, Cream,</u>
    <u>Soldiers: final evaluation report on the</u>
    <u>Rowntree Schools Cultural Studies Project</u>, New
    University of Ulster Education Centre.
Jessop, B. (1978) 'Capitalism & Democracy: the best
    possible political shell?' in Littlejohn, G.
    et. al., <u>Power and the State</u>, Croom Helm,
    London.
Jessop, B. (1979) 'The Transformation of the State
    in Post-War Britain' in Scase, R. (ed.) <u>The</u>
    <u>State in Western Europe</u>, Croom Helm, London.
King, R. (1980) 'Weberian Perspectives and the Study
    of Education', <u>British Journal of Sociology of</u>
    <u>Education</u>, Vol. 1, no. 1.
King, R. (1982) 'Organizational choice in Secondary
    Schools' <u>British Journal of Sociology of</u>
    <u>Education</u>, Vol. 3, No. 1.
Kogan, M. (1975) <u>Educational Policy-Making</u>, Allen
    & Unwin, London.
Kogan, M. (1978) <u>The Politics of Educational Change</u>,
    Fontana, London.
Lawton, D. (1980) <u>The Politics of the School</u>
    <u>Curriculum</u>, Routlege & Kegan Paul, London.

McDonald, M. (1980) 'Schooling and the Reproduction of Class and Gender Relations' in Barton, L. & Walker, S., Schooling, Ideology and the Curriculum, Falmer Press, Lewes.

Marsden, D. (1971) 'Politicians, Equality and Comprehensives', Fabian Tract 411, Fabian Society, London.

Marsh, C. (1973) 'The Emergence of the English Middle School', Dudley Journal of Education, Vol. 1, No. 3.

Marsh, C. (1980) 'The Emergence of Nine-Thirteen Middle Schools in Worcestershire' in Hargreaves & Tickle, op. cit.

Mason, S. (1964) The Leicestershire Experiment and Plan, Council and Education Press, London.

Parkinson, M. (1970) The Labour Party and the Organization of Secondary Education 1918-1965, Routledge & Kegan Paul, London.

Peschek, D. and Brand, D. (1966) 'Policies and Politics in Secondary Education', Greater London Papers No. 11, London School of Economics.

Poulantras, N. Political Power and Social Classes, New Left Books, London.

Riseborough, G. (1981) 'Teacher Careers and Comprehensive Schooling: an empirical study', Sociology Vol. 15, No. 3.

Robinson, P. (1977) Education and Poverty, Methuen, London.

Salter, B. and Tapper, T. (1981) Education, Politics and the State, Grant McIntyre, London.

Saran, R. (1973) Policy Making in Secondary Education: a Case Study, Oxford University Press, Oxford.

Scase, R. (1980) The State in Western Europe, Croom Helm, London.

Seaborne and Lowe, R. (1977) The English School: its architecture and organisation 1870-1970, Routledge & Kegan Paul, London.

Silver, H. (1980) Education and the Social Condition Methuen, London.

Stone, J.A. (1978) 'The Age of Transfer', in Department of Education and Science, Comprehensive Education - report of a conference held at the invitation of the Secretary of State for Education and Science, University of York.

Tapper, T. and Salter, B. (1978) Education and the Political Order, McMillan, London.

West Riding Yorkshire Education Committee Reports (1975) The Organization of Comprehensive Schooling in Certain Areas of the West Riding.

Whitty, G. and Young, M. (1976) <u>Society, State and Schooling</u>, Falmer Press, Lewes.
Williams, R. (1976) <u>Keywords</u>, Fontana, London.
Williams, R. (1978) <u>Marxism and Literature</u>, Oxford University Press, Oxford.
Wright, E.O. (1979) <u>Class, Crisis and the State</u>, New Left Books, London.

3. AN ELITE TRANSFORMED: CONTINUITY AND CHANGE IN 16-19 EDUCATIONAL POLICY

A. D. Edwards

INTRODUCTION

After the immediate post-war onslaught on selection had subsided, the Times Educational Supplement published a celebratory survey of the grammar school sixth form in which the brilliance of 'this most precious jewel in the crown of English secondary education' was attributed to a unique combination of 'rigorous intellectual discipline through the medium of advanced academic studies and practical training in adult responsibility' (TES 1949). It was at this stage that the benefits of 'selection by differentiation' were most clearly displayed, the ablest pupils being carried forward to higher education and the professions.

The formal and informal processes of selection which produced those benefits were severe. Even ten years later, at the time of the Crowther Report '15-18', less than 40% of those who had been judged capable of 'academic studies' stayed on in the sixth form, and only 12% of 17-year olds were involved in any form of full-time education. The Committee's own approval of the traditional sixth form was qualified by its concern at the inadequacy of all the alternatives. The few pages describing the emergence of less academic 'sixth forms with a difference' were a realistic reflection of their rarity. Opportunities for part-time education and training were described as being erratically distributed across the country, too confined to the training of skilled male workers, and too dependent on the whims of employers. Worse still, the great majority of those aged 15-18 were receiving no education at all. Progress towards a more efficient and more equal society demanded the raising of the school leaving age to 16, a marked increase in voluntary staying on, and compulsory part-time education for young workers in revised versions of the county colleges which had been envisaged in the 1944 Act. 'Morally and materially, we are compelled to go forward...If we are to build a higher standard of life, and if we are to have higher standards in life, we shall need a firmer educational base than we have today' (Central Advisory Council 1959, pp.3-5).

Crowther hoped that by 1980, half of all 17-year olds would be receiving full-time education. That target has not been achieved, and the admitted difficulties of making international comparisons only blur the edges of an obvious gap in age-participation rates between this country and almost all its industrial competitors. But it is the meagreness of the total provision for post-compulsory education which represents the real failure of Crowther's aspirations.

Table 1: Proportion of 17-year olds receiving full- and part-time education

	1957-58 Boys	1957-58 Girls	1979-80 Boys and Girls
Full-time at school	11	9	18
Full-time non-advanced FE	2	2	9
Part-time (day) FE	25	6	16
Employed without part-time day education, or unemployed	72	83	57

Note: a. The 1979-80 figure includes those on YOP programmes.

Sources: Central Advisory Council, 15-18 (HMSO, London, 1959), p.7; Parliamentary Answer April 30, 1981, cited in the Labour Party, 16-19: Learning for Life (London, 1982), p.12.

While its title at least reflects the raising of the school leaving age (some years later than Crowther had intended), the Macfarlane Report on 'Education for 16-19 Year Olds' (1981) offered a bleak commentary on the hopes of its predecessor.

It noted a still 'urgent need' to provide more vocational training for those entering work at 16,
continued to deplore the low rates of day-release
(especially for girls), and was forced to comment on
if not confront the problems of that growing minority 'without work or immediate prospect of work'.
Youth employment on the present scale could not have
been envisaged by Crowther, though it recognised
that competition for jobs within a rapidly rising
population of young workers was becoming more intense. That Report was published when the post-war
'bulge' in the birth-rate was already affecting
secondary schools, and its recommendations had to
take account of an imminent 30% increase in the
number of 16-year olds. It was also able to refer
to an already established 'trend' to longer school
life which had been causing sixth forms to grow by
about 6% a year. 'Bulge' and 'trend' were about to
coincide in a society apparently prepared to increase its investment in education because wider
access to general and specific qualifications was
accepted as being beneficial to both national and
individual prosperity (pp.45-53). Its successor
was an altogether meaner document. Although published when the number of 16-19 year olds was
reaching another peak, the Macfarlane Report was
produced in the hope of coordinating LEAs' responses
to an imminent 30% fall in the age-group and of re-
considering 'the institutional basis of their provision'. Nor was the drop in numbers likely to be
offset by any trend towards longer periods of schooling. Indeed, there had been a 'falling-back' in
full-time participation. Where the whole tone of
the Crowther Report had been expansionist,
Macfarlane's keynotes were rationalisation, resource-
management and cost-effectiveness.
     Much of this chapter too will be concerned with
different approaches to the rationalisation of 16-19
provision. But there is also a view of the scope
of that provision in which the two Reports at least
superficially concur. While neither offers a single
institutional solution to the problem of reconciling
a sufficient diversity of courses with an avoidance
of wasteful duplication, both refer repeatedly to
the importance of blurring the boundary between
Schools and Further Education. That 'gradual but
substantial' convergence between them which
Macfarlane describes was already becoming apparent
in 1959. So was the need for 'new style' and
'practical' courses for the less academically-
inclined 'new sixth formers' (the terms are all

Crowther's). Both Reports express concern at the limited scope and quality of vocational (especially technical) education, and at the extreme difficulty of winning esteem for any radical departures from traditional academic courses. The resulting deficiencies and inequalities have recently been identified as the main betrayal of comprehensive reorganisation, and attributed to the consistent priority given to 'middle class sixth formers in grammar and private schools who then enter higher education to take academic degree courses' (Labour Party 1982, p.5). As a demonstration of resistance to the traditional order of priorities, that Labour Party discussion document begins with the half of the age-group who have suffered a 'long history of neglect'. My own account, however, will follow the actual chronology of policy preoccupations, beginning with arguments about how the academic sixth form could be broadened, and ending with proposals for a comprehensive 'tertiary' stage of education and training.

AN ACADEMIC ELITE AND A SPECIALISED CURRICULUM

The provision for post-compulsory education which Crowther judged to be so inadequate was highly traditional in form. Those seeking academic courses oriented towards higher education entered a sixth form, and most who did so simply stayed on in the grammar school in which they had spent the previous four or five years. Those wanting more directly vocational training went to further education colleges, normally as part-time students. The two routes were distinct in organisation and almost entirely distinct in content. The great majority of the age-group followed neither.
     In Crowther's view, it was 'the education of our brightest children' which the English system did best (p.472). As the Head Masters Association had pointed out in its memorandum to the Committee, the proper function of the sixth form was to train pupils of high ability 'for a particular type of career by means of a particular type of course' (TES 28 December, 1956). Since that 'type of career' was in government, management and the professions, and since the social survey carried out as part of Crowther's enquiry indicated that over 60% sixth formers had fathers who had themselves left school at the earliest possible age, it could be argued that the sixth form represented most clearly those opportunities for the advancement of the able which the grammar school had made accessible to all.

Crowther's own list of the 'essential marks' of a sixth form displayed the conventional view of an academic elite being prepared for higher education and high-status occupations through the intensive study of a few subjects. But it was followed by a question - whether such a model might not be 'a luxury of the past...a privilege which cannot extend beyond the leading schools...which cannot of its nature be generalised' (pp.222-225).

As I have argued elsewhere, the grammar school sixth form never had that homogeneity of capacity and purpose so often and nostalgically ascribed to it (Edwards, 1982; 1970, ch. 3 and 7). Despite its own elite definition of the 'essential' sixth form, the Crowther Committee was forced to add to already longstanding complaints that many pupils were forced into the unsuitably narrow mould of 'study in depth'. Twenty years later, the proportion of maintained school pupils staying on had risen from 8% to 18%, and a growing minority of them lacked the conventional academic passport of 4-5 O-levels (e.g. Taylor, Reid and Holley, 1974, p.14). Taken together, these facts surely indicated something other than 'a training ground for a narrow and clearly defined band of professions', and made it necessary to 'radically revise a former generation's concept of the sixth form as being almost entirely composed of scholars moving forward to University' (Schools Council 1972). Yet the normal pattern of sixth form studies described by Crowther remains remarkably intact. Of those who stay two years, 95% take two or three A-level subjects, and almost three-quarters of the entries are in the same nine subjects which produced some 80% entries in 1960 (English, French, History, Geography, Economics, Mathematics, Physics, Chemistry and Biology/Zoology). While the range of subjects is certainly wider, only 6% of all 1979 entries came from the 'modern' list of subjects like business and computer studies. Study in depth is still likely to be complemented either by General Studies as an additional qualification, or by general studies likely to be offered and received as a distraction from the serious business of achieving high grades at A-level. Of the 25-30% staying on who can certainly be characterised as 'non-traditional' sixth formers, the great majority leave after one year having found few courses devised to match their 'modest 16+ examination achievements' and few 'intermediate' qualifications to lure them on (Dept. of Education & Science 1980). The Government's declared intention of abandoning the

Certificate of Extended Education, though still strongly challenged, leaves still more uncertain what should be provided 'between' A-level and either specific or unified vocational preparation. Some schools are certainly experimenting with pre-vocational education, and with the general components of TEC, BEC and City and Guilds courses. But while the expansion of FE into 'academic' territories once reserved for schools has been both rapid and extensive, there has been relatively little movement the other way. It is not only the 'new' sixth formers who suffer the consequences. A considerable minority of those who stay two years leave without higher qualifications. From a credentialist perspective, they may be disadvantaged in competition for jobs with their contemporaries, having neither accredited knowledge nor experience to offer possible employers (Barker 1974).

It can be argued that the sixth form curriculum illustrates with particular vividness a general failure to reconstruct the content of secondary education as its organisation has been transformed. Although the curriculum implications of defining sixth formers by age rather than as supposed members of an academic elite were given a high priority in the early programme of the Schools Council, that 'variety in breadth and depth' called for in Working Papers 5 (1966) and 16 (1967) is hardly planned, yet alone achieved. While the justification for this diversity is often taken as obvious, the obstacles to its achievement seem rather less so. Indeed, recent proposals for Normal and Further 18+ examinations, and especially the DES suggestion of a free-standing Intermediate-level, display a considerable insensitivity to the fate of their predecessors, that of being devalued as an evident second-best in a context still seen in predominantly 'academic' terms (Drake and Edwards 1979; Edwards 1982).

A main obstacle to any radical reshaping of the post-16 curriculum has been the fact that staying-on remains such a minority experience. There is nothing resembling that 'mass' move forward to an upper-secondary stage (or the substantial further move to higher education) which occurs in many comparable countries (Cerych and Colton 1980; Halls 1982; Haywood 1979). In 1959, it was easy to regard 70,000 sixth formers in maintained schools as the ablest of an already selected intake. The 300,000 sixth formers of 1979 were much more difficult to categorise. Yet it was apparently still

possible to ignore their substantial 'fringes' and
so continue to regard sixth forms as being essentially the selective route to highly selective forms
of higher education. For example, the universities'
rejection of N and F as a preparation for degree
work rested on assumptions that two-year sixth
formers were 'reasonably homogeneous' in aspiration
and had interests largely 'coincident' with their
own (Schools Council 1980, p.29). Similarly, the
schools' response expressed concern that a necessary
broadening of the curriculum should not be achieved
by abandoning those 'real' standards of academic
achievement of which A-level had served as custodian.
     These responses are obviously much more than
institutional inertia. The continued predominance
of degree courses which by international standards
are both unusually specialised and unusually short
has seemed to justify counting back from what
universities require of their entrants. Despite the
post-Robbins growth and the rapid expansion of
alternative forms of higher education, entry to
those courses has remained so competitive that universities need apparently objective information on
which to base their selections from within the ranks
of the qualified. Inclusion has therefore continued
to depend on reaching prescribed levels of performance in a few subjects, the selectors' normal
emphasis being on traditional subjects traditionally
assessed (Reid 1972; Edwards 1982). While critics
have complained that all sixth formers suffer from
the consequent over-specialisation, their main concern has been for that majority even among 'traditional' sixth formers who are unlikely to take a
degree course of any kind. Yet as in other countries, demands to separate university selection from
the provision of a more generally appropriate
'superior' leaving certificate have to recognise
the inter-relationship of these functions (Hearnden,
1973; McPherson and Neave, 1976). If it is misleading to regard the minority of 'scholars moving
forward to University' as representing the 'true'
function of that stage of secondary education, it is
also important not to exaggerate the extent to which
many others have been dragged unwillingly in their
wake. The power of A-level as a multi-purpose credential has maintained the pressure on schools not
to select by differentiation, and reduced the
pressure to find more general and more directly
vocational alternatives. The Macfarlane Committee
called for a 'stronger public commitment' from
employers to the 'relevance' of courses with a

'strong pre-employment character' as a necessary
condition for their development (pp. 16-18). What
many employers recruiting at 18+ have done is to
treat A-level results in much the same way as the
universities do - either as direct evidence of
educationally-created skills or as indirect evidence
of persistence or ambition (Drake and Edwards, 1979).
Given the strongly calculative view of staying-on so
often expressed by sixth formers and their parents
(King 1976, pp.27-8; Dean, Bradley, Choppin and
Vincent, 1979, pp.125-42), there has been an understandable reluctance in the schools to limit access
to those opportunities associated with A-level.
Certainly Neave's (1975) study failed to show any
consistently larger provision of general and 'practical' courses in comprehensive schools, though he
found evidence of more systematic provision of
'second chance' qualifications for 'new' sixth
formers in those schools which were new, mixed and
'egalitarian' in ethos.

Compared with the continuing hold of 'study in
depth', such provision remains slight. But there
are now reasons however for expecting it to increase. Growing doubts about the value of A-level as
a many-sided predictor of 'trainability' are part of
a larger scepticism about the benefits of being
qualified. While recognising the lure of high
wages to many youngsters, the Crowther Committee
(p.47) felt able to assert both a steady trend towards attesting special skills before entry to
employment and the increasing value placed on general qualifications. It then seemed apparent that
'education pays, always in the long run and often
quite quickly'. That confidence has been greatly
eroded by a spectacular increase in youth unemployment which has placed even the 'qualified' in
jeopardy, and has seemed to enhance the value of
specialised training for specific occupations
(Holland, 1979; Dean et al, 1979, pp.252-63). Such
credentials are much more easily found in Further
Education. Thus the present Government both insists
on the need for more vocationally-oriented courses,
especially for 'young people of broadly average
ability with modest examination achievements at 16+',
and seems to find in FE (and in the work of the FE
Curriculum Review and Development Unit) the appropriate models for them (Department of Education and
Science 1980).

Commenting on differences between comprehensives of different types, Neave (1975) suggested that
'structural changes' were more likely to bring inno-

vations in sixth form provision than were more direct attempts to reshape the curriculum. It is
certainly doubtful whether grammar schools catering
for 'the ablest pupils in a stratified society'
could have introduced radically different forms of
curriculum at what was their <u>most</u> selective stage
(Macfarlane, 1978, p.6). It is also understandable
that many otherwise 'egalitarian' comprehensives
seem to have regarded their sixth forms as requiring
more 'meritocratic' treatment (Taylor et al, 1974,
pp.121-5; King, 1976). The recent and rapid blurring of the boundary between the schools and Further
Education may therefore be an organisational change
with potentially much greater impact on the sixth
form curriculum than the transition from selective
to non-selective schools, even though the immediate
justification for challenging their long-established
separation may be a more mundane concern with the
'economical' use of resources. Thus the vocationalising of CEE proposed by the Keohane Committee was
rejected by the DES as insufficient. Preference was
given to a combination of more general 'Intermediate'
courses to complement A-level and one-year courses
of unified and specialised vocational preparation
for students 'of modest 16+ examination achievements' who would enter work a year later (DES 1980).
The vocational courses should be available in colleges and schools, but their form and validation
would follow the FE pattern.

THE RATIONALISATION OF POST-COMPULSORY SCHOOLING

My own short history (1970) of the impact of changes
in scale and scope on traditional assumptions about
the sixth form ended with a tentative prediction
that the years 16-18 might become 'a natural third
stage of education'. In the same year, the Exeter
LEA introduced its organisationally radical solution
to the problems of accommodating that third stage.
As part of a comprehensive plan, all sixth form
teaching in the city's two maintained grammar schools
was to be transferred to the College of Further
Education. I have begun with this earliest example
of a tertiary college because what has often been
advocated as the logical last step in comprehensive
reorganisation was then given a severely utilitarian
justification, as the most effective way of combining 'a wide choice of courses with economy of means'
(Edwards, 1970b; Webster, 1974, pp.42-51; King 1976,
pp.130-35). The Authority's lack of educational
commitment to a comprehensive tertiary stage, and

perhaps some doubts about the academic consequences of its own creation, were evident in its 1973 decision to take up sixth form places in the city's two direct-grant schools for selected pupils 'fit to follow A-level courses in three subjects'. That escape route disappeared with the city's disappearance as a separate LEA, and the comprehensiveness intended from the outset by the College's principal is available for its present 4000 full- and part-time students in the form of 37 A-level subjects (including Business Studies, Computing and Design and Technology) with a wide choice of vocational and general courses (O'Connor 1980).

It is claimed that such diversity is only possible through a concentration of post-16 provision in specialised institutions (MacFarlane, 1978; Janes and Miles, 1979). I want to return briefly however to less recent and radical proposals. Advanced work has never been more than a thin topsoil in most secondary schools (it is worth recalling that the typical sixth form in the 1930s was unlikely to have more than thirty pupils altogether), and there has been a striking consistency in the arguments against spreading that topsoil too thinly. For example, the introduction in 1917 of special grants for advanced courses was accompanied by warnings from the President of the Board of Education (H.A.L. Fisher) that a choice of courses could only be offered within each 'area of accessibility' because of the short supply of subject specialists. Over sixty years later, the Macfarlane Committee was still deploring the practice of counting the A-levels available in individual schools. What mattered was the number 'accessible in the area', and it was essential to avoid 'a scatter of small sixth forms offering an inadequate range of options at high cost' (p.15 and 36). The response of headteachers to Fisher's 'areas of access' was to foresee a loss of able teachers, status and morale from these schools forced to surrender their academic elite, while a 1922 policy statement by the Assistant Master's Association called for every grammar school to be 'so equipped as to provide to the age of 18 in all branches of the curriculum' (Edwards, 1970a, pp. 14-15). Fifty years later, a more local plan to coordinate provision was eliciting similar objections from the heads of schools threatened with 'beheading'. An ILEA working party report (1969) on 'Sixth Form Opportunities' commented on the frequent lack of opportunities, especially in the 1/4 of the Authority's secondary schools which had fewer than

thirty sixth formers. It proposed the temporary
concentration of all advanced work in some areas in
a single school, common provision between pairs of
schools, and longer-term arrangements for consortia
of up to four schools with their sixth form curriculum and teaching coordinated by a single Director of
Studies. Fears were immediately expressed that some
comprehensive schools would then lapse back into
secondary moderns, and that the elimination of
A-level work in main subjects would depress their
status and intake and remove that academic influence
which even a small sixth form could exert (TES 31
January and 4 July 1969). Then and since, the
'obvious' case for avoiding duplication and providing a reasonable breadth of subject-choice has been
countered by references to the material and less
tangible advantages of developing advanced work, and
to its significance as a touchstone of a school's
worth. As a TES editorial remarked (21 November
1980), taking up a reference from the paper's
archives, it is not possible to 'spend eighty or
ninety years making the sixth form the jewel in the
crown of secondary education...without creating a
strong professional assumption that every school
should have one'.

Despite frequent references in debates over
comprehensive reorganisation to the size of non-
selective intake needed to support a viable sixth
form, there is no doubt that sixth forms have
tended to emerge 'in default of a positive decision
to the contrary' (Wilcock, 1977) and that most comprehensives have been intended to provide (at least
eventually) 'to the age of 18 in all the main
branches to the curriculum'. There is no doubt
either that many have failed to do so. The following table indicates what proportion of maintained
schools in 1978 failed to meet various numerical
tests of viability.

Such criteria usually reflect a mixture of
economic and educational considerations. Small
sixth forms are said to consume too large a share of
their schools' resources, and to deny those schools
and their Authorities economies of scale. A national average staff-student ratio of 1:10 conceals
wide variations between schools (and is itself
significantly lower than at equivalent levels in
FE). Even where the 'advanced' curriculum extends
no further than the eight 'mainstream' subjects
which continue to produce over 70% A-level entries,
serious staffing problems arise from a general unwillingness to move from class-teaching as the core

Table 2: Size of Sixth Forms in Maintained Schools 1978 with Some Pupils Studying at A-level or Beyond

Total numbers below	11-18 Comprehensives % (n=1585)	13/14-18 Comprehensives % (n=476)	Grammar School % (n=319)
50[a]	26	17	4
100[b]	63	49	29
200[c]	89	88	86
300[d]	99	98	99

Notes:

a. Criterion adopted by the ILEA Working Party on 'Sixth Form Opportunities (1969).
b. The preferred minimum suggested by Mrs Shirley Williams to 'provide an adequate range of courses without uneconomic staffing or at the expense of the rest of the school', House of Commons, 18 April 1978.
c. Criterion suggested by Alec Peterson for The Sixth Form of the Future (Routledge, 1973).
d. Minimum suggested by R. Wearing King in his advocacy of The English Sixth Form College (Pergamon 1968).

Source of figures: Secretaries of State for Education and Science and for Wales, Providing Better Opportunities for 16-18 Year Olds, Department of Education and Science, April 1979.

of instruction, and from the consequent assumption that each subject demands a normal allocation of 5-7 teaching periods each week. Despite a passing reference to more use of 'tutorial methods' to off-set the disadvantages of small sixth forms, the Macfarlane Committee's conclusion was that 'educational considerations point strongly though not without exception towards the concentration of 16-19 pupils and students into large groups' (Report, p. 28), those considerations including the need to avoid classes too small to offer their members sufficient mutual stimulation, and to provide a reasonable choice from 12-16 A-level subjects.

It should be clear that in discussions of viability, priority may be given to the rational use of resources or to opportunity or to their inseparabi-

lity. Before turning to the currently compelling
constraints of resource-management, I want to indicate some considerable uncertainties even in an
overtly opportunity-view. When the Croydon LEA
proposed in 1954 what would have been the first
sixth form college, heavy emphasis was placed on the
impossibility of matching the academic opportunities
available in the Borough's independent schools with
the 'lamentably amateurish' sixth form provision
scattered through the public sector. Reflecting on
the failure of the plan in which he had been closely
involved, Wearing King (1968, p.122) reinforced his
list of the 'almost overwhelming logistic arguments'
for it with a reference to the folly of offering
'pre-University work as a kind of luxurious extra
with an inadequate number of pupils, inadequate time
and inadequate resources'. Similar arguments have
been used on behalf of sixth form consortia, and
especially of sixth form colleges (Dawson, 1980;
Macfarlane, 1978). Opposition to them is too easily
dismissed as a display of vested interest by teachers. As even the Macfarlane Committee recognised,
there is no 'proven connection' between A-level
successes and the size or selectivity of the post-16
unit, while the whole preoccupation with the results
of an academic minority can itself be dismissed as
institutionalised inertia. In defence of continuity,
it has been argued that working-class pupils are
especially likely to need the guidance of teachers
who know them well, and the visible example of even
small numbers staying on (Clark and Eavis, 1980;
Semmens, 1981). In defence of a break at 16, the
attractions of a move to a more 'adult' environment
may be even greater for pupils especially likely to
have become 'incurably tired of school' (Crowther
Report, p.422). Yet despite inferences from DES and
HMI statistics that separate post-16 provision
'tends to increase participation' (Macfarlane
Report, p.30), it is advisable to recall the failure
of the NFER team (despite its declared preference
for tertiary colleges as being 'more closely attuned
with the mood of today's 16-19 year olds') to discern any consistent effects on decisions to stay on
of either a break at 16 or of the particular organisational alternatives available (Dean et al, 1979).
In its reflections on various ways of 'Providing
Educational Opportunities' for this age-group, the
DES consultative paper (April 1979, pp.4-5) was able
to do no more than suggest that consensus had been
reached on some critical but still unanswered questions, for example about the diversity of academic

and vocational courses which should be available and
the minimum size for viable teaching groups. The
answers themselves would have to be obtained 'within
the discipline imposed by limited resources'.

It was the increasing discipline imposed on
LEAs by falling rolls and still more rapidly diminishing financial resources which led to the formation of the Macfarlane Committee. Its task was to
report on common problems which it would be inefficient for LEAs to face in isolation. Those problems
can be illustrated from two of the older metropolitan areas where rolls are falling especially far and
fast. In 1979, there were 719 sixth formers in
Newcastle's twelve comprehensive schools, and an
LEA consultative document was already indicating 556
'unused' places. Six of the city's schools had
fewer than 100 in the sixth form, 48% of all its
sixthformers were being taught in groups smaller
than five, and staff shortages in some subjects were
acute. It was 'already difficult to describe what
is on offer in some schools as genuine sixth form
education'; it was also difficult to balance the
benefits of retaining it against the costs in larger
classes and restricted curriculum options in the
main school. A tertiary college solution to these
problems would have been favoured 'given a completely clean slate', but the technical college had only
recently been reorganised and there were powerful
arguments against further upheaval. A proposal for
two sixth form colleges was strongly supported by
some LEA officials, but was opposed both by those
resistant to the beheading of schools and by some
Labour Party denunciations of such colleges as
elitist. The eventual solution to reduce the
number of schools to ten, but to retain sixth forms
in each - a solution which would still leave six of
them with projected sixth forms in 1990 of fewer
than a hundred. In Manchester, fiercer controversy
was roused by a more radical response to an even
greater problem. The number of children born within
the city fell from 13,600 in 1962 to only 5660 in
1978, and the expectations of a trend to longer
school life which had accompanied comprehensive reorganisation had been strikingly unfulfilled. Some
schools were recruiting only half the number of
sixth formers they had been intended to take, two-
thirds of all A-level groups had fewer than six
students, and the existing low numbers were expected
to decline by a further 40% by 1994. Informal pressure on schools to cooperate had achieved little,
and the LEA's response to 'the logic of the situa-

tion' was to propose the closure of sixth forms in all its schools, and their replacement by three sixth form colleges which would have close links with Further Education and which it was hoped would evolve into fully-fledged tertiary colleges (Tomlinson, 1980).

The DES response to the Manchester plan was eagerly awaited because it was ahead in time of, for example, Birmingham's plans for sixth form colleges, Sheffield's and Croydon's for tertiary colleges, and the ILEA's for more extensive rationalisation after an initial reduction in the number of 11-18 schools. Apparently siding with the parental pressure groups which had formed to 'save the sixth forms' in the large academically-oriented comprehensives in the southern suburbs, Sir Keith Joseph's rejection of the plan insisted that 'only in exceptional circumstances can it be right to reduce good schools from 11-18 to 11-16'. In doing so, he was contradicting the Macfarlane Committee's overt support for treating 16-19 provision 'as a totality', though he was perhaps expressing that commitment to sixth forms which many commentators discerned within the Committee and to which they attributed a delay in its appearance while conclusions too favourable to tertiary colleges were being qualified into blandness. A more general justification for rejecting the plan was a scepticism about all 'doctrinaire' solutions to the admittedly grave problems presented by rapidly falling rolls (Ranson and Walsh, 1982). It is doubtful whether either Labour-controlled Manchester or Conservative-controlled Croydon whose tertiary scheme was also rejected, would admit that they were doing more than establish the most 'rational' form of 16-19 provision. Yet 'doctrinaire' policies in Sir Keith's sense are not hard to find.

PROSPECTS OF A COMPREHENSIVE TERTIARY STAGE

Even if the empirical cases for and against competing policies had been less uncertain, 16-19 provision would still have attracted overtly 'normative' theory i.e. theory about phenomena defined by the values and objectives of the investigator (Horton, 1966). Beyond the frame of reference constituted by disputes over the reality of economies of scale or the relative costs of retaining sixth forms in schools, sixth form colleges have been defended as the most effective means of retaining and broadening 'academic' provision (Dawson, 1980). They have been attacked as 'error institutionalised' because they perpetuate the separation of study from work, the 'academic' from the 'vocational' (Judge, 1980). Tertiary colleges have seemed to threaten the sub-mergence of the expressive, community-oriented and 'liberal' values associated with schools in the more instrumental, associational and 'utilitarian' envir-onments of Further Education (King, 1976). They have been defended as the only way of avoiding a mere delay in the processes of educational and social selection. Those who see 16+ as 'the most significant educational frontier' are less likely to do so because of urgent decisions about allocat-ing resources than because they wish to see the 'logical' completion of comprehensive reorganisation (Benn, 1978). The required blurring of traditional boundaries between full-time students on 'academic' courses and part-time workers on 'practical' courses may be sought in a single type of tertiary institu-tion for which fourteen somewhat assorted models now exist. But given the variety of local circumstances, and the often entrenched positions of the sixth forms and colleges which they would replace, it might seem more realistic to accept a continued organisational diversity within a comprehensive system in which all barriers to cooperation between institutions would be steadily removed. The neces-sary conditions for such a system, however, include finding ways of combining functional diversity with parity of esteem and transforming the traditional view of substantial 16-19 education as being only appropriate to or possible for a minority.

Within the traditional boundaries of post-16 provision, there have been persistently close con-nections between socio-economic status and distinct educational channels. Sociological mapping of the distribution of 'opportunity' has long shown a strong tendency among middle-class pupils to follow extended academic tracks, and among working-class pupils to leave school as early as possible or to enter part-time further education (Halsey, Heath and Ridge, 1980). Even from an emphatically meritocratic perspective, it has to be recognised that the post-Robbins expansion of universities brought no significant increase in the proportion of working-class students, that it seems recently to have fallen, and that the increasingly severe com-petition for places as higher education contracts is likely to diminish it still further (Halls, 1982). Those working-class pupils who stayed on into the sixth form had already survived a long process of attrition, and evidence that the main wastage of ability occurred before or at the point of entry to that stage made it 'strange that maintenance allowances for sixth formers have been the cinderella of the grants system'. Financial need 'may be only one reason for early leaving, but it is more easily visible and more easily remedied than most' (Edwards 1970a, p.65). It was not until 1979 however that allowances for full-time study 16-18 were proposed by a Labour Government, to be introduced experimentally in areas where unemployment was especially high and age-participation rates low. Even that cautious trailer for a more extensive scheme was abandoned at the change of government. While the Macfarlane Committee recognised that the prospect of supplementary benefit and even more of the YOP training allowance might well lure many 16-year olds from full-time education, it declined to speculate further on possible relationships between grants and participation-rates because of the evident impracticality of any widespread provision.

As was suggested earlier, claims that school environments as such may deter working-class pupils from staying on have to be balanced against egalitarian arguments for continuity, and also against the likelihood that differences in ethos between organisational categories may be less than those within them. And while there is certainly evidence that Further Education has been less socially selective than post-16 schooling (Schools Council, 1970, Vol. 1, p.66 and Vol. 2, p.27; Dean et al, 1979, pp.125-42; Halsey et al, 1980, pp.178-86), those effects are slight compared with the close association between socio-economic status and all forms of post-16 provision. Two-thirds of the variation between LEAs in age-participation rates 'can be explained statistically by a simple linear relationship with a measure of social class' (DES 1979, p.4), and the range extended 1976-7 from 8% - 29% in maintained schools and from 5% - 16% in non-advanced FE. Nor did one form of provision compensate for another. In many inner-city Authorities, high rates of school leaving (and of leaving without formal qualifications) were accompanied by low rates of day-release. Overall, more than half of those aged 16-18 from working-class backgrounds receive no education at all or nothing beyond the training offered to the young unemployed.

I began this chapter by recalling the Crowther Committee's concern for the 'majority without education'. Any realistic review of post-compulsory schooling since that time has to recognise a con-

tinuing emphasis on the needs of the 'academic'
minority and, beyond them, on the training of tech-
nicians and craftsmen. It is likely, however, that
a similar review written in ten years time would
begin with successive Governments' proposals for
vocationalising a significant part of 16-19 education (DES 1979a; 1979b; 1980), and with the introduction in 1978 of the Youth Opportunities
Programme. Longstanding concern for those who
sever all connection with the education system at
16 has been massively reinforced by alarm at their
'unpreparedness' for work and by even greater alarm
at a more than threefold increase 1979-81 in the
numbers of young unemployed. The result has been
the first large-scale attempt in this country to
treat the years 16-18 as being primarily a period
of training.

    As with the occasional coincidence of pragma-
tism and principle in support of tertiary colleges,
so an even larger coincidence may be discernible in
recent proposals for a comprehensive tertiary stage
in which all would have a common status of trainee
whether they were full-time at school or college,
being trained as they worked, or being prepared for
work. For the increasing minority 'without education' who are also without work, an Opportunities
Programme intended as a temporary measure of limited
scope enlisted its millionth trainee in September
1981 and is expected to have catered for some
550,000 in the year ending April 1982. Yet the
Macfarlane Committee's brief reference to its rapid
expansion at a time of educational contraction is
matched by even briefer 'educational' references in
two major publications by the Manpower Services
Commission (1980; 1981). In an account of 16-19
provision written from a broadly educationist perspective, the Programme can only appear as a formi-
dable late challenge to traditional preoccupations.
It has certainly encouraged emphatically normative
analyses and predictions. Does it represent a
belated but necessary diversion of resources to a
large and previously neglected minority, or a per-
petuation of old divisions between 'education' and
'training'? Of those school leavers involved in the
Programme 1979-80, 55% had no formal qualifications
(compared with 20% in the whole age-group), and
their involvement has therefore been seen as an
attempt to educate through work experience a group
who had previously been largely cast adrift (MSC
1981). The Programme has also been attacked, not
only as an evasion and partial concealment of

structural unemployment, but also as a further betrayal of the victims of a history of neglect who
are now offered a bleak diet of 'social and life
skills' and of 'preparation for work' designed to
fit them still more rigidly into the remaining
niches in unskilled and semi-skilled employment
(Baron, Finn, Grant, Green and Johnson 1981, chapter
11).

A proposal common to the 'realism' of the
MSC's (1981) insistence on learning for work and
to the 'radicalism' of the Labour Party's (1982)
emphasis on 'learning for life' is that all those
aged 16-19 should have the status of trainees. The
Labour Party document is especially insistent on the
statutory obligations of LEAs and employers to provide comprehensive educational opportunities, and
on trainees' rights to the same allowances 'regardless of attainment and background' (p.17). It is
less clear about the obligations of the young to
use those opportunities than is the Government's
own proposal (December 1981) to replace Youth
Opportunities by 1983 with a compulsory one-year
Youth Training Scheme for all unemployed 16+ school-
leavers. That proposal can again be interpreted as
an educationally unprincipled response to politically unacceptable levels of unemployment, or as a
further belated move to the kind of tertiary
training stage available in other industrial countries. Any optimism that this will complete or even
extend the 'logic' of comprehensive reorganisation
must depend on how the 'broad foundation of generic
skills and knowledge' relevant to vocational preparation is defined in practice, and on whether the
'common' status of trainee can place on any 'equal
footing' the long-separated categories of students,
trainees, workers and 'unqualified' searchers for
work.

REFERENCES

Barker, G. (1974) 'Career Prospects' in R. Watkins
    (ed), The New Sixth Form, Ward Lock, London,
    pp.40-49.
Baron, S., Finn, D., Grant, N., Green, M., and
    Johnson, R., (1981) Unpopular Education:
    Schooling and Social Democracy in England
    since 1944, Hutchinson, London (in collabora-
    tion with the Centre for Contemporary Cultural
    Studies).

Benn, C. (1978) '16 to 19: Wanted - a New Will',
    Forum 21, 5-11.
Central Advisory Council for Education (England)
    (1959) 15 to 18, HMSO, London.
Cerych, L. and Colton, S. (1980) 'Summarising recent
    student flows' European Journal of Education
    15, pp.15-33.
Clark, M. and Eavis, P. (1980) 'The Urban Comprehen-
    sive School', Durham and Newcastle Research
    Review 9.44, 104-6.
Cox, A. (1980) 'The Grammar School Sixth Form',
    Durham and Newcastle Research Review 9.44, 98-
    103.
Dawson, K. (1980) 'The Sixth Form College' Durham
    and Newcastle Research Review 9.44, 93-7.
Dean, J., Bradley, K., Choppin, B., and Vincent, D.
    (1979) The Sixth Form and Its Alternatives,
    National Foundation for Educational Research,
    Windsor.
Department of Education and Science (1979a) A Better
    Start in Working Life, Consultative Paper
    presented by the Secretaries of State for
    Employment, Education and Science, Industry,
    Scotland and Wales, DES, London.
Department of Education and Science (1979b)
    Providing Opportunities for 16-18 Year Olds,
    Consultative Paper presented by Secretaries of
    State for Education and Science and for Wales.
Department of Education and Science (1980) Examina-
    tions 16-18, Consultative Paper presented by
    the Secretaries of State for Education and
    Science and for Wales, DES, London.
Drake, K. and Edwards, A. (1979) '18+ Examinations:
    Innovation without Change' Educational Studies
    5.3, 217-24.
Edwards, A. (1970a) The Changing Sixth Form,
    Routledge and Kegan Paul, London.
Edwards, A. (1970b) 'Exeter's Sixth Form Solution',
    New Society 23 July, 151-2.
Edwards, A. (1982) 'Specialisation under Constraint:
    the Universities and the Sixth Form Curriculum'
    in O. Anweiler and A. Hearnden (eds)
    Sekundarschulbildung und Hochschule (From
    Secondary to Higher Education), Bohlau Verlag.
Further Education Curriculum Review and Development
    Unit (1979) A Basis for Choice: Post-16 Pre-
    Employment Courses FEU, London.
Further Education Curriculum Review and Development
    Unit (1980) Signposts: A Map of 16-19 Educa-
    tional Provision, FEU, London.

Further Education Curriculum Review and Development Unit (1981) Vocational Preparation, FEU, London.

Halls, W. (1982) 'Access to University: Educational Policy and Cultural Considerations', in Anweiler and Hearnden (eds), Sekunderschulbildung und Hochschule.

Halsey, A., Heath, A., and Ridge, J. (1980) Origins and Destinations: Family, Class and Education in Modern Britain, Clarendon Press, Oxford.

Haywood, R. (1979) 'Recent Reforms in the Organisation and Curricula of Norwegian Secondary Schools' Comparative Education 15, 123-42.

Hearnden, A. (1973) Paths to University: Preparation, Assessment, Selection, Macmillan, London.

Holland, G. (1979) 'More than Half our Future: 16-19 Year Olds in Employment', Oxford Review of Education 5, 147-56.

Horton, J. (1966) 'Order and Conflict Theories of Social Problems as Competing Ideologies', American Journal of Sociology 71, 701-13.

Janes, F. and Miles, J. (1979) Tertiary Colleges, Tertiary College Panel, Bridgwater.

Judge, H. (1980) 'Education at 16', Paper given at the North of England Education Conference 3 January 1980.

King, R. (1976) School and College: Studies of Post-16 Education, Routledge and Kegan Paul, London.

King, R. Wearing (1968) The English Sixth Form College, Pergamon, London.

Labour Party (1982) 16-19: Learning for Life, Labour Party Discussion Document, London.

Macfarlane, E. (1978) Sixth Form Colleges, Heinemann Educational, London.

Macfarlane, N. (Chairman) (1981) Education for 16-19 Year Olds, Review undertaken for Her Majesty's Government and the Local Authority Associations, HMSO, London.

McPherson, A. and Neave, G. (1976) The Scottish Sixth, NFER, London.

Manpower Services Commission (1980) Outlook on Training: Review of the Employment and Training Act 1973, MSC, London.

Manpower Services Commission (1981) A New Training Initiative, Consultative Document, MSC, London.

Neave, G. (1975) How They Fared: The Impact of the Comprehensive School upon the University, Routledge and Kegan Paul, London.

O'Connor, M. (1980) 'The College of All the Talents' Guardian 2 December, p.11.

Peterson, A. (1973) The Future of the Sixth Form, Routledge and Kegan Paul, London.

Ranson, S. and Walsh, K. (1982) 'For the Greater Good of the Few', Guardian 12 January.

Reid, W. (1972) The Universities and the Sixth Form Curriculum, Macmillan, London (Schools Council Research Studies).

Schools Council (1970) Sixth Form Survey: Vol.1 Sixth Form Teachers and Pupils; Vol. 2 Students in Full-Time Courses in Further Education, Schools Council Publications, London.

Schools Council (1972) 16-19: Growth and Response (Working Paper 45), Evans/Methuen, London.

Schools Council (1978) Examinations at 18+: the N and F Studies (Working Paper 60), Evans/ Methuen, London.

Schools Council (1980) Examinations at 18+: Report on the N and F Debate (Working Paper 66), Methuen, London.

Semmens, G. (1981) 'A Member's Response to 16-19 Reorganisation', Journal of the Socialist Educational Association 8.2, 18-19.

Taylor, P., Reid, W., and Holley, B. (1974) The English Sixth Form: A Case Study in Curriculum Research, NFER, Windsor.

Times Educational Supplement (1949) 'The Sixth Form in Grammar Schools', TES pp. 481, 523 and 585; also published as a separate pamphlet.

Tomlinson, H. (1980) 'How Manchester came to Accept the Tertiary System', Education 21 November, pp.482-3.

Webster, J. (1974) 16-19: the Educational Explosion, Exeter University School of Education Themes in Education No.33.

Wilcock, R. (1977), 'Co-operation or Separation', TES 4 November.

4. EDUCATION AND LOCAL GOVERNMENT IN THE LIGHT OF CENTRAL GOVERNMENT POLICY

Colin Hunter

INTRODUCTION

The present contraction in pupil and student numbers and the squeezing of economic resources available, in nursery through to higher education, is particularly painful in a service which since the Second World War has experienced expansion in all areas.
   This paper looks at the managerial and education problems which accrue in schools due to the effect of the cutbacks in public spending of Central Government policy. It particularly encompasses the effects of the changing power position and structure of Local Authorities. Theirs is an uncomfortable mediating position for, on the one hand, they try to absorb Central Government financial constraints while on the other they attempt to retain some autonomy in the level of services offered to their electorate. Their problem can be encapsulated in the fact that since 1974 their share of public expenditure has gone down by 16% while Central Government spending has risen by 7%.
   Education is the major spending service of Local Authorities and it is at the forefront of being affected by decisions made at Whitehall or City Hall which, as resources become more scarce, are being based increasingly on political rather than educational criteria. Some of the possible positive and negative consequences of this trend are discussed at the end of the paper.

SCHOOLS, TEACHERS AND CUTS

I suggest elsewhere (Hunter, 1981) that 1974 is a suitable date to mark the commencement of a significant shift in the definition of the career of teach-

ing and the place of the educational system in our
society. Due to such events as the oil crisis and
the rise in inflation, there slowly emerged in the
Labour Government policy a shift to containing
public expenditure and positive support for industry.
The twin goals of justice and efficiency presented
by Anthony Crosland in the previous Labour administration in his advocacy for comprehensive schooling
became increasingly telescoped into the goal of
efficiency in the Great Debate.

The present Conservative Government took this
trend even further, spurred by its ideological
commitment to monetarism and the need to regenerate
the wealth-producing sector in order to finance more
securely the public service expenditure. However,
it could be argued that the present Government has
reversed the post-war political consensus that there
should be some positive attempt to make Britain a
more equal society by redistributing wealth through
a graded tax system and welfare state services, in
that the balance of both has tilted to accentuate
even more the difference between the richest and
poorest in society.

The cutback in real terms of public expenditure
has severely affected the education services to the
extent that basic requirements are often at risk.
In May 1981 Northamptonshire and Surrey parents
challenged the Education Minister as to whether the
education service offered to their children via the
Local Authority was able to fulfil the requirements
of the 1944 Education Act. In October later that
year, a Peterborough Head advised parents that he
believed the school was now operating illegally
under the 1944 Act because it could not provide the
books and equipment to maintain required educational
standards.

While these may be celebrated media cases, they
reflect a growing concern about the resources available to schools. It is also a reflection of the way
that Local Authorities have approached the management of implementing the cuts. Even in the
Comprehensive School debate there had been a broad
political consensus between Labour and Tory Councillors that education was 'a good thing' and that
changes in school organisation under their juris-
diction was based on educational rather than political criteria. When the necessity for cuts came,
there was no political basis for the prioritising of
where they should be located. There tended to be an
incremental cutting back over the whole budget by
officers, with the agreement of Councillors - a

holding operation to maintain the whole service until
better times re-emerged. However, except for a
modest up-turn in the pre-election year of 1978, as
the availability of funds became tighter and the
room for manoeuvre more restricted, Local Authorities
were forced to identify priorities for cuts on political rather than educational criteria. This process of education moving from a politically neutral
managerial service to one being dependent on overt
political decisions is clearly demonstrated in the
Officer Service Plan, Bradford Directorate of
Educational Services (December 1981).

> Unlike most other services, educational
> services are used by practically everybody
> in the District - rich and poor, able and
> less able, theatre-goer and remedial learner,
> squash player and city teenager. What we
> have largely done over the past few years is
> simply to trim and prune, still trying to
> keep all the services going. The result is
> that practically all the services are worse
> and we are feeling the public pressure
> about the cuts from parents in economically
> advantaged areas as well as unemployed
> teenagers who cannot get good grants to do
> further education...Some action can be taken
> within the Directorate itself. We are now,
> and will go on, re-directing our own
> resources and pursuing efficiency savings
> to release money for use in other areas.
> Re-direction takes time, but be under no
> illusions. A 're-direction' usually means
> a cut somewhere - in standards, or in a
> service, or in a part of the District. And
> internal re-direction can only go so far.
> Ultimately, there has to be an overall
> political decision by the Labour Group. An
> answer to the question 'What is your strategy
> for Educational Services in the future?'

Perhaps this appeal identifies the culmination of
possible exercises that can be done with trimming
the whole range of the budget, and shows the critical period education is entering into if cuts are
to be extended further, for since 1974 there has
been extensive surgery in both staffing and resources. With regard to staffing, there have been many
ways found of slimming down the teaching force without resorting to compulsory redundancies, and inci-
dentally avoiding large redundancy payments. This

is often done by voluntary or compulsory redeployment and is closely connected with the issue of falling roles and a strict observance of pupil/teacher ratios. If a school is over-staffed then those willing to move are encouraged to do so, often with help with travelling expenses incurred because of the move and with undertakings of security in their new school. Where no one volunteers, there is the necessity in many Authorities for the Head with Governors and advisers to nominate who will become compulsorily redeployed. Having been involved as a Chairman of Governors in this exercise I can testify to its effect on the morale of staff rooms - particularly in smaller schools. There is also the problem that other schools look with some suspicion on those teachers who are asked to leave their previous school in that it is thought that they may be one of the weaker members of that school. There were some teachers who not only had the stigma of being asked to leave, but have not been accepted by any other schools where vacancies had occurred. Such a policy therefore may save money by making internal appointments within the Authority, though would cause   great problems of insecurity and lack of morale among staff, and prevent new blood coming into the Authority.

Another policy for slimming down staff numbers and saving money is that of early retirement in that DES regulations allow Local Authorities to retire teachers over the age of 50, with up to 10 years' enhancement of their pension rights. In practice, because of the expense involved, few will allow teachers to retire until 55, or even 59 or 60. An aspect of financial gain to the administrators of this policy is that if the teachers are replaced by younger teachers then they are cheaper to employ.

Again, some Authorities have instituted large in-service schemes, particularly where there are schools which have over-establishment; nine-tenths of their salary is paid by the DES during their secondment, thereby saving the Local Authority some money. One Authority, for example, supplemented this policy by raising the First School pupil/teacher ratios from 28:1 to 29:1 in order to take out more teachers who are in service and not have to replace all of them because of the higher teacher/pupil ratio, thereby saving money. In this volatile financial climate, many Authorities have extended the temporary appointment policy so that if the need arises they could be shed from the staffing without redundancy payments being necessary. This in turn creates great problems in the management of schools and the pupils do not get the continuity of teaching, and Headmasters claim there is a lack of commitment in staff who do not see any long-term career prospects at the school.

The important point, however, is that all the above staff trimming policies can no longer be relied on to reduce the size of the teaching force as fast as the Government requires. A confidential DES Report leaked to the Guardian (1/9/81) calculated that between January 1981 and January 1984 there would have to be a loss of 43,000 teachers if the Public Spending White Paper targets of 1981 are to be achieved without breaking Government commitments to increase spending per pupil on books and equipment by 2% per year. Of these teachers, it is calculated that 10,000 might have to be made compulsorily redundant as well as pupil/teacher ratios raised. Given that these figures may be too high for implementation at operational levels within the identified timescale, the probability remains that many teachers are to be made compulsorily redundant given the present Government policy. Having exhausted the possibilities of the trimming mechanisms, education officers then turned to the politicians to legitimise necessary but unpopular steps.

This process is mirrored in school closure policies. The Bradford Educational Service Plan says:

> We have all seen the reaction to, for instance, threatened school closures, from the public, parents and the Government and the feelings that changes in grass cutting policy has produced. If we are to face the problems and make even more radical decisions about the future of our services, it will call for strong nerve and not a little resolve, together with solid and sustained political backing for our officers. (1982)

The resources available to schools are also under pressure. Headteachers of upper schools in Bradford in a special report - Education Cuts, Financial Support, September 1981 - highlighted the declining purchasing power of capitation.

> The increase has been smallest over the last four years, from 1978 to 1981; for lower school pupils the rate has risen from £16 to £18.70, an annual increase of 4.2%,

and for post sixteen the increase has been
from £22.50 to £27.60 at an annual rate of
4.5%. In real terms since 1975 there has
been a decline of at least 27% in spending
capacity, with a higher figure over the last
four years. Over the same period, general
price inflation has been in the order of 200%.
(p.1)

After specifying in detail problems that now accrue
in the practical areas of teaching they conclude -

A 13 year old entering an Upper School now
will find fewer adults, poor maintenance of
the fabric, inadequate furniture and a
restricted curriculum. There will be less
practical work, fewer games activities, no
books to take home, less stimulation in
lessons and fewer contacts with the community.
The examination courses to be encountered may
well be inappropriate and the preparation for
them less thorough than expected. This most
unsatisfactory state of affairs is to be
expected with the completely inadequate level
of capitation averaging considerably less
than 10p a day per pupil, and much of that
diverted to non-class purposes. (p.4)

Detailed information could be given regarding the
difficulties of nursery education which remains
a marginal service reaching only 20% of three to
four year olds; or student grants (up to 4% for
1982-83 which is a 6% below the Government's own
estimate of inflation for that time period); or
universities (average cuts of 15% in 1982-83, though
administered unequally between institutions, e.g.
34% for Salford, 7% for York); and the public sector
higher education (cuts of 6½% in real terms 1982-83
on the 1980-81 actual expenditure).
        All of these reductions are strains which the
educational service is now experiencing and often
can be directly linked to the present Conservative
policy as reflected in their economic policy.

PRESENT GOVERNMENT ECONOMIC POLICY UNDER DEPARTMENT
OF THE ENVIRONMENT

The reasoning behind the educational cuts is a
reflection of the interpretation of Government policy by the Department of the Environment. Indeed,
this is one of the key Government areas in which

public expenditure has to be held back, to the
extent that it could be argued that it is the
Department of the Environment, not the DES, which is
making the decisions with regard to education.

The Government has always had some degree of
influence over Local Authority spending in that the
greatest percentage of relevant expenditure has come
from the Rate Support Grant. However, since the
1980 Local Government Planning and Land Act (No. 2),
the trend of Government intervention in Local
Authority spending has reached a quite different
qualitative level which threatens the traditional
constitutional relationship between Central and
Local Government by transforming the financial
framework and which directly affects education as
the largest service spender.

The extent of the cuts has meant that Councillors are afraid that the Government's determination
to curb local spending will soon mean that they will
be no more than agents of Central Government and
unable to put into practice local programmes on
which they were elected. There is a conflict betwe-
en Central Government's wishes and local democracy;
an impasse between two elected bodies in which one
has greater and growing power over the other. For
example, since 1975-76 to 1981-82, the total Central
Government spending has gone up by 8% while Local
Authority spending has decreased by 21%. (See
Association of County Councils, 1982)

It is a conflict which is being enacted at the
centre of the political stage and is mirrored by
diametrically opposing rhetorics. For example, the
Minister of the Department of the Environment, Mr.
Heseltine, described in the House of Commons (Times,
3.6.81) the new and projected legislation as creating 'an environment of freedom subject to national
policy' and 'a vindication of the tradition of
voluntary co-operation between Central and Local
Government to ensure that Local Government expenditure as a whole remains within what the national
economy can afford'(Guardian, 4.9.81).

These are countered by the Shadow Secretary
for the Environment (Mr. Gerald Kaufaum) claiming
that 'all the 456 Councils will become the puppets
dangling from the strings of Whitehall' (Guardian,
12.11.81) while Mr. Jack Smart, Chairman of the
Association of Metropolitan Authorities talks of
the shackling of Local Government (Guardian, 17.12.
81).

The principle behind the new legislation is
that Local Authorities must act reasonably - but the

87

definition of reasonableness is shifted away from
the concept of the rates being an element of the
social wage which redistributes wealth through expenditure on services to that of efficiently administering those services in a cost effective way to a
quite different level of adequacy·than was envisaged
in the post-war development of the welfare state.
Ken Livingstone, the GLC leader, put it succinctly after the loss in the House of Lords of the
principle of the right to subsidise transport fares.

> The decision shifts the whole balance of
> every decision in Local Government, massively,
> against expenditure. It takes us back to the
> '20s. Since the Second World War, both
> parties have accepted that Local Government
> is there to provide a substantial part of the
> services of the welfare state. Now the law
> lords have affirmed, in straight language,
> their primary duty is to the relationship
> like that between directors of a company and
> shareholders. It is to make the least expend-
> iture and the best profit. Services are
> secondary. Now that changes the whole atti-
> tude of Local Government since I was borne.
> (Guardian, 21.12.81)

This rationale is repeated in the knowledge of the
Council house sale case where Mr. Heseltine, under
the powers of the 1980 Housing Act, sent agents to
sell the houses because the Council had been too
slow in satisfying tenants' purchase rights. This
action was upheld by Lord Denning (one of the bus
fare law lords), though he described the intervention as 'a very drastic action' and went on to
say that 'this default power enabled Central Government to interfere with a high hand over Local
Authorities. Local Government is such an important
part of the constitution that, to my mind, the
Courts should see that the power of the Government
is not overused' (Guardian 10.2.82). Jack Smart
blames the lack of consultation between Central and
Local Government leading to the intolerable situation of too many issues decided in the Court while
Professor John Griffiths (1981) says that neither
Judges nor Parliament has established the principle
of administrative law regulating when Judges should
not overturn the decision of bureaucrats and politicians so that the whole thing has become a dis-
graceful lottery and much may depend on which
Judges happen to hear the cases. So we have the

case of the Merseyside fares Court decision being different to the London one (a different interpretation of a different Act) and Camden successfully took the Department of the Environment to Court for clawing back grant under the 1980 Act without consultation.

These current events mirror the great tension and uncertainty in the Central and Local Government relations which is directly mirrored in the DES policy and in the cash limits that Local Authorities have to meet in educational spending. The greater control of the expenditure is encapsulated in the 1980 Local Government Planning and Land Act No. 2 and in the proposed Local Government Finance No. 2 Act currently at Committee stage (March 1982).

Basically, the 1980 Act defines in a more precise way than ever before what Local Authorities should spend. The total exchequer grant still includes (a) specific grants (13.2% of total 1981-82) for police services, urban programmes, Commonwealth immigrants, probation and after care, Magistrates' Courts and improvement grants; (b) supplementary grants (3.8% of total in 1981-82) for transport and national parks and (c) domestic rate relief grant (6.4% of 1981-82 total) which is a grant to relieve the burden on domestic ratepayers while allowing Local Government spending to increase. This element has been decreasing as a total of the Rate Support Grant from 9.4% in 1975-76 to 5.7% in 1982-83.

By far the largest element is the block grant (76.6%) and it is this around which most of the controversy lies, for one of the main aims is to control Local Government spending. There are four main concepts involved in understanding the block grant - grant related expenditure; grant related poundage; volume targets and penalties, and these are interlocked in a complicated system.

GRANT RELATED EXPENDITURE

The basic building blocks are the assessments made by Civil Servants of what each Council needs to spend to provide a standard level of service. It is built up by analysing unit costs of each Local Authority service and the number of 'clients' receiving the service and making allowance for factors such as the size, type and sparsity of population.

Over half (53%) of the GRE is based on educational need calculations. These include -

1) Nursery Education:

The number of children under 5 in the Authority x
unit cost. The unit cost is derived by dividing the
national assumed nursery expenditure by the national
total of the children under 5. This favours such
Authorities as Oxfordshire which has no nursery
education provision.

2) Schools - Primary and Secondary:

Based on the latest statistics of pupil numbers.
The assessment assumes that 15% of pupils nationally will have such special educational needs. Of
the 1.8% in each educational Authority are assumed
to require education at a unit cost $4\frac{1}{2}$ times the
average ordinary school pupils. The number of the
remaining 13.2% at 1.5 x the usual unit cost is
related to a number of socio-economic factors, which
is derived from the estimated number of children in
each Authority who are - (a) born outside UK or
belong to non-white ethnic groups; (b) living in
households whose head is a semi-skilled manual
worker; (c) living in a household lacking exclusive
use of standard amenities or occupational density is
greater than 1.5 persons per room; (d) in one parent
families with dependent children; (e) in families
with four or more children, and (f) receiving free
school meals.

3) Schools - pupils over school leaving age

4) Adult Education

5) Number having free school meals:

All of these are based on total numbers in the
Authority.

6) Non-advanced Further Education:

This is weighted according to whether the students
are on laboratory or classroom based courses, under
or over 19, from home or overseas.

7) Advanced Further Education:

Equals the contribution to the AFE pool.

8) Youth Service:

Half is determined by the total population 11-17 in
each area and the other half allocated on the special needs indication used for the socio-economic
factors in the GRE for schools.

The rest of the GRE total is calculated on
Housing, Social Services and other services using
similar indicators. It can be seen that the basis
of the allocation is relatively crude and does not
take into account the level of spending or priority
given to services previously; nor to the extent of
the particular, as opposed to broad, special needs
of districts. When it is taken into account that
the total GRE had already been formulated, based on
what the Government felt they could afford in the
present economic circumstances, i.e. the needs were
retrospectively made to fit the total, it is not
surprising that the GRE represented a cut for the
majority of Local Authorities.

The relationship between the GRE and what an
Authority actually decides to spend determines its
grant related poundage (GRP). This increased as an
Authority's total expenditure grows in relation to
its GRE. For example, if an Authority decides to
spend more than 10% above its GRE, the schedule of
GRP becomes steeper. That is, ratepayers have to
pay more towards each pound of spending beyond the
10% threshold. This is done to discourage spending.
We therefore end up with an equation: block grant =
total expenditure - (GRP x rateable value).

If this were the end of the story, it would be
a great relief to many people (including, I am sure,
the reader). An additional feature in the above are
multipliers which when applied can (and do) penalise
Authorities which overspend current expenditure
targets. Another feature is the 'close ending' of
the grant. If the total claims exceed the amount
available as defined by the Government, it reduces
the allocations to each Authority by a common percentage or a common rate poundage - another constraint on the Local Authorities concerned.

However, as the 1981/82 planned Authority
spending became known, it was evident that this
block grant system had failed to control Local
Government spending. To add to the confusion, the
Government introduced another target in January
1981, only one month after the Rate Support Grant
settlement based on GREs. This was that Authorities
should cut their current expenditure to 5.6% below
its out-turn spending in 1978-79 (the inflation
since that time was taken into account). This tar-

get was in many respects more achievable to many
Councils than the first calculation of GREs. It was
based on a different price base, a different definition of spending, and starting from a quite different point. Because Authorities overspent both GRE
and volume target, some (notably GLC, Merseyside and
West Midlands) had some of their grant held back
although the total Council expenditure still remained above the Government's required level. In 1982-
83, this hold back is calculated within the block
grant so that Councils know what the shortfall will
be from the beginning of the finance year; and
again there are two targets - GRE and volume target,
though it is the higher of the two that is the target accepted by the Government.

Added to this in 1982/83 budgeting is that the
percentage of grant to rates falls from 59.1% to
56%; that they assume a 6% rise in wages and a 9%
for inflation, and a fall in special grants for
housing subsidy has to be made up by a £2.50 rise
in Council rents. On top of all this is the threat
of the 1982 Local Government Finance Bill (No. 2).
Originally, this was to involve referenda before
levying supplementary rates and 'super hold backs'
of rate support; but after opposition from all
parties it now simply makes it illegal from 1982-83
to levy supplementary rates.

Part 2 of the Bill introduces greater explicit
powers to vary the block grant entitlement of individual Authorities. The other main strand of the
Bill is a reform of Local Government audit. A new
Audit Commission will be established 'to bring new
strength and impact to Local Government audit and
to contribute substantially to improving the efficiency of Local Authorities'. Understandably,
Local Authorities are worried about losing the right
to appoint their own auditors. Labour Councils are
particularly concerned that auditors may be encouraged to challenge spending decisions which they
believe are entirely political in character.

The powers, therefore, which the Government has
added to itself in the last two years to reduce
Local Authority expenditure are extensive and complex. The tighter the grip on the spending, the less
flexibility Local Authorities have in their allocation of resources. In the first section of this
paper we have already seen some of the outcomes at
the school level of the financial arrangements at
national level described in this section. It is also
mirrored in the policy decisions made by the DES in
that standards are required to be maintained while

resources are cut back. One of the consequences
that stems from this is that as the real levels of
resources go down, more and more decisions are based
on political priorities. We are therefore seeing
the growing politicalisation of education as a consequence of more intensive politicalisation of the
Central and Local Government relationship. The
resultant educational policy, stemming from this
economic policy, is now considered.

PRESENT EDUCATION POLICY

There is some tension between the Conservative 1979
Manifesto promise of raising standards in education
and the effect of cuts. The White Paper The
Government's Expenditure Plans 1981-82 to 1983-84
of March 1981 states:

> The Government remain committed to the
> objective of maintaining and improving the
> quality of education. In the present economic
> situation, it has however been necessary to
> restrict the aggregate level of public expend-
> iture on all services including education to
> what the country can afford at the present
> time. The Government accept that this will
> have some impact on educational provision but
> believe that Local Authorities and their other
> partners in education will wish to secure the
> maximum educational value for money within
> the substantial resources which will continue
> to be at their disposal: and to ensure that the
> quality of education offered to all children
> and students reaches the best standard possible,
> so that it can serve as the foundation for
> further educational development and improve-
> ments, not all of which need more resources.

Sir Keith Joseph at Leeds in January 1982 was more
explicit in relating economic priorities to educational policy. He said:

> There is a balance to be sought between the
> level of public spending on the one hand and
> the implications in terms of tax levels and,
> other things being equal, interest rates and
> inflation on the other. If Ministers were
> to accept continuing growth in real spending
> on education then there would be higher
> taxation and/or higher interest rates than
> if they did not. The higher taxation and/or

> the higher interest rates would damage the
> trading base and reduce the number of jobs
> that directly and, in the public sector for
> which it largely pays, indirectly, it supports.

He concluded on the basis of this judgement (of
what the country can afford) that assessments of
grant related expenditure on education represent a
fair distribution of expenditure among Local
Education Authorities.

The effects of this in expenditure terms in
education for 1982-83 were presented to the House of
Commons on 21 December 1981 by the Education
Secretary. He basically said that current expenditure on schools is to fall by 3½% between 1978/79
and 1981/82 and 6½% between 1978/79 and 1983/84
while pupil numbers are falling by 7½% and 13% over
the same period. The implied reduction of 700,000
places by 1983/84 will cause some redundancies.
Savings on school milk and meals services should be
used to protect more essential services such as
books and equipment. The planned contraction of
Higher Education up to 1984 is to be maintained and
capital expenditure on education to fall from
£536 million to £479 million. (See Education,
1.1.82)

Much of the above is a reflection of the spending patterns allowed for in the Rate Support Grant
already discussed. One of the major elements involved is the savings calculated for the effects of
falling rolls for grant is reduced on the assumption
that the surplus places will be in fact taken out.

The DES Circular 2/81 (June 1981) Falling Rolls
and Surplus Places asserts that the total school
population in England and Wales is 'likely to fall
from a little under nine million in 1979 to eight
million by 1983, with the prospect of a further fall
to below seven and a half million before the end of
the decade'. The estimates they work on (using
'bench marks' of surplus space as 3.7 sq. m. gross
area per Primary place and 6.5 sq. m. gross area
for Secondary places) are three million surplus
Primary and Secondary places by 1986. Taking into
consideration local variables and eventual up-turn
in school population, 1.3 million should be removed
by 1986. Sir Keith Joseph's revised plans however
have fallen from 700,000 to 470,000 surplus places
removed by March 1983 to make allowances for the
fact that only 230,000 have been removed by March
1982.

This again mirrors some of the difficulties that Local Authorities experience in having to fulfil Central Government requirements which are mirrored in grants, though the fulfilling of the requirements are often very difficult at the local level in political and/or educational and/or community grounds. The Circular calculates that every 100,000 surplus school places should, on average, yield savings approaching £10 m. - excluding any savings on teachers' salaries. These savings are necessary in order that 'a better range of educational provision be made for the pupils...and the money saved can be put to more effective use in meeting important educational needs' (page 2).

Both Education Secretaries, Mrs Shirley Williams and Mr. Mark Carlisle, had followed the premise that if staffing follows precisely the fall in pupil numbers in the school there would be damage done to the curriculum and allowances were therefore made for this. As we have seen in the calculation of GRE, the latest calculations assume a pro-rata drop. In school terms, this means that as number drops there may not be sufficient class hours to provide for minority subjects - or that school numbers of staff adjust themselves by natural wastage, putting at risk a balanced curriculum. It is coming to the point in some schools that if the constraints on staff/pupil ratios continue then in order to keep a balanced or full curriculum vital specialist staff may have to be replaced at the same time as other members of the school staff are made to be redeployed - or made redundant.

There is too the great problem of a community backlash to the closing of schools which the Local Authority has to face. The Circular 2/81 states that:

> The Secretary of State recognises the problems, political and practical, involved in closing schools. He appreciates that proposals for closure almost invariably arouse opposition... but he intends to play his part in the common task of bringing home to the general public the very real benefits that can arise from taking places out of use (p.2).

This has not always been reflected in any quickening of school closures being processed through the DES - and there are examples of the DES succumbing to influential pressure in refusing to close some schools Local Authorities had deemed necessary to

fulfil the DES demands (Powys and Bradford are two
examples which come immediately to mind).

There is, however, a more insidious contradiction within the recent DES policy decisions which
give rise to some fears of greater central control
over school policy which overrides the wish for
savings due to surplus places being taken out of the
system. It involves particularly the reorganisation
of the Secondary systems of Manchester and Croydon.

Manchester particularly was faced with rapidly
falling rolls. In 1966 there were 12,600 children
but by 1980 this had fallen to 5,400. The Authority
calculated that in 1982 there would be surplus
capacity amounting to 77 old forms of entry - equivalent to eight schools. So as to maximise the
opportunities for all 16 year olds, they decided on
one uniform system throughout the city, having to
take into account that the staying-on rate had not
grown as anticipated, and the size of most sixth
forms had become worryingly small. Although some
of the larger schools (11-18) would have been able
to sustain their own sixth forms, many others would
not and many were in fact borrowing from the lower
school to sustain a range of options in the sixth
form. After a great deal of public consultation,
the final decision that there should be a break at
16 and an evolutionary solution of sixth form colleges consulting with the city's FE colleges was
approved. This was in line with the 1980 Education
Act (Sections 12-16) which suggests that, where
possible, the determination of plans should be
produced locally.

However, the Secretary of State for Education,
Sir Keith Joseph, rejected the plan and supported
a minority interest of some of the parents of three
schools in the largely middle class south of the
city. He wrote:

> The Secretary of State is not satisfied that
> on balance the potential educational advan-
> tages...for the majority of pupils are
> sufficiently certain to justify the damage
> which will be done to some schools which have
> proved their worth...only in exceptional
> circumstances can it be right to reduce good
> schools from 11-18 to 11-16.

This decision immediately had an impact on the Tory
controlled Croydon Education Authority which was
waiting for the Manchester proposals to be passed
before submitting their own tertiary college system

proposals to replace school sixth forms, which was subsequently also refused. It was argued by the DES that the new 11-16 schools proposed would be too small to offer an appropriate curriculum and sufficient teaching groups without much more generous pupil/teacher ratios, and a novel and untried tertiary system raised doubts about the ability of the Education Authority to maintain educational standards.

The immediate effect was that Croydon was faced with extra costs from September 1982 unless an alternative system could be rushed through. The longer term effects are more insidious. No specific criteria as a basis for reorganisation to secure the withdrawal of surplus places had been given in Circular 2/81. David Hart, General Secretary of the National Association of Head Teachers, immediately commented (Guardian 8.2.82) 'Sir Keith is now proposing new ground rules which means that his personal views about the way schools should be organised would take preference over plans best suited to individual local circumstances'.

By siding with particular local interests against an elected Authority, the Secretary of State undermines that Authority and therefore it could be argued diminishes the responsibility of Local Government. It is an example of 'centralism' with the DES or Government taking on more responsibility and negating local decisions when it suits them. It could be argued that Local Authorities are being made publicly accountable, though it seems that public accountability and central political control need not be synonymous in a school system which, though publicly controlled, must be professionally operated at the local level.

Ransom & Walsh (1982) argue that the 'mushroom' system whereby some schools feed into the sixth forms of others is the most inequitable of all systems which seems to be favoured by the Secretary of State in that it could be interpreted to be an attempt to create first and second class schools.

> Clearly the Secretary of State...believes
> that the whole enterprise of stratifying
> young people would be more securely achieved
> within separate institutions. It might be
> a little difficult for the same institution
> to encourage a minority to study the horizon
> (to be given expectations) while the majority
> were taught to be realistic, stare at their
> boots, and acquire the virtues of place (Ransom

& Walsh, 1982).

This seems to fit in well with Sir Keith's own
philosophy which he outlined in his January 1982
speech at Leeds.

> For those who are unsuited to an academic
> curriculum, whether they leave at 16 or 17,
> education will be effective only if it
> directly prepares for life and for the world
> that the pupils themselves can be enabled to
> see it.

This will involved for many a curriculum which will

> provide a broad programme of general
> education, but with a practical slant that
> will develop young people's personal attri-
> butes such as a sense of responsibility and
> the capacity for independent work, and help
> them to discover what kind of job they might
> expect to tackle with success.

This philosophy is directly in line with the thinking behind the MSC new training initiative. Indeed,
by going out of the educational system, the Government have strengthened their control of the process
which is based on training for jobs as opposed to
education in furthering the 'needs of the economy'.
Sir Keith stated that:

> The more effective we make education at
> school, the more we ensure a firm grasp of
> basic skills, knowledge and understanding,
> the better for the children concerned and
> the better for society and the economy.
> Norman Tebbit and the MSC are seeking to
> provide a wider network of training and
> the schools are one of the most important
> agencies in equipping their pupils to be
> ready for it.

Emphasis is here placed on the training, rather than
a broader education, and the local authority associations are given definite boundaries within which
they should work.
    The M.S.C. Pamphlet 'The Youth Opportunities
Programme and the Local Education Authority' (May
1981) in Section 1.10 specifically states that
'The Head Office of Special Programmes Division is
responsible for setting out the broad requirement of

courses and for issuing guidelines within which the
curricula and courses are approved and monitored by
SPD and Training Service Division local staff'. The
utilitarian emphasis of such requirements is mirrored in The Profile Report of a northern FE College
whose courses begin in September 1983. Attainment
is recorded on the following skills only - reading,
writing, listening/talking, calculations, measure-
ment, graphs and tables, visual understanding,
dexterity, problem solving, coping skills and learning skills.

A tightening of the entry into higher education
by the slimming-down of both University and advanced
HE places for lower expenditure; the mechanism for
taking out and refusing new courses in the advanced
higher education; and the possible growth of
Government involvement in the curriculum are all
ways in which centralism in education is becoming
clearly seen as a trend. This extends also into
the retraction of grants for research and in defining the incompetent teacher.

But while the accountability of the education
system, and particularly Local Government, is emphasised, the Government do not acknowledge the consequences of the effects of their own decisions. When
parent groups in Northamptonshire and Surrey tried
to use Section 68 of the 1944 Act to fight off
'unreasonable cuts in education spending' the DES
refused to accept the complaints for investigation
on the ground that the Section was inapplicable to
the circumstances, namely, whether or not the LEAs
were being reasonable in not providing a sufficient
educational service under the 1944 Act.

In referring to the Tameside judgement as to
what amounted to unreasonableness, it was argued
that the Secretary of State had to have all relevant
information before him about an issue and that he
had to adhere to a legal standard of reasonableness.
He could not just act on whether he agreed or dis-
agreed with the local policy.

So we have the current situation where a
Minister can use legislation to act or not act
against Local Authorities depending on how he uses
his interpretation of powers. Whether on economic
or legal criteria, there seems to have been a significant shift in Central and Local Government relationships which could have critical consequences for
education in the future.

EDUCATION AND CORPORATENESS

One other significant aspect needs to be taken into
account concerning the present administrative and
policy processes of education at the local level.
This is the introduction of corporate planning
management techniques. The theory of corporateness
is based on a rational approach for attaining the
most efficient workings of large scale organisations.
It was first used in practice by private companies
in the United States during the late 1950s and later
it spread to the larger United Kingdom companies
before being taken into account in the early 1960s
by Central Government, particularly with regard to
the approach towards the study of urban problems
and the forward planning of public expenditure
(Hambleton, 1978, p.49-55). The approach also began
to influence Local Government reorganisation. The
London Local Government reorganisation of 1963 based
on the findings of the Herbert Commission, the Maud
Report (1967) on management of Local Authorities,
and the Mallaby Report (1967) on staffing, set the
scene for the Redcliffe-Maud Report of 1969. Although much of the detailed proposals of the last
report were rejected by the Conservative Government
of 1970, many of the broad principles were established in the Local Government Act 1972 which created
the two tier system of Counties and Districts. The
implementation of the Act on 1 April 1974 was guided
to a great degree by the Bains Report (1972).
    Basically, the ideas underlying the approach
involved taking an overall view of a Local
Authority's activities, i.e. it should consider its
resources and activities as a whole and that it
should plan and review them in relation to the
changing needs and problems of its environment. It
was argued that the problems facing Local Authorities
were not conveniently divisible into the designated
services as they were then organised and that
issues such as unemployment, homelessness, community
development, the elderly and the under-5s, needed to
be approached from a more coherent and comprehensive
combination of organisational structures and processes.
    This directly attacks the traditional Local
Government structures of separate specialised departments manned by specialist professionals, and the
inefficiencies of deploying resources without over-
arching management systems. The new management
structures, based on models from the Bains Report,
centred therefore on the post of Chief Executive with

the Management Team of chief officers who would secure overall co-ordination and control. They would service the main Policy and Resources Committees where elected Members would set Authority objectives and priorities, co-ordinate policy, allocate resources and review performance (see Jennings, 1979; Stewart, 1974). From this it can be seen that the traditional positions of the separated individual services, including education, would become less autonomous and would work to fit into the policy plans and action plans of total Authority objectives rather than initiating policy independently in their own sphere.

In practice, however, there were many problems and opposition to implementing the theory. Much of the Bains structure models were implemented on reorganisation without the full commitment and the necessary skills of many of the main officers concerned - that is the chief officers who constituted the Management Team. The strength of their separatist professionalism was underestimated so that there was a clash between the co-ordination and integration of activities across the Authority and the vertical functions of separate service departments (see Jennings, 1979, p.11; Hunter, 1982). Hence, tensions developed between the centre and the periphery of the Authorities.

Reorganisation also took place in a time of cutbacks and financial stringency and the resultant crisis situations were not conducive to the orderly development of corporate approaches. Indeed, it seemed to many in education, the biggest spending service, that the new procedures were being used to cut its allocation, for decisions with regard to education's resources were now being made by Committees other than the traditional Education Committees. Indeed, the implementation of corporate structures (as opposed to processes) meant that many important decisions were being made by a small caucus of officers and members of the controlling party who may not have grasped the differing emphases of needs of services or taking into account the subtle factors of flexibility, pacing and differential support affecting the quality of education in particular.

Since reorganisation, the position and style of the Chief Education Officer became more that of an implementer and administrator rather than that of policy initiator and formulator. Miriam David (1977), in a study of Local Authority Education Departments in the early 1970s, identified a useful

analytical distinction of chief education officer
styles, that of between 'conciliator' and 'educator'.
The former tends to stress the mediator or broker-
age role of the officers, to arbitrate between the
conflicting interests and demands on the system:
'Essentially they are professionals, but predominantly in generalist administration' (p. 41). The
educator is one who pursues educational objectives,
chosen as a result of professional training and
experience, and is the teachers' representative:
'Theirs is a commitment to the substance of the task
rather than to its organisation. They are professional educators' (p. 41).

Since this study was researched, there has been
a definite shift of emphasis in structure so that
the 'conciliator' rather than the 'educator' is the
more relevant style given the shift of the locus of
power in Local Authorities towards the centre. Also,
as has been argued earlier in this paper, in a situation of declining resources, decisions are being
made by the more centralised administration using
political values to differentiate between competing
demands rather than professionally based criteria
per se. Again, it needs to be stressed that these
politicised decisions are essentially re-active
rather than pro-active in that the context in which
they are made in response to decisions made elsewhere by Central Government. The new Block Grant
System for regularising grant allocations involves
the Department of the Environment in needing and
receiving greater information of what the Local
Authority is doing before it decides the level of
rate support. John Cretton (1980) remarks: 'The
more Central Government looks in detail at what
each Authority is doing, the greater its capacity
for control, and the direr the threat to local
independence'.

It seems then that education is entangled in
a changing system of loci of power within Local
Government and between Local and Central Government
so that increasingly priorities other than educational priorities are being used to condition and,
in some respects, determine what should be done by
and for education.

SOME THEORETICAL CONSIDERATIONS

Much of the evidence above of the changing emphasis
of education policy making could be taken as vindi-
cating the clear-cut view of Cockburn (1977) that
Councils are expressions at a local level of the

state.

> We need an analysis that sets Local Government
> in the context of the real economic situation
> of the period in which we live and ask what is
> its job? Such an approach involves stepping
> outside the conventional frame of reference
> and seeing Local Government, our old red brick
> town hall, for what it really is; a key part
> of the state in capitalist society. (p.49)

The main function of the state according to Cockburn
is to secure conditions favourable to capital accumulation by contributing to both capitalist production and capitalist reproduction. From this, it
could be argued that the main task of the Local
Authority is reproduction and that in a fiscal
crisis the process of capital accumulation (mostly
private accumulation) takes relative precedence over
the social wage elements of public expenditure.
This is facilitated by the growing extent of centralisation of power and resources towards Central
Government and mirrored in education by the growing
utilitarianism of the Labour Party's Great Debate
(1976-77) with its emphasis on accountability, needs
of industry and standards (see Fynn et al., 1977;
Hunter, 1981) to the direct cuts mentioned in the
earlier part of this paper. The systems of corporate management and planning with their emphasis on
the mechanics of efficient administration are most
useful in implementing the actual cuts within the
given parameters of cash limits.
  Corrigan (1979) does not take such a pessimistic view and indeed sees a possible scenario where
such savage attacks on the social wage and services
could lead to erasing of class consciousness which
could be the basis of a potent reaction in that the
local state is

> an arena for class struggle in the locality.
> It provides the opportunity for organising
> pressure and change in the local area of
> struggle, at all times recognising the
> influence of Central Government and the power
> of the multi-nationals in the struggle but
> underlining that the consciousness of the
> great mass of working people is around
> local issues (p.204).

He does not, however, see this as unproblematic for
he argues that the growth in the social wage by an

increasingly bureaucratic state has de-politicised
sections of the working class in that they have
become passive recipients of aid. Bassett (1980)
describes this in that:

> Insofar as the process of reform has failed
> to provide any continuing democratic exper-
> ience for working people, it has proved
> difficult to mobilise mass support for the
> defence of these reforms now that they are
> under attack as part of the cutback in state
> expenditure (p.55).

Indeed, it could be argued further that the Thatcher
Government has transferred the fiscal crisis of the
state on to the local state in that much of the
tension has been placed between services in Local
Authorities in their fight to keep their own cuts to
the minimum. Educationalists have been at the forefront of such infights with regard to school closures, trying to keep teachers' posts to the detriment of materials, and for the different sections
of the educational services competing against each
other for the shrinking resources. The Falklands
dispute and the rise of the SDP cannot entirely
account for the present popularity of the Government
and the relatively poor showing of the Labour vote
in the municipal elections of May 1982.

But perhaps Cockburn and Corrigan, with their
theoretical clarity, have not taken into account
the complexity, the ambiguity and confusion that
still exists with regard to understanding the
relationship between Central and Local Government.
In education and other services, there remain wide
variations in patterns of expenditure and the way in
which Central Government policies are implemented
between different Authorities, and while Central
Government powers may have increased, it is still
an empirical question as to how effective they are
in practice.

I argue elsewhere (Hunter, 1981) that there are
contradictions and unintended consequences which
stem from the present Government's educational policies, for example with regard to the Education
Bills of 1979 and 1980 and their policies of school
closures, 16-19 year old education, curriculum
development, and their defence of 'standards'. It
is suggested that there are possible spaces for manoeuvre for meeting alternative goals within the
broad parameters which are set by Central Government.

Saunders (1980) argues on a similar line that
Local Authorities have some relative autonomy from
state control and points out the different Local
Authorities appear to enjoy different degrees of
autonomy over different policies at different times.
One example of this relative autonomy at the present
time is the nuclear free zone policy of many
Authorities in direct opposition to the official
Government defence policy. Saunders identifies the
tension between social and economic priorities
(social need and private profit) as being institu-
tionally insulated in the division between local and
central state agencies.

Local Government in Britain is typically concerned with provision of social consumption
through competitive modes of political media-
tion and organised around the principle of
citizenship rights and social need. Central
and regional levels of government, on the
other hand, are typically the agencies through
which social investment and fiscal policies
are developed within a relatively exclusive
corporate sector of politics organised around
the principal of private property rights and
the need to maintain private sector profitability (p. 31).

It is this same tension which exists in education
between the irreconcilable goals of striving for
greater efficiency and social justice. The present
Government have considerably reduced this tension
by strongly emphasising the former almost to the
exclusion of the latter.

However, it is perhaps constraining to tie
these tensions to class struggles in that there is
a distinction between the struggles relating to
capital and labour (class) and those around distribution and consumption which is where local political struggles take place. It is to argue for a
pluralistic theoretical model rather than an
economically based model. This would be underlined
by a Weberian rather than a Marxist approach. Weber
denied the 'necessary' supremacy of the economic
factors in any historical stage of development
(Weber, 1948, p.68). He does not maintain that
economic considerations are unimportant, but he
would not make a definite choice as to whether economic or non-economic factors were decisive in the
last resort in any given situation or epoch. What
he did was to underline the potential importance of

political, religious, military or economic interests, and that historically all were bases of power which were significant in themselves.

If this is accepted, it should be possible to explore alternative processes involving education vis-a-vis the Local Authority and the increasing centralisation of Central Government. The latter process involves both main parties for the Labour Party too has recently suggested that education expenditure should be removed from the control of Local Authorities and given over to a new Government body responsible for the allocation of specific grants (Education, 13.4.82). This is consistent with the Labour Party's growing emphasis since the Second World War of the role of a strong central state with regard to reform relative to the local community or 'local state'. It is argued here, though, that there is evidence of movements in society which involve a raising of consciousness which challenges accepted norms and institutions and which, if the present argument is correct, could effect structural changes in society. At the institutional level, Donald Schon (1971) believes:

> We must become able not only to transform our institutions, in response to changing situations and requirements, we must invent and develop institutions which are 'learning systems', that is to say, capable of bringing about their own continuing transformation (p. 30).

These would include schools, Local Authorities and Central Government organisations and would entail systems that can change as rapidly as the environment in which they operate while remaining internally stable. There is a need for this for, whether we are ready for it or not, the opportunities and the problems of the imminent technological revolution will radically alter the definition of work, the communication system and many aspects of every-day living. Technically, it would be possible for control to reside in the hands of a few, or for greater opportunities to be made available for participation in communal life with a more rigorous interpretation of democracy. These movements can be seen in the ways in which new definitions of communality are being highlighted in community politics, in various forms of industrial democracy, in the women's and anti-racialist organisations, in the conservation lobbies and in the agitation for

peace. In some schools and parts of higher education it is present in the debate of what constitutes
open education, with its emphasis on teaching 'how'
rather than 'what' to think (Hunter, 1979).
At the present time, however, the weight of
evidence suggests that it is a more centralised process that is in the ascendancy. Perhaps if alternatives are supported, especially with regard to
education, this will involve committed political
action rather than discussions of theoretical nice-
ties.

BIBLIOGRAPHY

Association of County Councils et al.,(1982) Rate
    Support Grant 1982/83, County Hall, Chichester.
Bains Committee (1972) The New Local Government:
    Management and Structure, HMSO.
Cockburn, C. (1977) The Local State: Management of
    Cities and People, Pluto Press.
Corrigan, P. (1979) The Local State: The struggle
    for democracy, Marxism Today (July).
Cretton, J. (1980) Quantifying the dire threat to
    local independence, Education, Nov. 11th, p.441.
David, E. (1977) Reform, Reaction and Resources:
    the 3R's of Educational Planning, NFER.
Finn, D. et al. (1977) Social Democracy, Education
    and the Crisis in 'On Ideology', Hutchinson.
Griffiths, J. (1981) Lord Denning rolls the dice
    against London, New Society Vol. 58, No. 992
    (19.11.81).
Hambleton, R. (1978) Policy Planning and Local
    Government, Hutchinson.
Hunter, C. (1979) The Politics of Participation -
    with specific reference to Teacher-pupil
    relationships in Teacher Strategies, ed. by
    Wood, P., Croom-Helm.
Hunter, C. (1981) Politicians Rule O.K.? Implications
    for Teacher Careers and School Management, in
    Schools, Teachers and Teaching, ed. by Barton,
    L. and Walker, S., The Falmer Press.
Hunter, C. (1982) Draft Discussion Document:
    Performance Review of Policy Unit, Bradford
    Metropolitan City Council.
Jennings, R. (1980) Corporateness and Education:
    Changing power relationships in local govern-
    ment, Sheffield City Polytechnic Department of
    Education Management.
Mallaby Report (1967) Report of the Committee on the
    staffing of local government, HMSO.

Maud Report (1967) Report of the Committee on the management of local government, HMSO.

Redcliffe-Maud Report (1969) Report of The Royal Commission on Local Government in England, HMSO.

Saunders, P. (1981) Notes on the Specificity of the Local State in The Local State: Theory and Practice, ed. Boddy, M., Fudge, C., School for Advanced Urban Studies, University of Bristol.

Schon, D. (1971) Beyond the Stable State, Temple Smith.

Stewart, J. (1974) Corporate Management and The Education Service, Educational Administration Bulletin, Vol. 3 No. 1.

Weber, M. (1948) The Methodology of the Social Sciences, Glencoe.

5. TEACHERS' RESPONSES TO THE CUTS

G. Wallace, H.D.R. Miller, M. Ginsburg

INRODUCTION

This chapter is about changes in schooling. It
attempts to relate administrative interventions to
teacher responses over a period of time. The task
inevitably poses problems of interpretation and
explanation, and we suggest that Habermas (1976)
provides some useful insights into these. His
theoretical schema makes use of both the systems
perspective on the control of nature for profit, and
the interactionist perspective, with its focus on
the symbolic construction of a meaningful social
world by active participants.

In what he calls a 'rough diagnosis' of advanced capitalism, Habermas argues that the liberal
exchange relations of the market have been replaced
by administrative structures. The fundamental task
of all administrative systems is to help safeguard
the process of 'growth' and profit through the kind
of forward planning which can provide stability and
predictable outcomes for capital. Nevertheless,
competing capitalist interests are inherently anarchic, and within such an anarchic environment, the
planning bureaucracies find themselves reacting to
crisis, rather than pursuing rational outcomes.

From the interactionist perspective, our major
concern here is with the way in which the consequences of such reactive movements are interpreted. For
as part of his critique of systems theory, Habermas
argues that it is within the processes of interaction that participants find the meaning for
events, call for legitimation of political actions,
and constitute their own ego and group identities in
ways which motivate them to act within specific
social situations (Habermas, 1976, p.120).

One of the links which unites the two perspectives comes from the use, by the political system of administration, of traditional 'world views' at the rhetorical level, in order to legitimate administrative activity which serves capitals. However, it is Habermas' claim that administrative systems cannot produce meanings as these must be generated through socio-cultural interaction. Thus those 'world views' which are appropriated are irreparably harmed and opened up to question.

As an alternative to the rhetorical legitimation of policy, there is also a process orientated towards 'buying off' participants on the basis of occupational and educational achievement. However, this process generates a 'crisis of expectations' which the State cannot meet.

The consequence of these processes as diagnosed by Habermas, is a crisis of legitimation. Given this diagnosis, the survival of the class-based capitalist structure depends upon the State's ability to detach its decision making processes from the interactive process of meaningful participation. Whilst systems theorists, like Luhman (1970), have argued that legitimacy may be vested in the law alone, it has been Habermas' contention that it is the interactive processes which ultimately provide the meaning and purpose for action, and that a crisis of legitimation will bring about a transformation of class relations. He has not explored the mechanism by which the meanings and purposes generated through interactive processes may react back upon administrative systems in order to affect the fundamental ways in which class relations are structured. This may be a weakness in the theory which may only be filled by the working out of the relationship in particular historical contexts.

For the present, we intend to situate our study of teachers' responses to administrative interventions, and the consequences generated by the totality of these processes, within the schema of Habermas' 'rough diagnosis'. We begin therefore, by placing our study in its historical context.

THE HISTORICAL CONTEXT

Reviewing the longer, historical view, Grace has argued that nineteenth century schooling was circumscribed by policies governing space, time and the demand for measurable results based on prescribed curricula. The imposition of a culture of silence and immobility upon pupils was a necessary response by teachers to the physical setting as well as to official intentions governing pupil sociali- sation.

The pattern was modified significantly after 1926 when conservative fear of centralised, social- ist control encouraged de-centralisation and a dispersal of power. Implicitly teachers were per- ceived as inherently conservative (Grace, 1978, pp. 98-99; White, 1975).

In the 1960s at least in the realm of pedagogy, teachers appeared to reach a high level of school- based autonomy. The Plowden Report (1967), and the teacher training establishments encouraged progres- sive approaches. Through the Certificate of Secondary Education, teachers even gained a legiti- mate say in the pupil assessment process. The rhetoric which developed matched triple pressures from politicians, parents and the economy. Firstly, both social democrats and progressive conservatives viewed the socialisation process within schools as a mechanism of social reform, aimed at the equali- sation of opportunities. Secondly, parentaly expec- tations centred on schooling as a means of promoting the social mobility of their children (Goldthorpe et al., 1969). Thirdly, there was the political hope, typified in the Wilson Government of a more efficient and expanding economy geared to techno- logical advancement. Investment in education was seen as essential for social and economic success. At a time when more, better educated manpower, was perceived as the key to 'growth' the doubt cast on the validity of the 11+ examinations as a predictor of pupils' future potential (Jackson and Marsden, 1953) played a part in undermining the traditional tripartite division of secondary schooling. (See also Newsom, 1963; Robbins 1963; Donnison, 1970). A further, but complementary pressure for change derived from the need to provide new schools for the contemporary 'bulge' in the pre-teen population. With the post war movement of population to the suburbs and new towns, new secondary schools were needed in areas where there were frequently no existing grammar schools. The building of compre- hensive schools offered a cost-effective solution (Bryan and Hardcastle, 1977).

The degree of apparent consensus in educational and economic thinking, produced strong pressures towards the comprehensivisation of secondary school- ing. In some areas, out of the historical conjunc- ture of pressures, middle schools emerged, with a clearly 'progressive' mandate derived from the

Plowden Report (Blyth and Derricot, 1977; Hargreaves and Tickle, 1980).

Nonetheless in the wake of the oil crisis of 1973, the prospects for any sustained economic growth came to an abrupt end. The educational service was subject to its share of cuts; demand management gave way to monetarism and the 'failures' of centrist policies gave way to the right.

Begun as a defence of the elitist grammar school (Cox and Dyson, 1969) the conservative educational backlash, which had at first struggled for legitimacy, developed in the later 1970s into a direct attack on comprehensive schooling, on the grounds of falling standards and rising disorder (Cox and Boyson, 1975). The drive against progressive practices in schools strengthened and exploded into the public arena amplified by media interest.

The general outburst in the media virulently attacked teaching standards (Crutcher, 1979). Neville Bennett's (1976) research into teaching styles was (mistakenly) taken to indicate that 'traditional' teaching methods were superior to 'progressive' approaches. The then Prime Minister, James Callaghan launched the 'Great Debate' on education at Ruskin College, Oxford in October 1976. The major issues were identified and elaborated in a Green Paper published in the summer of 1977. Education was called upon to be the efficient servant of a managed economy (DES, 1977, para. 1.16; Simon, 1977). Furthermore, the newly demanded improvements in 'standards' had to be brought about without additional resources.

The local government reorganisation of 1974, and the development of corporate management techniques (Cockburn, 1978) had shifted the focus of power at County Hall tightening the control of policy through the allocation and distribution of finance tied to specific policies. The decline of the birth rate and the reduction in school rolls in some areas offered a readily available 'problem' which could be 'solved' by school closures and the employment of fewer teachers. The government's orientation to schooling had altered significantly. (Finn, et al., 1977; Ginsburg, et al., 1979). Analysing the discourse of the 1977 Green Paper, Donald claimed (1979:14):

> What education is for is being redefined and, at the same time, the institutions of the education system are being restructured to achieve these new goals and to fit new patterns

of state expenditure...

This administrative process of redefinition as it
has developed since the 1977 Green Paper may be
understood as a response to two inter-related
structural imperatives. The first imperative is
derived from the instrumental requirement to maintain economic returns to capital, in the context of
declining rates of profit and a world-wide crisis.
Schooling in its presently organised form is therefore called upon to be more efficient and more
accountable to the economic demands of the social
system. The financial constraints are portrayed as
the inevitable consequence of 'market forces' and
the 'natural' consequence of a failure to 'live
within our means'. Schools must therefore take a
'share' of the 'cuts' and teachers must work harder
and to better effect. The second structural imperative is concerned with the role of the administrative system in the organisation and management of
the reproduction of social relationships appropriate
to the means of production. The establishment of
the administration's right to intervene and determine the particular kinds of knowledge, skill and
disposition required of the workforce had to be
legitimated. Redefinitions are not merely a question of financial limitations on what may be spent
on schooling, but also a question of authority,
hierarchy and discipline: a question of cooling out
on a mass scale those 'enhanced quality of life
expectations' which cannot be met, and a question of
meeting head on the problem of 'ungovernability'
which was perceived as reaching crisis point in the
schools (Taylor, 1980:10). We turn now to the
working out of these policies at local authority
level, drawing on data which relates particularly to
the County in which the field studies were carried
out.

THE PROCESS OF MANAGEMENT: WHO RULES WHOM?

It is important to note that although local authorities faced unprecedented cuts in expenditure following the oil crisis, money for capital projects has
always been scarce. In particular the space available for schooling had been declining throughout the
1960s (Wallace, 1980). As the largest single item
of expenditure of local government, state educational policies have always been tied to the level of
generosity shown by the government in allocating
finance, although the form of the allocation has

changed over time. Since the Local Government Act
of 1966, the necessary support has been incorporated
into the process devised for allocating the Rate
Support Grant (RSG). The crucial months of decision-
making between allocation of the RSG and the final
decisions of the budget, came between the announcement of the level of RSG by the Government, usually
in November and the final County Council ratifica-
tion of budget decisions usually in February. Taken
with the fact that this period also covered important months of negotiation over teachers' salaries,
the early months of the year tended to be periods of
heightened interest in policy making for teachers,
and the months in which teacher union activity was
at its most visible.

Administrative changes under corporate management had wide implications for negotiative procedures, fragmenting educational interests which were
once under the direct control of the Local Education
Committee and significantly undermining informal
interactions. In the County studied, crucial economic decisions were vested in the powerful Policy,
Resources and Finance Committee. Educational buildings became the concern of the Property Committee
and teachers interests were made part of the task of
the Personnel Committee. These shifts in the loci
of the decision making have tended to elevate financial considerations, including such matters as the
possible financial return on the sale of school
buildings, and to devalue the influence of social
and educational criteria in policy deliberations
about local schools (Cooke, TES, 18 February, 1980).

Locally, in the authority under study we obser-
ved significant changes in the relation between the
members of the Education Committee and the elected
representatives of teachers. Before reorganisation
of the authority the latter had even held voting
rights in one of the authorities. Under amalgamat-
ion and with the reorganised system of local government these rights were denied and the role of
Teacher Representative was redefined as consultative
only. The next major move occurred in the autumn of
1979, when representatives were informed that they
should not imply that they represented anyone, as
they were no more than individual teachers from whom
the Committee might or might not wish to have an
opinion. By this time negotiations were also under
way for the setting up of a new joing negotiating
body of teacher representatives; negotiations which
culminated at the end of the summer in a committee
which brought together sixteen representatives of

the employers' side. The latter consisted mainly of councillors from the education committee and the personnel committee, but also included relevant officials and the Chairman of PRAF. In this way teachers' representatives found themselves having to consider specific options placed before them by their employers rather than comment on, or raise objections to, proposals for policy, and it was noted in one union meeting that, given the position of sharing in management, teachers now had to show that they could 'act professionally'. The freedom to debate, and if necessary oppose, had become a responsibility to negotiate 'options' on management terms, with the corollary that the union leadership now had to sell the agreements to their members. Avid scrutiny of management consultative documents became a primary necessity for union officers. One of the first tasks of the new committee was to nego- tiate a package deal on early retirement which teachers wanted and on redeployment which they didn't.

A further area of change in relationships con- cerns the breakdown of the 'informal networks' of communication which were once the means whereby individuals responsible for educational interests, from the heads of schools, through officials and County Education Officers even up to the Minister of State, had been able to solve the day-to-day diffi- culties involved in making the education system work. Not only did the institution of Corporate Management block direct informal communications be- tween County Education interests and the Department of State, but also it blocked many of the methods whereby schools had been able to get informal deci- sions made about their particular problems through the informal telephone calls from heads to county officials. Further pressure came from an increase in directives from the CEO, containing instructions to be followed 'without exception' and the use of the Health and Safety at Work Act to regulate such activities as school outings. For example, insur- ance and parental permission were required before pupils could be taken beyond the school gates. In addition heads were required to aid economies by undertaking such activities as the supervision of the use of cleaning materials and the regulation of the opening of windows and the use of heating oil.

Local Consultative Committees, made up of the Local District Inspectorate and Councillors were set up to make decisions about local schools without necessarily consulting teachers at all, although any

school's respective Head and Chairman of the
Governors could be invited to attend specific meetings. Most recently in 1981 heads were required to
seek the permission of such a committee if they
wished to spend more than £100 on one item. In one
instance a head reported that in spite of an initial
call to the local inspector, whom he knew to be
sympathetic, his request to spend money which the
school had as part of its capitation allowance had
been refused.

Alongside these new apparatuses of constraint
there were developments in a rhetorical line of discourse, directed to defining the legitimate limits
of democracy. This rhetoric has been in evidence
at Central Government and County levels. This
stance is well illustrated by a report in The
Teacher (28 November, 1981) and comes from the Chief
Education Officer of Staffordshire:

> The input teachers have at every level of
> policy making from national level downwards
> is considerable and important. But once
> decisions are taken, teachers have to do the
> best they can with them. Teachers do not
> have the right to take active political
> stances on educational issues.

In a similar vein a County Councillor in the authority under study stated that heads ought not to be
using parents in a campaign against the legitimately
decided policies of local government; this when some
heads sought to defend their own particular schools
against particular decisions by rousing parental
protest. This stance may be contrasted with the
free-market notion embodied in the 1980 Education
Act that parents had the right to choose the school
they wanted their children to attend.

A further example of the trends is identifiable
in the justification given by the Conservative Party
for the overweighting of committees after their
majority was reduced to a handful following the 1981
County Council elections. The claim then was that,
as the party had been 'elected to govern' it must
be able to get its policies through. A general
complaint by the opposition, which surfaced in letters to the press and was taken up by members of
the public was that educational decisions were being
pre-decided, before committee meetings, and that
councillors were merely 'voting the party ticket'
without regard to the issues. Education had been
thoroughly politicised, but in terms of 'Who has the

right to decide?' rather than 'On what social principles should the decision be made?'

The evidence so far suggests no attempt to
establish any moral criteria, even at the rhetorical
level, to guide educational decision making. Rather
legitimacy was being located in a definition of the
power structure which asserted power itself, obtained through the ballot box, but detached from any
mandate of social principles, as the defining criterion. The 'self-evident' necessity of financial
constraint brought about by monetarist economic
management, was presented as justification for the
need to restrict spending. The new apparatuses of
control ensured that the money which was available
was directed according to management priorities.
Opposition to policies formulated by democratically
elected councillors could be defined as illegitimate
without regard to the social and educational issues
at all.

THE TEACHERS' RESPONSE

We move now to two related research projects which
focussed on six suburban and new town middle schools
with pupils aged 9-13 years, in this Midlands county.
The first project involved five of the six schools
used overall, and participant observation fieldwork
was undertaken during the period from November 1976 -
July, 1978 (Ginsburg, et al., 1977). Interviews
were conducted with 18 members of staff in June and
July, 1977, including heads and those holding office
or active in the NUT and NAS/UWT. These interviews
focussed upon teachers' responses to the 'Great
Debate' and the education cuts, particularly as
these were being experienced in schools. Related
questions about attitudes to professionalism and
trade unionism also formed part of the discussions.
The second project involved all six schools and
the data is based upon responses of 49 members of
staff interviewed twice. The sample covered heads,
deputies and senior teachers (hereafter designated
administrators), year group coordinators, subject
advisors and classroom teachers. Participant observation in the schools and more widely in the county
served to contextualise the findings. The first set
of interviews took place between December 1979 and
April, 1980; the second set ran approximately in
parallel a year later. The interviews followed a
scheduled pattern of both open and closed questions
and elicited responses about the issues involved in

the 'Great Debate' and its aftermath, without refer-
encing it as the source of the central concerns.
Matters covered included teaching styles and organisation, resources, curriculum, testing, standards,
the 'gifted' child, perceived pressures for change,
relations with the neighbourhood, perceptions of the
power of teachers to influence policies and opinions
about union activities.

The findings of the first project have already
been published elsewhere (Ginsburg et al., 1977,
1979). What we will do here is merely summarise the
changes which were occurring in the middle schools
studied, insofar as they appear relevant to the
processes set in train by the range of interventions
surrounding the Great Debate.

Undoubtedly teachers felt they were being made
scapegoats by the media and that their work was
under attack. Some accepted that there were incompetent teachers who should go, but there were doubts
about bringing schools into line with industry and
claims that it was society that needed changing. In
general, teachers saw 'standards' in terms of individual pupil 'potential' and had some doubts about
how national 'standards' might be set or measured.
Cuts in ancillary help, in-service training and
capitation had already occurred, with some complaint,
but teachers felt they could cope with these providing the pupil-teacher ratio was maintained. Perc-
eiving a County threat to cut the ratio in January
1977, many teachers united to support a half-day
protest, organised by the NUT which included a
demonstration outside County Hall as the rate precept was being decided. The pupil-teacher ratio
was maintained but further cuts in ancillary hours
and capitation were made. Even so, the half-day
protest provoked division and controversy amongst
the teachers including those who supported it.
Reactions ranged from those who thought the action
too weak, through those who felt that the unions
themselves were divided or 'lacked muscle', to those
who argued that teacher protests had a bad effect on
pupils.

Several important administrative changes in the
schools were occurring however, as teachers responded to pressures to move away from mixed-ability
teaching and to 'set' pupils by ability for the
'basics' of English, Maths and French. Similarly,
integrated work was declining in favour of time-
tabled subjects. On the whole there was sufficient
disagreement amongst these teachers over mixed-
ability teaching and other innovations such as team

teaching, for administrative changes to be adopted
as 'necessary', given declining resources. Teachers
varied widely in their opinions however. The promotion of standardised testing by the County, for
example, met with a welcome from some but total
rejection by others, who saw their own knowledge of
the child as providing a better measure of progress.
    In terms of the theoretical perspective inform-
ing Habermas' 'rough diagnosis' we would suggest
that administrative actions to exert new influences
on classroom teachers were clearly in train. At
this stage, however, rather than serve to provoke
processes of interaction amongst teachers which
might have led them to unite in a redefinition of
their own purposes, the changed policies met with
differentiated responses and sometimes individualised resentments and unease. The unity expressed in
protest was at the level of common fear of job loss.
There was little awareness anywhere of the broad
implications of the rhetoric of the Great Debate.
The main focus was on the 'cuts'.
    The set of interviews conducted late in 1979,
and early in 1980 for the second project, followed
a period of considerable union activity centred on
salary negotiations begun in the spring of 1978. In
connection with this, NUT members had refused to do
'voluntary' tasks such as supervise lunch breaks,
and NAS/UWT members had argued (on the basis of
hourly rates paid to part-time staff) that they were
within their rights in leaving the premises before
the official end to the school day. Both these
actions had caused considerable conflict within
schools, and a number of staff claimed to have left
their unions as a result. Nevertheless, the
Government had set up the Clegg Commission to carry
out a comparability exercise on teacher pay and this
body was still sitting throughout the 1979/80 interviews. The message which came to teachers from
media pronouncements, was that a large increase in
pay would mean a cut in teacher employment. Furthermore, the Rate Support Grant had been cut again. The
Education Committee had proposed savings totalling
£3 million but were being pressured to find a further
£2 million. With attendance at local union meetings
no higher than 10% - 20% there could be no guarantee
of support from teachers for action.
    The County Council's budget proposals to cut
capitation yet again, and to reduce the amount spent
on school cleaning, were passed in January 1980, but
County proposals to charge pupils for school transport were defeated later, at national level in the

House of Lords. An attempt to levy charges for
individual music tuition also had to be dropped when
legal action was taken against it by the NUT. The
eventual court judgement was that tuition charges
were illegal under the 1944 Act. With the acceptance of the Report of the Clegg Commission early in
August 1980, and the subsequent pay rise for teachers, it appeared increasingly likely that teachers'
jobs would be axed.

During the winter of 1979-80 for example, two
management consultative documents on staffing a
basic curriculum had been made available to union
officers and heads of schools, but by midsummer the
Chief Education Officer had announced that whatever
agreements might be reached in negotiations, there
could be no guarantee that the curriculum could be
staffed according to subject needs. In October,
1980, the local authority announced that 550 teachers' jobs would have to go, only 250 of which would
be matched by falling rolls. Unions stood by permanent staff and accepted the loss of temporary
teachers who had been appointed to fill vacancies
over the previous year or so. In addition some
older staff welcomed the prospect of early retirement. This time, uncertain of mass support for
action, the NUT opted for personal representations
to councillors, urged all members to write to their
own councillor and stirred up the matter in the
local press, urging parents to act.

Middle school heads who had been meeting occasionally for about a year to discuss the changes
which were occurring, decided to write to the press,
under the safeguard of an association. They chose
to argue for the safeguarding of High School examination curriculum, reasoning that this was an issue
which would command parental support. In the event
they were proved correct and had found a suitable
strategy for opposing the county.

The County backed down over examination pupils
and instituted an appeals procedure for heads who
lost specialist staff engaged in examination
courses. Temporary staffing appointments were permitted to fill these gaps until after the summer
examinations. Furthermore, the Education Committee
meeting in January 1981, was lobbied by parents
and 300 of the teachers who were to have been axed,
over and above falling rolls, kept their jobs.
Teachers sometimes cited this experience as evidence
that they had 'won' their case, by the County claimed that the jobs had been saved by a 'windfall' Rate
Support Grant. The latter was the result of Central

Government alternations in the basis for calculating the Grant in a way which benefitted counties rather than urban areas, and was seen by some to be related to the forthcoming County Council elections. Nonetheless, the Authority also raised the rate precept and took £500,000 from Further Education. With the budget settled, plans for united action by all the teachers' unions lost their impetus and were abandoned in February.

The major effect of staff cuts in the schools in the study was felt in the need to re-timetable classes at the start of the spring term. In some cases staff opted for increased class-contact time rather than 'unsettle' pupils by reorganising them in new classes. In one case, it was the end of February before the staffing situation was finally clarified. In some cases organisation of pupils into different 'ability sets' for basic subjects was perceived as unavoidable, and it was this aspect of the process which teachers debated.

In responding to the interview and in the staff room, the problem of allocating pupils to what were rationalised as 'ability' groupings, caused teachers considerable soul searching. In at least two of the schools, pupils were re-tested across one full year, and in one of these, staff eventually settled for 'parallel' sets, rather than make arbitrary decisions between them. Whereas in one of the schools with rapidly declining rolls, teachers had argued in December that they might be forced to give up setting, by March teachers in other schools who had been through the re-setting process were arguing that it would be easier to cope with arbitrary losses of staff if they taught their own mixed-ability classes. In the school with rising rolls staff began to debate whether it might not be a good thing if they taught their own classes more, as the big increase in pupils was unsettling children, and more class teaching would improve discipline.

It became apparent that local advisers were discussing the problems with heads, and that a move away from setting and towards more mixed-ability class teaching was perceived as a practical step which could aid stability. At County level the prospect of an end to middle schools and a reversion to the 11+ divide as High School rolls dropped, would be easier to implement. Thus different rationales, backed up the change.

Reid, et al. (1981) recently noted that the swing to setting of 11-year olds between 1975 and 1980 (from 9% to 23%) was going into reverse, 'as shrinking numbers in secondary schools meant more teachers were likely soon to have mixed groups thrust upon them'. Furthermore, teachers were being encouraged by HMI (1981) in a review of the 11-16 curriculum, to cooperate over the teaching of skills across the subject divide. If the 'Great Debate' set in train a move to differentiate in order to improve 'standards' events now appeared to be pushing teachers back to mixed-ability work and cooperation.

It is surprising that during the first set of interviews teachers showed little concern with attacks upon teachers' autonomy. On the whole, teachers had adapted to the pressures of change by accepting increased setting policies, more rigid timetabling of 'subjects', less cooperation, and a general reorientation of curricula in line with the demands of High Schools, and had made some sense of them as necessary internal policy decisions in response to particular problems. Admittedly a major problem which concerned all teachers was the level of resourcing, and this was readily applied as a rationale of any policy decision. The other, readily available rationale was that of, 'what works with pupils'. In discussing their work, more than half the teachers raised the issue at some point in the first interview of deteriorating pupil behaviour. The teachers were asked specifically if they saw their job changing at all. The pattern of responses to this is presented in Table 1. The range of responses in the second set of interviews demonstrates some of the changes.

One teacher in the second set of responses argued for a particular set of changes which he personally intended to initiate or pursue. Otherwise, two changes stand out. The first is the extent to which teachers became aware that policies being pursued at county level were affecting their work with pupils. The second demonstrates that the handful of teachers who in 1980 had some idea of the 'middle school identity' as a central reason for the way in which they operated had virtually abandoned any ideological commitment to it. Interestingly, four out of these five responses came from teachers who were under thirty-five and who were, in general, more idealistic. (See also for example, Barker-Lunn 1970).

It is noteworthy that 60% of the teachers who argued that pupils were changing (and were taking more time in pastoral care) had more than 15 years teaching experience. The teachers of older pupils were most likely to associate the changes in middle schools with the call for better tests and examination results, and hence with the obligation on them to liaise more with High School staff and prepare pupils for High School examination courses. They varied, however, in the extent to which they welcomed this development and they also had reason to associate some policy interventions with fear for their jobs.

However, attempts to make standardised testing a basis for making teachers more accountable had met with little success. Whilst two heads took to them enthusiastically as a guide to making judgements about pupils, two had adopted them reluctantly and two had actively resisted them. Similarly, teachers in their turn argued either that tests could be useful as a means of discovering whether or not pupils were underachieving or declared that tests failed to support what they 'knew' about individual pupils. Only in one of the schools had a year team concluded that they were falling down in their teaching of graphs after testing across the year, because their pupils in general might have been expected to have done better on those tests given their performance on the whole Richmond battery. In the course of the first set of interviews, it became apparent, for example, that the major use of tests was claimed by teachers tobe that of ranking pupils in order of 'ability' prior to transfer to the High Schools. However, in practice, teachers in one of the middle schools also administered a 'guided choice' of options for High School courses before transfer. From other schools too a variety of ways of ranking pupils occurred. By the second set of interviews two middle schools were using their English tests only, whilst one school used a variety of different tests, together with teacher assessments. Only one of the High Schools operated a policy of testing on entry and staff in one of its contributary middle schools who had initially rejected testing, had organised pupil tests for 'practice'. As in each case two middle schools contributed to one High School, the main pressure at this stage was perceived to be the need to gain more pupil places in the High Schools' 'top band' than the other contributing middle school. The objective was to be perceived as 'successful' by parents who might exercise their right of choice under the 1980 Education Act.

A wide variation in belief about what was happening to 'standards' not only between teachers in the same school, but also between interviews, suggested that teachers were unclear as to what was

being required of them. If 'standards' includes not
only 'knowledge' and 'skills' but also attitudes and
dispositions, the question of assessment by test is
overlaid by evaluative criteria concerned with
broader human qualities.

In addition the messages from the media tended
to confuse both behavioural and academic aspects of
'standards' whilst at the same time appearing to
blame teachers both for not getting more pupils
through 'A' levels and for not teaching them to cope
with the 'basics'. One way around the problem of
catering for the range of pupils and one which appeared to be gaining in popularity for use with the
nine and ten year olds, was to use individualised,
graded work exercises. Speed of progress then indicated not only that the exercises had been completed
satisfactorily, but also that the pupils had applied
themselves to the task in an appropriate manner.
This process compares with the technical control of
pupils, through curricula objectives, current in
America (Apple, 1981). Nonetheless, such exercises
bored pupils and left teachers with the problem of
motivating them.

During the interviews, teachers were asked if,
during their experience at the school 'standards'
had 'improved', 'worsened' or 'stayed the same'. An
additional category to take account of some teachers
claims that overall standards of each annual intake
varied had to be added. (See Table TT)

Whilst there is no significant difference between the two sets of responses overall, there is
evidence of teachers changing their individual perceptions. For example, 20.5% responded in terms
which suggested standards had worsened in 1980, and
18.2% claimed this in 1981, but only 6.2% of the
sample claimed standards had worsened on both occasions. 60% of the responses in the first interviews, and 62.5% of the second which fell into the
'worsened' category came from teachers with more
than 15 years of teaching experience; teachers who
might have been expected to recognise 'standards'
when they saw them. Even amongst this group,
however, there was obvious variation in response
from one set of interviews to another. There is no
apparent reason for this kind of change available
within any of the data, and teachers' choice of
category bears no significant relationship to measures of sex, qualifications, type of experience,
status or training. It may be pertinent to note
that almost a quarter of the teachers (22.4%) stayed
with the non-judgemental categories of 'stayed the

same' or 'varies yearly'.

The dominant view in both these latter categories was that 'standards' depended on small variations in pupils at the 'top' and 'bottom' of the
year group; a conclusion hardly surprising from
teachers who, when first working in these schools
had been required to grade pupils for High School
transfer as though they could be fitted into the
normal curve of distribution (Ginsburg et al., 1977).
If the expression of support for the education of
'gifted children' in separate schools may be taken
as a measure of elitism (approximately a third of
teachers each time) we can also claim that there was
no political dimension which could be significantly
related to these observations. The only clue may
come from the second set of interviews, where ten
out of the fifteen respondents who opted for 'stayed
the same' were teaching pupils in the top two years
of the schools. We may speculate that for these
teachers to claim that standards had fallen might be
construed as a judgement on their teaching. That
does not, however, take account for the fact that
the remaining five responses from these teachers
fell into the 'worsened' category. It appears that
the notion of 'standards' had little meaning for
these teachers, and it is noteworthy that no-one
suggested that 'standards' were a matter of individual 'potential' as they had for the first project.

Many of the interview responses, particularly
on the second occasion, indicated that teachers
were actively engaged in gathering and interpreting
messages from the media, from reports and county
'directives' as to what they were actually expected
to be doing. At the same time, they were also
interpreting messages from pupils' attitudes and
behaviour about what they were doing. Both of these
processes are intersubjective and identify forming
and serve to socialise teachers. We need to take
account of both if we are to understand the conflicts and contradictions to which teachers are
subject (See Lortie, 1975).

We may, recall, for example, that in January
1977 some teachers argued that pupils' interests
would be harmed by the half-day stoppage while some
teachers argued that pupils' interests would be
harmed if the LEA cut teachers' jobs. Caught by
these irresolvable dilemmas the very idea that
teachers were pursuing their own interests in pro-
testing against the cuts, could only provoke denials
and moral outrage. What then might be the course
and consequences of the cuts in terms of the meaning

teachers gave to events given the dilemmas inherent in the identity of the teacher? The question must concern the network of social relationships with pupils as well as the context of formal role relations defined through media messages and by the bureaucracy.

Important for both kinds of relationships are teachers perceptions of their own power. Attempts to measure the way in which respondents perceived 'teachers in general' to have some degree of autonomy and power over policy decisions which affected their working situation, were made by asking respondents to assign to the different levels of policy-making (school, county, central government) a category which suggested how they saw 'teachers in general' as in a position to influence policy decisions. Results scored on a five point scale provided a range of statistics which indicated on both occasions that more than 70% of respondents felt that they had either 'considerable power' or 'some power' to influence school policy making. At central government level, the reverse was the case, and a similar percentage opted for either 'very little power' or 'no power at all'. Whilst there were some changes in these figures between interviews, the overall relationship did not alter significantly, but again there were interesting changes within the overall framework. (See Table III)

In each case the lower the mean score, the more highly teachers ranked their power to influence events. The most pertinent results, bearing in mind that the teachers' most direct contact with administrative pressures stemmed from the local authority, are those which show teacher attitudes towards the County. Here, the final means show about a fifth of the teachers claiming 'some power' and more than half opting for 'very little' or 'no power at all'. We might conclude from this that the majority of these teachers were well aware that there were features of schooling over which they had very little influence. The comments on these issues suggested that this was less a case of taken-for-granted constraints, and more a matter of impotence in the face of powerful administrators.

However, there was a tendency amongst younger staff to believe that heads could have an influence with county officials, and it was a view observably encouraged by some heads. It also had some basis in the historical fact that heads had been able to obtain direct help with problems, on occasions, via the telephone calls to the LEA officials. As the

power relationship with the county changed heads and
deputies were to be found instituting surveillance
measures which ensured county directives were being
followed. Furthermore, the LEA increasingly followed the principles of hierarchical authority noted
earlier, in their ideological rhetoric. Thus heads
were encouraged to see themselves in schools as
'managers' and were required to 'manage' with appropriate authority. This could place heads and deputies (who were the mediators between county directives and staff complaints), at the point of conflict
making them less the people who could deal effectively with teachers' problems. The major effect on
action was a general increase in the administrative
workloads of all staff. Some were conscious of
feelings of stress and disillusion.
    In terms of the cut-backs however, some teach-
ers were willing to look for excuses for the behaviour of the local authority, and these saw the LEA
as 'doing its best' in the face of Central Government constraints. Others cited the reprieve of the
300 teaching jobs in January 1981, as evidence of
ways in which the local authority was still responsive to public pressure.
    What the results show overall is that during
the period of the project women drew closer to men
in a recognition of County power and that the more
highly qualified staff were more aware of the
administrative pressures than the less well qualified. Interestingly however, teachers with more
than 15 years of teaching experience were inclined
to believe that they were getting more rather than
less power to influence policy at County and
Government levels over the period (Table IV).
    If we recall (Table 1) that this group was the
one most concerned that their jobs were changing
because pupils were changing, (in their 1979/80
responses) that they made up the majority of those
who perceived 'standards' worsening, and that they
were also shown to be significantly more likely than
the other age groups to place a high value on
teaching from textbooks, then it seems there are
grounds for concluding that here was a relatively
conservative group who felt that their views were
shared by the policy makers. They were also the
ones who were most likely to benefit from early
retirement schemes.
    What makes the implementation of county poli-
cies in the schools problematic, however, is the
fact that the most highly qualified, most disillusioned and most sceptical group, was the group with

5-15 years experience. Trained since the mix-sixties
they found their ideas being challenged and their
promotion prospects blocked by retrenchment. Sad-
dled with mortgages and family commitments, it was
they who most feared redeployment or total job loss.
Moreover, Table V suggests that status did not
relate significantly to teacher perceptions of
power.

As far as union activity was concerned the pre-
dominant feeling echoed those of the first project.
'Lack of muscle', unwillingness to do anything which
might harm pupils, and above all a sense that the
unions were divided and engaged in petty squabbles,
merged with a sense of 'if only'. Teachers who dis-
liked what was happening to them, tended to perceive
themselves as 'battling against people who don't
really understand education...', who 'don't understands schools', who 'don't care...'. If only 'the
unions got together', 'the authority understood
teachers' problems...', 'if only they asked us...'.
These were some of the sentiments expressed. Something of the nature of the dilemma came across in a
union official's advice to a small association
meeting in July, 1981. Concerned to defend education from further attack, the group looked to the
official for guidance and leadership. The official
was reduced to rousing them to action as individuals.

> We can play our part as citizens...put
> plenty of pressure on our elected members...
> whoever they are. We are up against media
> attacks and a climate has been built up
> which presents Trades Unions as a disease.
> Yet we are talking about people within our
> committees, people who wouldn't dream of
> abusing the individual...In our communities
> is where we can get support...

The last point eas emphasised with the assertion
that some individual schools had been defended by
parental support - a potential form of alliance
taken up by teachers in threatened schools, but
traditionally shunned by teacher unions for fear of
parental 'interference' in the teachers' professional role. Further, this was a line of defence which
was being actively undermined by the media attacks
upon teachers and by the teachers' view that parental choice would be based upon competitive test
results.

128

SUMMARY AND DISCUSSION

We can now relate the process of change to changes
in three different sets of relationships. Firstly,
there was the changing nature of the relationship
between education and other administrative concerns,
with the financial constraints on local authorities
elevated to such a central position that financial
interests became overtly dominant. Secondly, there
was the changing pattern of interrelationships between teachers and personnel administering the
system, so that hierarchy and bureaucratic relations
undermined the personal networks which had traditionally underpinned decisions about particular
schools. Thirdly, there was a similar formalisation
of the traditional consultative relationship between
the LEA and the teacher unions. All the changes
occurred at both ideological and <u>practical</u> levels,
with the rhetoric used both to support new measures
of constraint and to undermine the legitimacy of
any opposition.

Even so for teachers the overriding problem
remained the management of <u>pupils</u> on a day-to-day
basis. For those who were more aware of the effect
of constraining county and Government policies, the
major problem remained the one of coping with pupils
whilst responding adequately to the growing demands
of the administration.

If we return to the framework offered by Grace
(1978) we may note that the <u>form</u> if not the content
of the situation has parallels with the nineteenth
century (ibid : 30).

We may observe that there are still two different kinds of constraints operating on teachers. On
one side, we can place those rules, regulations and
resources which are the limiting framework <u>within</u>
which teachers must work. Whilst this is broadly
determined by the effects of administrative policy,
there is some obvious scope for stretching these
limits in schools where parents are able and willing
to provide additional monies and where teachers add
to stocks of materials by their own efforts. Nonetheless, the building, finance, hours, pupil-teacher
ratio and examination system, do create a recognis-
able structure which affects all schools. On the
other side of the constraining network we must
place the pupils themselves: the live and lively
material to be 'moulded' by the 'potter' or 'culti-
vated' by the 'gardener' according to the choice of
educational metaphor.

These are, however, people too. They and their parents bring to the schooling situation, habits, mores, expectations and demands, and they too have power to operate as a constraining force on what teachers do. In terms of both of these sets of constraining factors, it is the organisation of the space available, the breakdown of the available time, the perception of 'knowledge, skills and dispositions', to be conveyed through the curriculum, and the legitimate forms of assessment, which may be altered by decisions taken at one level or another of the administration.

What we have from the data then is a sense of increasing administrative constraint which appears difficult to resist because it involved changes in power relations as well as in ideology. We have provided here an example of a policy rhetoric based on a currently meaningless, albeit traditionally meaningful view of 'standards'. Set against the decline in resources and the increased administrative workload, the rhetoric failed to make much sense to those teachers whose major source of motivation and identity comes from their relationship with pupils.

Nonetheless, the opposition roused by the 'cuts' was fragmented and largely ineffective. Only on rare occasions was an issue sufficiently well defined and agreed for an effective counter-strategy to be mounted. Some 'cuts' could be accepted by some teachers on economic grounds, but as the power structure became more visible and the pressures on teachers grew, the policy makers at County Hall were perceived as people who either didn't understand or who didn't care about the teachers' day-to-day work with pupils. The placing of administrative responsibility upon heads for carrying out of policies made outside of school, rather than for creating a traditionally vague 'good' school, within administrative limits, was changing the nature of the relationship between heads and their staff, and was placing heads in positions of conflict and stress.

Under these circumstances contrary to Habermas' ideas that the administrative reaction to social and economic crisis would provoke a crisis of legitimacy we have seen interaction networks generally undermined. Furthermore, there was no 'buying off' of those willing to conform to administrative pressures, except for those willing to retire. For the rest, the threat of redundancy or redeployment served to suppress individual protest. The outcomes cannot, however, be determined. It appears that a crisis of legitimacy may for a time be dealt with by the use

of authority and power. But as teacher motivation
declines and morale sinks the ability of teachers to
handle the situations which arise in classrooms and
schools diminishes. If schooling itself loses its
legitimacy then the ultimate consequences have yet
to be worked out.

ACKNOWLEDGEMENTS

The second project was undertaken with the aid of a
grant from SSRC.

REFERENCES

Apple, M. (1981) 'Reproduction, contestation and
     curriculum' in New Directions in Education:
     Critical Perspectives, Occasional Paper, No. 8,
     State University of New York.
Barker-Lunn, J. (1970) Streaming in the Primary
     School, NFER, Slough.
Bennett, N. (1976) Teaching Styles and Pupil
     Progress, Open Books, London.
Blyth, W.A.L. and Derricot, R. (1977) The Social
     Significance of Middle Schools, Batsford,
     London.
Bryan, K. and Hardcastle, K. (1977) 'The growth of
     middle schools: educational rhetoric and
     economic reality', Journal of Educational
     Administration and History, Vol. IX, No. 1,
     University of Leeds.
Centre for Contemporary Cultural Studies (1981)
     Unpopular Education, Hutchinson, London.
Cockburn, C. (1978) The Local State, Pluto, London.
Crutcher, M. (1979) Education News and the Popular
     Press: The Daily Mail and the Daily Mirror,
     unpublished M.Sc. dissertation, Department of
     Educational Enquiry, University of Aston in
     Birmingham, England.
Cooke, G. (1980) 'Too tough at the top' Times
     Educational Supplement, 1 February, p.4.
Cox, C.B. and Dyson, A.E. (eds) (1970-1979) Black
     Papers One, Two and Three, Critical Quarterly
     Society, London.
Cox, C.B. and Boyson, R. (eds) The Fight for
     Education Black Paper, 1975, Dent, London.
Donald, J. (1979) 'Green Paper: noise of crisis'
     Screen Education, No. 30.
Donnison, Report (1970) Second Report of the Public
     Schools Commission, Vol. 1, Report on

Independent Day Schools and Direct Grant
Grammar Schools, HMSO, London.

Ginsburg, M.B., Meyenn, R.J., Miller, H.D.R. and
Ranceford-Hadley, C. (1977) The Role of the
Middle School Teacher, Aston Educational
Enquiry Monograph, No. 7, University of Aston
in Birmingham.

Ginsburg, M.B., Meyenn, R.J., and Miller, H.D.R.
(1979) 'Teachers, the 'Great Debate' and the
Education Cuts' in Westminster Studies in
Education, Vol. 2.

Goldthorpe, H.J., Lockwood, D. Bechofer, F., Platt,
J. (1968) The Affluent Worker in the Class
Structure, Cambridge University Press,
Cambridge.

Grace, G. (1978) Teachers, Ideology and Control,
RKP, London.

Green Paper (1977) Education in Schools: A
Consultative Document, July 1977, HMSO, London.

Habermas, J. (1976) Legitimation Crisis, Heinemann
Educational Books, London.

Hammersley, M. and Woods, P. (eds) (1976) The
Process of Schooling, RKP, London.

Hargreaves, A. and Tickle, L. (eds) (1980) Middle
Schools: Origins, Ideology and Practice,
Harper and Rowe, London.

HMI and LEA Study (1981) Curriculum 11 to 16, a
Review of Progress, DES, HMSO, London.

Jackson, B. and Marsden, D. (1962) Education and the
Working Class, RKP, London.

Lortie, D.C. (1975) School Teacher, University of
Chicago Press, Chicago.

Luhman, N. (1970) 'Positive Recht and Ideologie' in
Sociologische Aufklarung, Opladen, for example.
Quoted in Habermas, op. cit., p.98 and
critiqued pp.130-142.

Newsom Report (1963) Half Our Future, Report of the
Central Advisory Council for Education
(England) HMSO, London.

Reid, M.I., Clunies-Ross, L.R., Goacher, B. and
Vice, C., 'Mixed ability teaching, problems
and possibilities' in Educational Research,
Vol. 24, No. 1, November 1981, NFER, Slough.

Robbins Report (1963), Report of a Committee on
Higher Education, appointed by the Prime
Minister in 1961. Higher Education, HMSO,
London.

Simon, B. (1977) 'Marx and the crisis in education'
Marxism Today (July:195-205).

Taylor, W. (1980) Education: A Redefinition. Talk
given at a conference of local authority

inspectors and advisors, September 1980, Mimeo, London Institute of Education.

Wallace, G. (1980a) 'Architectural constraints on educational aims and organisations, with particular reference to middle schools'. In Journal of Educational Administration and History, Vol. XII, No. 2, July 1980, Leeds University.

Wallace, G. (1980b) 'The constraints of architecture on the aims and organisation of five middle schools'. In Hargreaves, A. and Tickle, L. (eds) Middle Schools: Origins, Ideology and Practice, Harper and Rowe, London.

Wallace, G. (1981) 'Countervailing strategies in the organisation of schooling' Paper presented at an international seminar, Teacher Education in the 1980's and 90's, Danbury Park Conference Centre, April 10-16, 1981.

Wallace, G. (forthcoming) Structural Limits and Teachers' Perspectives on Pedagogy. Unpublished Ph.D. thesis, University of Aston in Birmingham, England.

White, J. (1975) 'The end of the compulsory curriculum'. The Doris Lee Lectures, 1975, University of London, quoted in Grace, op. cit.

Table 1: Teachers Perceptions of Job Change

Broad category of response	Numbers		%	
	1979/80	1980/81	1979/80	1980/81
Generally a bureaucratic or top-down pressure (inc High Schools)	10	30	20.4	61.2
Job was always changing/need for constant adaptations	6	4	12.2	8.2
Increasing social problems/pastoral care work/pupil behaviour difficulties	15	7	30.6	14.3
No changes at all	9	5	18.4	10.2
Change directed to establishing a 'middle school identity' through school policies	5	0	10.2	0
Personal strategy for change	0	1	0	2.0
Missing	4	2	8.2	4.1
TOTAL	49	49	100	100

Table II: Teacher perception of changing 'standards'

	1980/81 Stayed the same	Improved	Worsened	Varies yearly	% Row Total
1979/1980					
Stayed the same	11.4	9.1	6.8	2.3	29.5
Improved	9.1	11.4	2.3	4.5	27.3
Worsened	9.1	0	6.8	4.5	20.5
Varies yearly	2.3	6.8	2.3	11.4	22.7
Column Total %	31.8	27.3	18.2	22.7	100.0

Missing observations 5

Table III: Teachers' perception of the power of 'teachers in general' to influence policy

% Response	IN SCHOOL		AT COUNTY LEVEL		AT CENTRAL GOVERNMENT LEVEL	
	1980	1981	1980	1981	1980	1981
1. Considerable power	38.1	32.7	0	2.0	0	2.0
2. Some power	42.9	38.8	20.4	20.4	4.1	8.2
3. There's a balance between different interests	12.2	10.2	14.3	8.2	2.0	4.1
4. Very little power	2.0	6.1	40.8	38.9	55.1	36.7
5. No power at all	2.0	0	16.3	14.3	28.6	32.7
*Missing observations	2.0	12.2	8.2	16.3	10.2	16.3

*Three respondents (6.1%) avoided replying directly to all but the first part of this question. The rest of the missing responses are accounted for by a failure to complete the schedule in the time available.

Table IV: Teachers' years of experience, related to their perception of teacher power to influence policy

Years of experience	School		County		Central government		N
	1979/80	1980/81	1978/80	1980/81	1979/80	1980/81	
Under 5	1.7*	2.2	3.5	3.1*	4.2	3.9	10
5 to 15	2.0	2.0	3.8	4.0	4.5	4.5	17
Over 15	1.4	1.6	3.4	3.0	4.7	3.6	14

*Difference significant at better than the 5% level.

137

Table V: Status positions and differences in teachers' perception of their power to influence events

	School		County		Government		N
	1979/80	1980/81	1979/80	1980/81	1979/80	1980/81	
Admin	1.3	1.6	2.9	3.0	4.4	3.6	8
Co-ords	1.8	1.8	3.8	3.7	4.7	4.2	11
Advisers	1.8	2.1	3.6	3.3	4.4	4.1	14
Cl teach	1.8	2.0	4.0	3.8	4.4	4.1	8

6. THE PERIPHERALISATION OF YOUTH IN THE LABOUR MARKET: PROBLEMS, ANALYSES AND OPPORTUNITIES: BRITAIN AND THE FEDERAL REPUBLIC OF GERMANY

Bill Williamson

INTRODUCTION

This paper considers the process of the transition from school to work in two societies, Britain and the Federal Republic of Germany. The economic fortunes of the two societies have been very different. In comparison with that of Britain the German economy, at least until the onset of the recession from 1973 onwards, experienced steady growth in output, productivity and earnings and all of this was achieved with one of the lowest rates of inflation in Western Europe and a strong currency.

But such differences nonetheless conceal some striking similarities. In both societies unemployment is increasing (Hanby and Jackson, 1979) and, with respect to the theme of this paper, a significant number of young people in the two societies are being driven to the periphery of labour market into unemployment or jobs which carry little promise for a secure future (O.E.C.D., 1980). In both societies young people affected in this way typically find little that is positive in their experience of school; they leave ill-equipped to face the obstacles and uncertainties of a labour market which no longer has any real need of their labour. The response of the governments of the two societies to the problems of rising youth unemployment have been remarkably similar, too. Schemes for subsidising the employment of young people, of vocational training and of strengthening the links between industry and schooling have developed rapidly in both societies just as they have done throughout the states of western Europe.

A closer inspection, however, reveals the differences again. The logic of the transformation of
the capitalist economy expresses itself in the same
way in the two societies, but the background in each
case is different. Demographic differences, institutional differences in education, apprenticeship
training, and differences in the structure of the
two labour markets result in patterns of transition
from school to work with marked contrasts between
the two societies and with the prospect of marked
differences in the future. And herein lies the
importance of comparative studies. Given that the
structural changes of the capitalist economy exert
themselves similarly in the two societies it is
nonetheless the case that the outcome of these pressures are different. Comparative studies help us to
qualify the generalisations which we must make about
how modern capitalist societies are changing.

The central claim which I seek to develop in
this paper is this: in both Britain and West Germany
some groups of young people, the unqualified and the
untrained, are being driven to the margins of the
economy with little prospect of decent jobs. One
aspect of this is that young people who, in the
1950s and 1960s might have taken up white collar
occupations or technical employment are now filling
jobs which the least qualified once filled. Youth
unemployment in both societies is high and likely
to remain so. In this way the disadvantaged young -
along with the sick, the old and those not well
organised - are bearing the real costs of the restructuring of the capitalist economy. The inabili-
ty of the formal system of schooling to prepare
young people adequately for the real situation they
face is one aspect of this and also part of the
reason for the increased activity of governments in
seeking to manage more carefully what happens to
young people after school.

The development of measures to prepare more
young people for work in all west European societies
is something which signals two quite distinct potentialities. On the one hand such measures can be
seen as attempts on the part of the state to discipline and control the unemployed, a series of crisis
measures to foster a belief among them that work
will eventually come available thereby securing
their continued support for the present social
order. On the other hand, such developments offer
new opportunities particularly, as I shall show, in
the field of youth work and vocational training to
challenge existing structures of employment in ways

THE PERIPHERALISATION OF YOUTH IN THE LABOUR MARKET

which could lead to more fundamental changes in
society. What the opportunities are varies, of
course, with context; one of the aims of this paper
is to identify what opportunities for change there
are in both Britain and the Federal Republic.

CONTEXTS

The background of this paper is the changing relationship between the system of education and vocational training which exists in the two societies of
Britain and West Germany and the needs of the labour
market for the labour of young people. Given the
present recession and the longer term restructuring
of industry which is part of it, it seems clear that
the link between schooling and working cannot be
left any longer to the chance play of market forces
or to the quiet unfolding of literally millions of
private decisions about what kind of training or
education to follow. The disjunction which currently exists between expectations developed since the
Second World War for steady employment and the
ability of the labour markets of West Europe to meet
those expectations is a serious social problem. And
not just for those who, in a formal educational
sense, are not well qualified. It is also a problem
for well-qualified school leavers who find themselves having to lower their expectations of the
kind of work they will seek. The argument can be
illustrated in the following diagram.

Diagram 1:   The Peripheralisation of Youth in the
             Labour Market

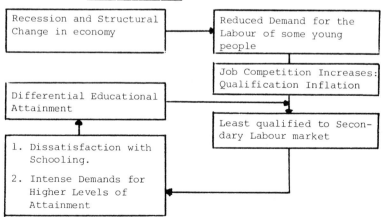

Each element in this model represents a complex set of social and economic processes in their own right and there is not sufficient space to elaborate each step in the argument. But it is necessary to clarify some of its assumptions concerning the present phase of the development of capitalist society. The reason is simple. Without a view of what the underlying structural transformations of the modern capitalist economy are, it is not possible to assess the significance of social policies for the unemployed young. Simply put, the assumptions I make are as follows. Firstly, in order to remain competitive and retain market shares and prevent the rate of profit from falling, firms in a capitalist society where labour costs have been high through trade union action, must seek to substitute machinery for labour. The consequences of not doing so include lower productivity relative to market competitors, rising real costs, diminishing market shares and unemployment. Secondly, through the world realignment of capitalist production effected through international companies the profit to investment in the developed capitalist societies comes not from the existence there of cheap labour but from the availability of scarce skills and scientific and technical knowledge. Investment in high technology industry is more likely because labour costs are high; where a production process requires a lot of labour then investment will be located where labour is relatively cheap. In this way societies on the European periphery or in the Third World can be exploited as reserves of cheap labour. Both pressures affect the employment structure of the developed capitalist societies. Unemployment among those not highly skilled rises to leave a growing pool of permanently unemployed. And there are structural reasons, connected with the historical success of organised labour in these societies in securing various forms of benefit from the state why these technical and economic changes will work most strongly against the interest of the young. Finally, because of the social stresses economic change generates, the state has to play a much more direct role in crisis management to stabilise both conflicts in society and its own fiscal base (Habermas, 1976).

The structural ramifications of these trends are legion. What concerns me here, however, are their effects on the system of the occupational placement of young people and the increasing involvement of the state in that system. The growth of youth unemployment among the states of Western Europe symbolises the issues very clearly.

The growth in the numbers of young people who are unemployed is as follows.

Table 1:   Youth Unemployment in the European Economic Community

	Total Million	Unemployed under 25	Youth unemployed as % of total
1974	7.4	0.8	33.3
1976	4.9	1.8	36.7
1978	5.7	2.1	36.8
1979	5.7	2.2	38.5

Source: Vocational Training 4, 1980.

In Britain and the Federal Republic the figures are as follows. They indicate a steady rise in the numbers of unemployed young people during the 1970s.

Table 2:   Proportion of Young People (i.e. less than 25) among the Unemployed

	U.K.	FRG	EEC
1970	27.3	18.7	26.0
1971	31.1	19.8	27.3
1972	31.7	19.8	28.2
1973	27.5	23.3	28.7
1974	30.4	23.1	30.2
1975	41.9	24.9	34.5
1976	43.9	25.6	36.7
1977	45.5	26.6	37.9
1978	44.9	25.6	43.3
1979	44.1	23.8	40.6

CEDEFOP 'Youth Unemployment and Alternance Training in the EEC' 1980 Conference Report (p.208)

It is important to note, however, that, high as these figures are they probably underestimate the real size of the problem. It has been estimated, for instance, in the Federal Republic that register-ed young unemployment constitutes only 60 per cent of the real figure because a significant group of young people simply do not bother to register (Schober, 1979). In addition the fact that there are in both societies schemes to subsidise the em-ployment of the young and to keep them off the registers in some form of training means that the real unemployment figure is inevitably always higher than the numbers registered as unemployed. In the U.K., for example, the numbers of young people en-rolled on the Youth Opportunities Scheme increased from 1 in 8 in 1978 to 1 in 3 in 1980 (i.e. from 162,000 in total to 360,000 in 1980) (MSC, Oct. 1981). A total of 630,000 places are being planned for 1982 (MSC, Jan. 1982). It amount to this: with-out the youth opportunities scheme 1 out of every 2 school leavers would be unemployed. These data raise fundamental questions about the long-term value of the kind of training young people are being offered in different government schemes and I shall come to these later. My point for the moment is that the employment market for a significant group of young people has collapsed.

The groups at greatest risk of unemployment are the least qualified school leavers (Department of Industry, 1977). The Holland report put it this way:

> The impact of unemployment is most severe on those young people who have few or no qualifications. In comparison with the better qualified they suffer longer duration of unemployment, are more frequently unemploy-ed and when employed they tend to work in lower status jobs with poorer prospects of promotion and fewer opportunities for training. Moreover, when there is a high level of unemployment, people with poor qualifications encounter increased competition for jobs from those of higher ability and with better qualifications.
> (MSC, 1977: 17)

Yet a significant proportion of the 17-18 year old age group in the EEC countries are neither in re-ceipt of vocational training or further education. The following table illustrates this point. It shows that 41 per cent of this age group were in this position in 1978:

Table 3:   Activities of the 16-18 age group 1978
            (U.K., FRG, EEC)

		% full-time educ. and training	% part-time educ. and training	% no education and training
FRG	16-17	50	35	15
	17-18	33	46	21
U.K.	16-17	60	7	33
	17-18	32	12	56
EEC	16-17	61	15	24
	17-18	41	18	41

Source: adapted from Vocational Training 4, 1980:
           71.

For the 'unqualified' and 'untrained', the risks of unemployment are high indeed. In addition, this group are more likely to experience extended periods of unemployment (Melvyn, 1977). But being trained and gaining skills is of itself no guarantee that work will be available. In 1977 in the Federal Republic, one third of those under 20 years of age who were unemployed were trained. This observation opens up the whole question of the relevance of training to the occupational life chances of young workers. I shall discuss this shortly but there is a real issue in whether the vocational training system in most European societies - even, perhaps particularly, in societies like West Germany where this system is very well developed - is at all in line with the long-term training needs of young workers. Are those currently being trained being trained for jobs which are likely to disappear?
      The problem for the moment though is the disc- repancy which clearly exists between the system of education and vocational training on the one hand and the needs of the labour market on the other. Unemployment for a growing number of young people is only one aspect of this. Stegman and Saterdag

have pointed to other aspects of it. Inadequate or unsuitable programmes of vocational training could result in young people changing jobs frequently. The risk that better qualified young people will lower their occupational aspirations and take over jobs which previously would have been filled by the less qualified is a real one. The pressure on schools to be more effective in their social selection is increasingly leading to both the phenomenon of both school stress and resignation (H. Stegman, H. Saterdag, 1978). Their work finds an echo in a comment by P. Melvyn reflecting on Europe-wide surveys of the attitudes of school leavers: 'Many young people', he writes 'and not only in the United Kingdom, seem to feel that the school system has little or nothing to offer them.' (1977, p.32).

It is not, however, just a question of the relationship between school and work which is a problem. The nature of the work young people have to do is also an issue. V. Koditz has noted that the underprivileged in work usually find themselves in smaller firms which are weak in the market and in which the threat of dismissal is great. It follows, he claims, that 'occupational indifference and instability and forms of diffused rebellion are more the consequences of the 'normal' work situation than the outcome of the changed employment situation.' (1978, p.14).

These problems of unemployment and the relevance of schooling to the world of work have come to occupy a central position in the policy deliberations of the E.E.C. In 1980, for example, the European social fund allocated 39 per cent of its total resources to measures designed to help young people. The amount thus allocated is double what was allocated in 1978 (European File 3/81, p.3). The Council of Ministers of the European Community have dealt frequently with the issues arising from high levels of youth unemployment and have recently endorsed the view that links between school life and work life ought to be strengthened throughout the EEC. They have endorsed a new concept to indicate the lines of policy they feel are necessary, the concept of alternance (see Vocational Training No. 4, 1980). It refers to the need, as the Ministers see it, to strengthen the dialogue between educators and employers to make the school curriculum more relevant to the pattern of vocational education and, ultimately, to the work young people will do in industry and commerce.

The responses of European states to these problems have been very similar and have taken the form of programmes of job creation and of vocational preparation. The Commission of the EEC reviewed these programmes in 1977 under the two headings, multilateral measures and unilateral measures. The second group are the most important and the Commission notes:

> All countries have, in one form or another, adopted measures of direct aid to job creation (including, where appropriate, tax relief or reduced social charges). The various procedures which implement these measures comprise three basic types of aid
>
> (a) premiums to undertakings to encourage them to increase their staff within the framework of their normal activity,
>
> (b) programmes of employment in the public sector in the context of general interest activities,
>
> (c) aids paid to undertakings to encourage them to organise periods of practical experience employing young job seekers.
>
> (Commission of the EEC, 1977)

The review of training measures which the Commission carried out included the following: vocational training programmes, vocational preparation programmes such as link courses, workshop courses, vocational guidance programmes and careers advisory services and placement programmes. These are the common patterns.

In Britain and the Federal Republic these programmes are managed mainly by, respectively, the Manpower Services Commission and the Bundesanstalt fur Arbeit working closely within a framework of employment policies and educational policies and in co-operation with employers, trades unions and voluntary bodies and local authorities. The resulting framework of policy is complex, rapidly changing and under-researched. I shall discuss some aspects of it in a moment. For the present, however, I want to indicate what such developments mean for an understanding of the school-work transition.

THE SCHOOL-WORK TRANSITION

Against such growing evidence of the involvement of
state agencies in the management of this aspect of
economic structure of modern societies, it would be
misleading to think of the process of entering the
labour market as one in which individuals adjust
their self-images to available opportunities and
make an occupational 'choice'. The literature on
occupational choice which grew in the 1960s in a
period of economic expansion now seems irrelevant to
a situation of recession and the collapse of work
for large numbers of young people. Notions like
'choice' have a hollow ring. The correspondence
between social class background and educational
attainment and entry into the labour market has
always, in any case, been high (Ashton and Field,
1976). Given this it seems clear that the notion
of choice was always an illusory one, a reflection
more of an idealised and, indeed, ideological view
of how labour markets were supposed to work than a
reflection of how they worked in practice. But the
rhetoric of choice is important; it gives credence
to an individualistic outlook and justifies a view
that what happens to people is the outcome, in large
part of how they manage themselves. Success and
failure, either in school or in the labour market
can then be explained in individual terms. And as
a corrollary, the aim of careers counselling for
the young is to assist them in making rational
choices consistent with their interests and inclin-
ations and think in the longer term to make sure the
investments they make in their education or training
will pay off handsomely in years to come; to make
sure, in short, that the first critical steps into
the world of work are taken rationally and purposefully.
So long as economic expansion could give some
credence to such a view the motivational problem
(Habermas, 1976) was a relatively straightforward
one of sustaining in young people a belief that
through hard work and educational achievement they
could realise in their own lives the important goals
which society held out for them. In the present
situation of recession the motivational problem,
even accepting that it will appear differently
according to standpoint, is essentially different.
For the unqualified whose work expectations were
never high the problem is one of compensating for
the absence in their lives of what would, in better
times, have been realised in work - namely, money

148

Diagram 2: The Transition from School to Work: Variables in a Process

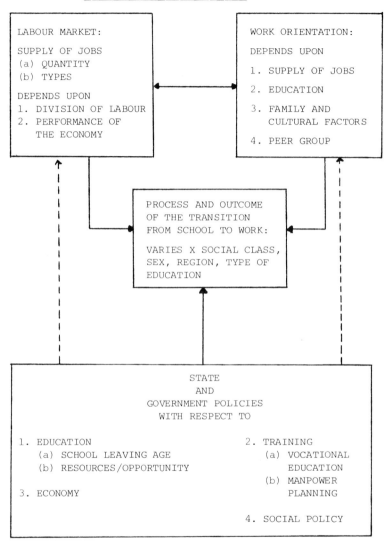

and the recognition of their peers and growing independence from the family. For the better qualified, given the growth of qualification inflation (Dore, 1976; OECD, 1977) there is the problem of adjusting expectations for high status work to the lack of such opportunities in the labour market. For the essential problem is this; expectations which have been built up in the thirty year period after the Second World War for ever-increasing standards of living fixated on the possession of ever more expensive consumer durables and lavishly indulged free time can now no longer be met.

For the young or, at least, some of them, such a discrepancy implies serious difficulties of a personal kind. For the state, however, the problem is different. The requirements of public order and social stability are pressing; disaffection must be contained and hopes kindled that the future still holds the promise of better things to come. How these two sets of expectations interact and with what outcomes is, of course, an open question. The outcomes will depend upon a range of factors including the demographic structure of different populations, the structure and outlook of trade unions and political parties, the actual performance of different economies and the consequences of different kinds of state policies for welfare and public order. I cannot speculate on these. But the point I wish to stress is this: the growth, all over Western Europe, of state involvement in the management of the school-work transition is likely to be a permanent feature of social policy for the foreseeable future. With this clearly in view it is obvious that the process of the transition from school to work is not one which can be represented adequately as a social process in which family and educational influences are in some way decisive. Such influences themselves are part of a more subtle mechanism of social reproduction in which the state itself plays a decisive role. The argument can be illustrated in Diagram 2.

The diagram does no more than suggest possible interconnections among the many factors which must be taken into account in assessing the different experiences of different groups of young people entering the labour market. Some of the relationships indicated have a great deal of empirical support. The variables connected with family and educational background are clearly of decisive importance. Reviewing research carried out on vocational guidance in several European states, V.

Koditz summarised the main findings thus: 'In nearly every member state vocational guidance (and job placement) plays only a secondary role as a source of information (and placement). The primary source of information (also the main placement instrument) remains the family or the immediate social environment.' (1978, p.12). For the less qualified, he writes; 'their concrete job expectations are more likely to be linked to the existing spectrum and distribution of jobs. A German study shows that a kind of synchronization of occupational aspiration and actual job distribution comes about quite independently of any vocational guidance' (1978, p.14). This same synchronization has been noted many times before. (See Ashton and Field, 1976; Willis, 1977; Saterdag and Stegman, 1979), although, of course, explanations of why it should occur differ significantly.

The connections between educational background and subsequent occupational attainment has, of course, been well known for a long time and has generated its own massive literature (see Collins, 1971; Bowles and Gintis, 1976; Halsey, Heath, Ridge, 1980). In suggesting a strong connection there is no suggestion that the school in some way prepares its students directly for the labour market. Indeed, quite the opposite is the case. Torsten Husen reflecting on research findings from an OECD committee looking into the link between education and the world of work, has noted an 'institutional mismatch between the two' with schools not providing the kind of 'functional participation' in the real world of jobs that he believes is vital to their future (Husen 1979: 155). And it is the recognition of this mismatch in several European states which explains the development of policies aimed at making schooling more directly relevant to the needs of young people entering work (Magnusson, 1977). In Britain the discussions which followed in the train of the 'Great Debate' opened up by Prime Minister Callaghan in his famous speech at Ruskin College, Oxford, and which focussed on such themes as the need for school leavers to appreciate more of the world of industry and to acquire the basic skills which would equip them in that world (Centre for Contemporary Cultural Studies, 1981) had their parallel in German discussions about the 'basic year of work education' (Berufsgrundschuljahr) and the notion of the 'mature citizen' (Mundige Burger). In both discussions the root question was how children could be better prepared for work.

The explanation for this common concern is to be found in the way in which some young people face difficulties in the labour market either in securing a job in the first place or in finding jobs which carry some prospect of security and further training. For there are structural pressures at work which discriminate against young people. Relative to workers who already possess marketable skills, young people are a less attractive proposition to employers of labour. Husen noted, for instance, that: 'Efforts to get students temporarily or permanently into the world of work are running up against the stumbling block represented by a highly rationalized and cost-effective economy. Youngsters coming direct from school - as well as workers close to retirement - are not considered profitable prospects by employers' (1979, p.156). P. Melvyn has suggested two reasons why this might be the case (1977). Quoting German research by Soltweden and Spinanger he argues 'The costs of employing young people are in the short term greater than the benefit to the firm'. And the reason for this is that the wage aspirations of young people are higher than their productivity. Secondly, he quotes evidence from the I.L.O. which, in the case of Britain, suggests that redundancy payment schemes have the effect 'to encourage cyclical shakeouts of the youngest workers, since in absolute and relative terms the cost to the economy of removing this type of worker was least' (1977: 27). If this is indeed the case then it is a good example of the unintended consequences of social action. Redundancy payments were never intended as a way of discriminating against the employment of young people.

The point I want to extract from this discussion, however, is that aspects of the structure of the labour market do shape the experience of young people entering the world of work. In this case there is an age segregation effect which feeds back on the attitudes and expectations of young people although, of course, in different ways, depending on circumstances. For some it increases the pressure they feel to do well at school to make sure of good school leaving certificates. Saterdag and Stegman refer to this as school stress. For others, the knowledge that jobs are in short supply can result in a lowering of expectations and a rejection of the values school supports (Boker, 1976). What is required, then, to appreciate what underlies the process of the transition from school to work and the pattern of occupational choice of different

groups of young people, is a sense of the interaction of economic, political and socio-cultural
conditions which define the structural locations of
different groups among them. It is within this set
of interacting forces that young people can arrive
at an understanding of their position in society.

VOCATIONAL TRAINING

I have already indicated that in Britain over fifty
per cent of young people in the 17-18 year age group
receive no further education or training. The figure for the Federal Republic is 21 per cent. This
reflects longstanding differences in the way in
which young people are filtered into training schemes for work. In the Federal Republic apprentices
account for 5.2 per cent of the civil employed population; the comparable figure for the United
Kingdom is 1.9 per cent (Vocational Training 1980,
p.75). Another way of looking at this is to be seen
in Table 4.

Table 4: Activities of Young People after
          Compulsory School Period

          Britain and FRG 1977

	% in: Full-time General Education	Full-time Vocational Education	Apprent- iceship	Work and/ or Unem- ployment
U.K.	32	10	14	44
FRG	21	19	50	9

Source: Hayes, C. (1980: 83)

     There is a clear difference in the pattern of
entry of young people into work and training. In
Germany a smaller percentage of young people remain
in formal schooling in comparison with Britain and
a much higher proportion enter some form of vocational training.
     The explanation of this is that in Germany it
is a legal requirement that children should complete
twelve years of education, the last three of which
can be completed in the form of part-time vocational
education. This is the so-called 'dual system' of

the FRG which caters for almost 60 per cent of the
age group. During this training young people have
the legal status of employees (OECD, 1980).

The differences between Britain and the FRG
reflect longstanding differences in emphasis on the
importance of a thorough training for work, in attitudes to education and in the values attached to
work in industry, to differences in the structure of
opportunity in the systems of secondary education
between the two societies and to some quite fundamental differences in the meaning attached to the
ideas of education (Bildung) and training (Ausbild-
ung). It amounts, however, to this: in Germany the
routes which young people follow into the worlds
either of work or higher education, have been much
more clearly defined in comparison with Britain.
The problem of what to do with the sixteen to nine-
teens, currently receiving so much attention in
Britain has not, until recently, been quite so acute
politically in the FRG.

This is not to say, however, that there is no
problem. The quality of the training offered in the
dual system, as well as the supply of places by the
private sector, have both been at the centre of
recent German discussions of vocational education.
Sixty per cent of apprentices receive their training
in enterprises which employ less than 50 employees
(Schmidt, 1981). And while, in 1979, there was a
surplus of 17,000 training places - about 4 per cent
more than demand - there were serious imbalances
between the two in some regions of the country and
in some sectors of the economy (European Commission
1981). And although the system, in principle, makes
training available in over four hundred different
trades, 70 per cent of trainees are concentrated in
the twenty most popular trades (OECD, 1980, p.119).
It has been argued, however, since firms will invest
in only those apprentices whose labour they can
actually use as part of current production the longer term training needs of those who will be required
in capital-intensive industry are not really being
met and that the most important consequence of this
is that those who are currently being trained are
being trained for jobs which might not exist in the
future or are being trained only to become unemployed when their training period is over (Lenhardt and
Schober, 198). Some support for this argument comes
from a report of the European Commission. Noting
that there had been some improvement in the number
of training places made available, the report nevertheless reported several critics - largely from

trades union sources - who argue that this improvement has been bought at the expense of quality
(European Commission, 1981, p.59). Moreover, claims
the Commission, some firms are unable to offer jobs
to apprentices when their formal period of training
is over and that this is one of the factors contributing to the growth of youth unemployment.

In both Britain and the FRG, however, the state
has come to play a far more positive role in relation to vocational preparation because in both cases
the labour market and traditional training systems
are inadequate to cope with the combined effects of
demographic change - more young people entering the
labour market - and recession. What has to be assessed therefore is the significance of the special
measures which have developed in the two societies.

SPECIAL MEASURES AND ALTERNATIVES

It is not possible to evaluate the importance of
special employment and training programmes without
some notion of an alternative to them (Lempert, W.,
1974). Seen in the context of the short-term
political goal of reducing unemployment or, indeed,
of giving to some young people a rudimentary training in work skills, such measures are of great
value. But questions do arise about their long-term
relevance and if these measures are evaluated
against some conceivable alternatives, it can be
seen how limited they really are.

It is difficult, however, to specify precisely
what the special measures aimed at the young really
are since they are in any case part of broader programmes including fiscal measures and regional
policies to maintain employment (Winterhager, 1980).
In Germany measures at both Federal and State level
under the legislation to promote employment - the
ArbeitsbeschaffungsMassnahmen under the
ArbeitsForderungsGesetz (AFG) of 1969 - are not
directed just at the young but necessarily the
affect this group. There are, however, special measures aimed at the young traceable through educational policy and employment policy. In Germany
measures in the former category include the development of the basic vocational educational year and
special measures to assist unemployed school leavers.
These include compensatory pre-vocational courses
for those who have found difficulty in finding
places in the dual system and special courses for
handicapped young people (OECD, 1980; Winterhager,
1980).

In the field of employment policy there is the law to encourage firms to maintain their quotas of apprenticeships. This is the Ausbildungsplatzforderungsgesetz of 1976 which imposes financial penalties of 0.25 per cent of a firm's total payroll if the number of training places offered falls below 12.5 per cent of the demand for places. Since its inception the penalty clauses of this legislation have not been invoked.

There is also a programme to develop apprenticeship training outside of particular firms in special centres. This is the programme of the uberbetriebliche Ausbildungsstatten. Overall, these programmes have added over 100,000 places annually or something like 5 per cent of the total (Winterhager, 1980). Without such schemes youth unemployment would have been twice as high as it actually was.

The figure for the contribution of such schemes to the reduction of unemployment among the young is comparable to that of Britain. But the emphasis among the various policies is different in the two societies. In Germany there is much more of an emphasis on combatting youth unemployment in the future through training. Until recently, on the other hand, the emphasis in Britain has been on temporary measures to reduce unemployment. Over 55 per cent of young people drawn into the net of special projects (including, for example, community industry programmes, community service projects, training workshop schemes and various work preparation schemes) are in the youth opportunities scheme working on employers' premises. Both the quality of the training given here and the level of remuneration under this programme have been quite severely criticised recently (e.g. Colin and Mog Ball, 1979; Centre for Contemporary Cultural Studies, 1980). And not just by experts; there have been demonstrations by young people against YOP programmes for their low pay and against the fact that many young people see the schemes as simply exploiting cheap labour. It seems as if a growing number of young people do not see temporary employment as 'proper work'. There is dissatisfaction in Germany, too. Many young workers without apprenticeships simply do not bother to attend part-time vocational schools and there is evidence of high truancy rates on the special courses for the unemployed (Aspen Institute, 1980, p.21). What is more, there is some slight evidence of young people becoming disillusioned with the training facilities on offer since they perceive few opportunities for themselves after the training is over

156

(Hanby and Jackson, 1979). Perhaps all that can be said unequivocally about such measures in both societies is that they have kept the level of youth unemployment lower than it would otherwise have been.

In addition to this outcome, however, there is a more fundamental common denominator. In both societies it is assumed that the solution to the crisis of unemployment among the young lies ultimately in the ability of private enterprise to regenerate itself. In this way most of the social policy initiatives referred to in this paper accept as an unquestioned premise that the problems can be solved within a given framework of society. A good example of this is given in the work of Reimut Jochimsen (1978) who has argued that the German measures for vocational training, taken together with the demographic fact that in the late 1980s the numbers in the younger age groups will fall, will ensure that the problem of youth unemployment will actually disappear. Such a view is inconsistent with other German assessments that capitalism actually needs a reserve army of disciplined unemployed to secure its future viability (Boker, 1979; Lenhardt, 1979). Conclusions about the value and effectiveness of employment and educational policies for the young depend, then, on particular analyses of how the capitalist economy functions and how it will change.

Such a conclusion, however, need not bring the argument about policy options to a close leaving people in different ideological camps. Rather it would open up questions about what the options for the present really are to effect changes in the life chances of the young people entering the labour market and to move beyond the ad hoc measures which are being taken at present in response to short-term political calculations and crisis management.

Three areas have received a great deal of discussion in this respect both in Britain and West Germany although the emphasis has been different in each case. They are (1) the field of youth work and the options which may exist here for new kinds of work with young people, (2) the period of the school work transition and the opportunities which exist to explore the new relationships between the last two or three years at school and the first few years of working life, and finally, (3) vocational training and the possibility of developing the general education of young people in the context of work itself.

The field of youth work is in both Britain and
the Federal Republic a small one with an overwhelming emphasis on the provision of leisure (Freizeit)
facilities for young people. But it has been the
experience of a growing number of youth workers
(sozialpadagogen) that helping unemployed young
people must involve more than just keeping them
entertained and off the streets. Radical youth
workers in Germany or, at least, some of them, are
moving towards a notion of youth work as a process
of political education among young people (Jordan, E.
1979; Boker, 1976). Their argument is that the problems young people face - particularly young people
who are unemployed - and including such things as
difficulties with parents, a sense of personal failure and worthlessness, boredom, conflict with the
police etc., cannot be detached from the overall
social and political context in which young people
find themselves. The task of the youth worker is
to help young people understand their position in
society and to know how to act positively and
creatively to change that position. Similar arguments have been developed in Britain and have come
to focus on what the conditions for radical youth
work are and involve discussions of how youth work
ought to relate to more broadly based strategies of
community work (Consultative Group on Youth and
Community Work Training, 1978). And at the heart
of such thinking is the aim of helping young people
develop a critical understanding of their position
and of the need to do so outside of existing institutions which have palpably failed to represent the
interests of the disadvantaged young (Robins and
Cohen, 1978).
The second area concerns the school to work
transition itself. This too has been at the centre
of much discussion recently. Colin and Mog Ball
have suggested that the link between school and work
should be much more flexible to allow young people
to experience the risks and challenges of work
directly. A similar argument has been developed by
Husen (1979). And they favour, too, breaking down
the barriers between schools and communities to
remove young people from the 'functionless vacuum'
which is the school. They argue for more diversity
of post-school provision and for continuous education and for a considerable broadening of the notion
of what it is to be educated. They believe it is
possible to build such flexible 'learning and
earning' systems but they are not naive about the
obstacles. And one of the greatest obstacles in the

world of work itself, the third and final area I wish to mention.

Technical change carries an ominous threat, that only relatively few people with high qualifications will be needed for the work which is available. The same process of change, however, creates many jobs which are menial and carry no hope of further personal development. The traditional craft-apprenticeship will become less important than the technician apprenticeship which demands higher skills and educational qualifications (Colin and Mog Ball, 1979, p.51). The question arises; given such possibilities what ought the shape of vocational education to look like? Is it reasonable to continue with a system of vocational training which prepares people for work when much of what they have to do is menial and requires only the barest minimum of skill? And is it reasonable to allow private industry and its training needs, geared as they are, necessarily, to the relatively short-term future and to existing technologies, to continue to determine the nature of the learning of young people in those decisive years immediately following school? Is there any way in which the work experience of young people can be changed to develop an environment conducive to further learning and development?

The answers to these questions vary considerably. Some writers, e.g. Gero Lenhardt, believe that apprenticeship training is the one area where reforms will be most difficult to affect since the control of labour is something capitalists will not give up (1978). Apprenticeship reform he says, 'entails deep inroads into capitalist property rights' and this is why governments have not been successful in this area. But he nonetheless recognises changes in vocational training for 'Capitalist ownership demands skill requirements which conflict with the worker's needs for personal growth and development' (1978, p.456).

Paradoxically it might be the case that the structural possibilities for change in vocational training are greater in Britain than in West Germany because vocational training in this country is, in a sense, not nearly so well developed. The Aspen Institute noted, for instance, in the case of the Federal Republic:

> ...the problem of designing training activites for the young unemployed...is made much more difficult by the existence of the highly developed and almost universal system of

apprenticeship which is adequate for those
within it but a major obstacle for those
outside it because they are so obviously
separated from mainstream provision (1980,p.21).

Perhaps what is needed, therefore, is a view of
the possibilities of change which might affect all
young people and which looks for new opportunities
for personal development in the world of work itself.
And here is the importance of the work of
Wolfgang Lempert of the Max Planck Institute of
Berlin (1974, 1978). It is too complex to discuss
in detail in such a short space. But its essential
vision is this: Much of the work available to
people in a capitalist society is fragmented, mono-
tonous and dehumanising. Because of the way in
which general education functions as a system of
social selection whose outcomes in terms of occupational placement are then reinforced by the system
of vocational training, it is essential to develop
an alternative to both. Education must, he argues,
countenance directly the world of work. It must
become polytechnical and reflect in its curricula
some of the skills which children will need in the
world of work. It must be non-selective so that
all children are introduced to these skills. It
should lead not simply to either further general
education for some and vocational education for the
majority but to work for all with further education
being woven into lifelong programmes of working and
learning. Work, he insists, is an area of personal
growth and development and its potentialities for
learning should be explored. This is the purpose of
the research with which Lempert is currently engaged
(1979), and through it he hopes to be able to influence the attitudes of trades unions towards what
vocational education could mean.
But such changes would be worthless in themselves were they not accompanied by quite fundamental changes in the division of labour itself to
reintegrate work tasks, humanize work and rotate
the essential tasks of planning and decision-making
so that all workers can take greater responsibilities, vary their experience and continue to develop
intellectually. What is required then, fundamentally, is a cultural revolution in attitudes to
work. Without the further development of such an
understanding, particularly among trade unionists
and educators then existing measures to cope with
the training needs of the young will continue to
play their present role, that of propping up a

system which can never offer any real hope of meeting the real interests of young workers.

CONCLUSION

What I have attempted to show in this paper is that there are processes of change in the capitalist economy which are common to all capitalist societies but which manifest themselves differently according to context. Differences between societies in such areas as the level of economic growth, the demographic structure of the populations, systems of vocational training and so on to ensure that the problems of, as in this case, young people are very different in different societies. But all the states of Western Europe have a problem of youth unemployment and all are seeking ways through special measures in the field of employment, education and training to overcome this problem. My argument, however, is that such problems are essentially intractable unless efforts are made to step outside the assumptions of existing social policies and to develop an alternative vision of what the prospects and options for the future really are. The three areas briefly discussed, education, youth work and vocational training all offer opportunities for change which must be explored. There can be no rational assessment of current policies unless the alternatives to them are clearly in view.

This paper arises out of research carried out in 1979-80 and made possible with financial help from the German Academic Exchange Service (D.A.A.D.). I would like formally to acknowledge their most generous help.

BIBLIOGRAPHY

Ashton, N., and Field, D. (1976), Young Workers, Hutchinson, London.
Aspen Institute for Humanistic Studies (Berlin), (1980), Youth Unemployment.
Ball, Cohn and Mog (1979), Fit for Work? Writers and Readers, London.
Boker, W. et al. (1976), Jugendarbeitslosigkeit: Reaktionen und Perspectiven der Sozialarbeit - Aspekte der Lebens - und Arbeitssituation Jugendlicher in der gegenwartige Krise. Neue Praxis, 6.

Bowles, S. and Gintis, H. (1976), Schooling in
    Capitalist America, Routledge and Kegan Paul,
    London.
Centre for Contemporary Cultural Studies (1981),
    Unpopular Education, Heinemann, London.
Collins, R., (1971), Functional and Conflict Theories
    of Educational Stratification, American
    Sociological Review, 36, No. 6.
Commission of the E.E.C. (1977), Bulletin of the
    European Communities, 4.
Consultative Group on Youth and Community Work
    Training (1978), Realities of Training, National
    Youth Bureau.
Department of Industry (1977), Untrained, Unqualified,
    Unemployed, H.M.S.O., London.
Dore, R., (1976), The Diploma Disease, Allen and
    Unwin, London.
European Economic Community (1981), European File.
Habermas, J. (1976), The Legitimation Crisis,
    Heinemann Education Books, London.
Halsey, A.H., Heath, A.F., Ridge, J. (1980) Origins
    and Destinations, Oxford University Press,
    London.
Hanby, V.J. and Jackson, M.P., An Evaluation of Job
    Creation in Germany in International Journal of
    Social Economics, Vol. 6, No. 2.
Hayes, C., (1981), Trends in Apprenticeship in the
    E.E.C. in C.E.D.E.F.O.P. Youth Unemployment and
    Alternance Training, E.E.C., Luxembourg.
Husen, T., (1979), The School in Question, Oxford
    University Press, London.
Jochimsen, R. (1978), Aims and Objectives of German
    Vocational and Professional Education in the
    Present European Context, Comparative Education,
    Vol. 14, No. 3, October.
Jordan, E., (1979), Jugendarbeitslosigkeit -
    Situation und Sozialpadagogische Moglichkeiten
    in Jugend, Beruf, Gesellschaft, Heft 1.
Koditz, V. (1978), Occupational Choice and Motiva-
    tion of Young People, Vocational Training, Vol.
    2.
Lempert, W. (1974), Berufliche Bildung als Beitrag
    zur Gesellschaftlichen Demokratisierung,
    Frankfurt am Main Suhrkamp verlag.
Lempert, W. (1979) Vocational Education, Division of
    Labour and Social Inequality, in Education and
    Working Life, Anglo-German Conference.
Lempert, W. (with Hoff, E. and Lappe, L.) (1979),
    Konzeptionen zur Analyse der Sozialisation
    durch Arbeit, Max Planck Institut, Berlin.

Lenhardt, G. (1979), Problems of Reforming Recurrent Education for Workers, Comparative Education Review, Vol. 22, No. 3.

Lenhardt, G., and Schober, K., (1980), Der schwierige Berufsstart: Jugendarbeitslosigkeit und Lehrstellenmarkt. in Max Planck Institut für Bildungsforschung (ed), Bildung in Der Bundesrepublik Deutschland, Rowohlt, Stuttgart.

Magnusson, O., (1977), Opportunity Structure for Early School Leavers, in Vocational Training, Vol. 1.

Manpower Services Commission, (1981, 1982) Special Project News.

Manpower Services Commission, (1977), Young People and Work.

Melvyn, P. (1977), Youth Unemployment in Industrialised Market Countries, International Labour Review, 116, No. 1, July-August 1977.

O.E.C.D. (Organisation for European Co-operation and Development) (1980) Youth Unemployment: The Causes and the Consequences, Paris.

O.E.C.D. (1977) Selection and Certification in Education and Employment, Paris.

Schmidt, H. (1981), Small and Medium Sized Enterprises determine the future of Vocational Training, Vocational Training, No. 7.

Schober, K. (1979), Jugendarbeitslosigkeit in Zahlen: Ausmass und Entwicklungstendenzen, in G. Lenhardt (Ed), Der Hilflose Sozialstaat. Jugendarbeitslosigkeit und Politik, Surkamp 1979, Frankfurt am main.

Stegman, H. and Saterdag, H., (1978), Jugendliche Beim Ubergang Vom Bildings - in Das Beschaftigungssystem (IAB Project 3 - 213E), Institut für Arbeitsmarkt und Berufsforschung der Bundesanstalt fur Arbeit.

Willis, P., (1977), Learning to Labour, Saxon House, London.

Winterhager, W.D. (1980), Berufsbildung und Jugendarbeitslosigkeit - Einschatzung der Situation in Max Planck Institut for Bildungsforschung (Ed) Bildung in Der Bundesrepublik Deutschland, Rowohlt, Stuttgart.

7. STATE POLICY AND SCHOOL EXAMINATIONS 1976--82: An exploration of some implications of the sixteen-plus controversy

Geoff Whitty

The research upon which this paper is based grew out
of an earlier study of the extent of teacher autonomy within CSE and GCE examinations, which was
carried out between 1973 and 1978. The latter
stages of that research coincided with a heightening
of the controversy that had been developing since
1970 over a proposed common system of examining at
16 plus and with the launching of the so-called
Great Debate on education. It also took place
during a period when the 'new sociology of
education' that had been in vogue during the early
1970s was increasingly being challenged by work with
a neo-Marxist theoretical orientation. I want to
argue in this paper that neither state policy
initiatives themselves, nor the cruder forms of neo-
Marxist analysis that have been used to explain
them, pay sufficient heed to the complexities of
policy implementation and the uncertainties
surrounding its outcomes. I also want to suggest
that a lack of interest in the detailed processes of
policy implementation has had unfortunate effects on
left policy and practice around education in recent
years. By discussing one relatively limited area of
educational policy and practice - school examining
at 16 plus - I hope to illustrate the more general
importance of exploring the specificities of
political and ideological practice in and around
education, whilst not abandoning a consideration of
the ways in which the demands of a capitalist
economy exert pressures, and perhaps set limits, on
the nature and significance of that practice.

BACKGROUND TO THE STUDY

The earlier research on teacher autonomy had begun

in a context where the common system of examining
was only a distant possibility, where the ideology
of teacher professionalism remained largely un-
challenged and where, within the sociology of education, phenomenological perspectives were at the
height of their influence. The research sought to
explore a view, later given formal expression by
Eggleston (1975), that the social control function
of education was secured largely through the
conservatism of 'teachers' own consciousness' rather
than through the more formal constraints imposed by
the work of curriculum development agencies or
examining boards. Concentrating on courses leading
to public examinations at 16 plus, the research
recognised that, while the majority of teachers
were content to operate well within any constraints
imposed by such agencies, a significant minority of
teachers sought to overcome such formal constraints
as did exist by utilising the Mode 3 regulations
within the CSE boards and, to a much lesser extent,
within the GCE boards. A much smaller minority of
these teachers, those who sought to use these
regulations for explicitly radical ends, became the
central focus of the study as constraints on their
practice clearly could <u>not</u> be understood purely in
terms of a theory of the conservatism of teacher
consciousness. The study (Whitty, 1976) revealed
that the boards exercised considerable constraints
upon the autonomy of these teachers and it seemed
to offer only limited support for Eggleston's claim
that, in exercising control of the educational
system via teacher consciousness, the system was
potentially vulnerable to a radicalisation of
teacher consciousness. In general terms, then, the
study offered more support for Sharp and Green's
argument that the phenomenological perspective was
flawed because 'what seems to be crucial is whether
in the last analysis one can control others and
bring sanctions to bear against others, irrespective of their definition of reality' (Sharp and
Green, 1975).

Yet although this research concluded that, in
practice, teachers had had only very limited autonomy even in this earlier period, it also revealed
that the limits to that autonomy were beginning to
be drawn significantly more tightly by the end of
the 1970s than they had been during the previous
decade. It was the changes in the relationship
between schools, examining boards and other
agencies, and the articulation of these changes with
broader attacks on the concept of professional auto-

nomy, that became the focus of the subsequent study
which is discussed in the present paper. This
research was carried out through observation and
interviewing in schools, examining boards and
various other relevant interest groups during the
period 1976-82. It also involved the scrutiny of
the minutes of a number of the examining boards, together with the regulations and circulars that they
issued to schools in this period. Increasingly,
however, the research developed an additional focus
by examining in some detail the developing controversy over the proposed new system of examining at
16 plus, and particularly over the degree of
teacher control that would be permitted under such a
system. This project involved the study of
official pronouncements about the proposed system,
the response to those pronouncements and the press
coverage of the ongoing debate. The research sought
to understand the effects of changes in policy discourse on the practices of the examination boards
and the implications of both for teachers within the
schools. At the same time, it sought to explore the
extent to which such changes in policy and practice
in school examinations could be related to broader
policy initiatives concerning professional autonomy,
accountability and the content and relevance of the
school curriculum to the needs of contemporary
society. Finally, it was concerned to examine the
ways in which such developments articulated with the
wider economic, political and ideological climate of
the period, thus exploring how far the ability 'to
control others and bring sanctions to bear against
others' in this particular arena could be seen to
derive from 'the distribution of power and authority
in the macro-structure' (Sharp and Green, 1975). The
intention here, then, was to utilise the research
data in an interrogation of the increasingly
fashionable neo-Marxist perspectives in the
sociology of education.

MODE 3 AND THE 16 PLUS CONTROVERSY

In themselves Mode 3 examinations, which give classroom teachers a greater degree of involvement in
designing and assessing examination courses than
they usually have within the more conventional Mode
1 system, are a relatively marginal aspect of the
English examination system. They certainly cannot
be said to have destroyed the effectiveness of the
external examination system as 'almost all that
remains of the "public" aspect of the school

curriculum' in Britain (Maclure, 1975). Most CSE
entries have continued to be made under the Mode 1
regulations and those Boards where this has not been
the case have generally been regarded as anomalies.
In most areas, teacher control of CSE examinations
has effectively meant formal control of the structures of the Boards by senior members of the
profession rather than a major devolution of power
to teachers on the classroom floor. Within the
high-status O-level sector, where teacher involvement even in the formal structures has remained more
limited, the penetration of Mode 3s in terms of
subject entries has been negligible in national
terms despite some significant institutional and
regional variations in this picture. Many of the
Mode 3s that do exist have been relatively conventional in the nature of their content and many of
those that can be seen as innovative have been
designed to bring into the examinable curriculum
practical or vocationally-orientated subjects
excluded from the Mode 1s on offer. In many
schools, the major motivation for introducing Mode
3s has been to extend the public examination system
beyond the top sixty per cent of pupils, not as a
way of challenging the legitimacy of that system,
but as a way of solving motivational and social control problems within the school. In view of this,
and the findings of my own earlier piece of
research, it may seem tempting to agree with Donald
(1978) that 'it remains puzzling that Mode 3s should
be regarded as subversive'.

Nevertheless, despite their relative mar-
ginality and the conservative nature of many Mode 3
schemes, the Mode 3 issue became during the 1970s a
symbol around which broader struggles over the
future content and control of the school examination
system could be fought out. As long as even a few
radical teachers celebrated Mode 3 as providing a
space within the educational system from which they
could initiate change, Mode 3 - as the fullest
extension of the principle of teacher control so far
permitted - could provide excellent ammunition for
those opposed to teacher control in general. It is
clear from a variety of statements from both the
left and the right that the Mode 3 facilities for
teachers to develop and assess their own courses at
examination level constitute a symbol of the possibilities open to teachers to utilise the state
educational system for radical purposes, however
limited such possibilities may actually be in
practice. In 1974, Murdock certainly viewed the

Mode 3 regulations as providing teachers with the
opportunity to establish courses which:

> encourage pupils to develop and articulate
> their own particular sense of themselves and
> their situation, over and against the
> definitions imposed on them from outside....
> (and) by moving pupils out of their role as
> consumers and enabling them to become
> producers....demystify the process of
> authorship and cut away the dominant
> definitions of 'cultural' production as some-
> thing separate from everyday life and best
> left to the experts. (Murdock, 1974)

Thus Mode 3 regulations seemed to offer the possibility of replacing a traditional concept of the
curriculum - what Young (1977) has termed
'curriculum as fact' - with an alternative and more
liberating conception of 'curriculum as practice'.
This resonated strongly with the themes of radical
community politics in the late 1960s and early
1970s, but Mode 3s have also received support from
the organised revolutionary left (Hurford, 1979)
even though it has sometimes been suspicious of the
sort of individualism that some Mode 3s seem to
encourage. Meanwhile, there are those on the right
who take equally seriously the idea that Mode 3
examinations pose a threat to the sort of society
that traditional forms of examination serve to
uphold. Cox has argued as follows:

> In recent years Left-wing teachers have
> exploited a more general dissatisfaction
> with GCE examinations to propose that
> external assessment should be replaced with
> teacher assessment, and that the present
> system of O & A levels should be abandoned.
> Some fanatics want to abolish all external
> controls on the school curriculum. Examina-
> tions are said to be "elitist", even
> "fascist", an essential part of a class-
> stratified, competitive society, a barrier
> to the emergence of a truly popular culture.
> (Cox, 1980)

It is evident, then, that teacher-assessment in
public examinations is an issue that can potentially
take us right to the heart of a debate about the
sort of society we aspire to and the role of
teachers in creating it. There is little doubt that

the issue of Mode 3 examinations formed an important
sub-plot in the considerable and widespread 'moral
panic' about education in the mid and late-1970s in
which teachers were seen as, at best, selling the
country short, or at worst, actually fostering
revolution in the classroom. If William Tyndale
School was made to provide the major pretext for the
subsequent reining in of teacher autonomy (Dale,
1981a), Mode 3 and the issue of teacher control of
examinations also played its part. A series of
articles by Christopher Rowlands in the Daily Mail
(e.g. Rowlands, 1977) helped to place the issue
before the public view, while a statement by Tom
Howarth to a meeting at the House of Commons to the
effect that 'we cannot afford to become a CSE Mode 3
nation' (T.E.S., 1977) symbolically linked the
issues of teacher power and national decline and
helped to legitimate attempts to restrict or abolish
Mode 3s and modify those parts of the Schools
Council's 16 plus proposals that seemed to point in
the direction of teacher control. Yet these were
only the most public manifestations of a campaign
that had been raging in political and educational
circles at least since the publication of the
Schools Council's recommendations about the new
examination in September 1975 (J.E.S.C., 1975).

Although by no means all the critics of the 16
plus proposals accepted Cox's claim that 'a main aim
of the reformers is that CSE Mode III (teacher
assessed) exams will become the norm' or even shared
his own suspicions of their 'underlying ideological
purpose' (Cox, 1980), the possibility that teacher-
assessed work would be a significant part of any new
examination arrangements did seem to provide a major
source of concern for many of those contributing to
the debate. Conservative politicians, leading
industrialists, senior university academics, as well
as some of the more traditional school examination
boards, joined in a massive establishment onslaught
on the initial proposals. During 1975 and 1976 the
press contained numerous letters, articles, and
reports of speeches attacking CSE standards and the
Mode 3 option and trying to ensure that such models
did not come to dominate the new examination, upon
whose credibility the legitimation of access to high
status occupations might depend. Norman St.John
Stevas, Lord Belstead, Lord Annan, the CBI, the
CVCP, and the London and Cambridge examination
boards were amongst those who publicly attacked the
16 plus proposals by citing the problems of teacher-
assessed elements or teacher control. It is hardly

surprising that, in the face of this sort of opposition, Shirley Williams, Secretary of State for
Education, chose, in October 1976, to delay the
implementation of the Schools Council's proposals
and submit them to a further round of deliberations
by the Waddell Committee. At this very time, the
Great Debate on education was in the process of
being launched with the preparation of the Government's Yellow Book and the now-famous speech by
Prime Minister Callaghan at Ruskin College on 18
October 1976. Hopkins (1978) has suggested that it
was 'partly because of the Schools Council's
injudicious exam proposals' - which 'seemed to imply
the most radical extension of teacher-power, with a
heavy reliance on the Mode III principle' - that
'teacher power was one of the main targets the
Yellow Paper (sic) shot at' and hence became one of
the central issues in the ensuing Great Debate. Even
the Waddell recommendations (D.E.S., 1978a) and the
government's subsequent White Paper (D.E.S., 1978b)
failed to satisfy the critics, despite the concessions that had been made to them, and since the
Conservatives came to power in 1979 and produced
further modifications, there has been continuing
pressure on the Secretaries of State to limit the
opportunities for teacher involvement in assessment
even further (Shaw, 1982).

EXISTING ACCOUNTS

One way of viewing recent developments within and
around school examinations is to see them as part of
a broader attempt to bring education into line with
the demands of the economy in a period of economic
crisis, a policy which is seen by its advocates and
critics alike as necessitating some limitation of
the freedom of teachers and particularly the closing
down of any "space" within the system which has
allowed politically radical teachers to flourish.
This can be seen in the demands made by leading
industrialists and in the official support given to
such demands by James Callaghan in launching the
Great Debate in 1976. Thus, in a now-famous
article, published early in 1976 and headed 'I blame
the teachers', Sir Arnold Weinstock, managing
director of GEC, wrote as follows:

> Teachers fulfil an essential function in the
> community but, having themselves chosen not
> to go into industry, they often deliberately
> or more usually unconsciously instil in their

> pupils a similar bias....And this is quite
> apart from the strong though unquantifiable
> impression an outsider receives that the
> teaching profession has more than its fair
> share of people who are actively politically
> committed to the overthrow of liberal
> institutions, democratic will or no democratic
> will.
>   The most insidious and "respectable" version
> of this anti-industry bias has impeccable
> antecedents. At least since Plato, there
> has been a deep-seated preference in Western
> culture (reinforced in Britain by our class
> structure) for the life of the mind over the
> practical life. But why should children be
> taught that the products of the brain will
> be valued more highly than the products of
> the hands? (Weinstock, 1976)

Such sentiments struck a cord with Callaghan who,
in announcing the opening of the Great Debate, made
the following observations:

> But I am concerned on my journeys to find
> complaints from industry that new recruits
> from the schools sometimes do not have the
> basic tools to do the job that is required.
>   I have been concerned to find that many
> of our best trained students who have com-
> pleted their higher levels of education at
> university or polytechnic have no desire to
> join industry. Their preferences are to stay
> in academic life or to find their way into
> the Civil Service. There seems to be a need
> for a more technological bias in science
> teaching that will lead towards practical
> applications to industry rather than toward
> academic studies. (Callaghan, 1976)

During the subsequent debate, there were frequent
charges that teachers had abused society's mandate
or had at least used the relative autonomy granted
to the educational system in the 1950s and 1960s for
purposes which, if not directly antagonistic to the
survival of capitalist industry, had certainly
become inappropriate in a period of economic crisis.
In the Green Paper that formally brought the first
phase of the Great Debate to an end (D.E.S., 1977),
it was stressed that the whole range of government
policies, including education, should 'contribute as
much as possible to improving industrial performance

and thereby increasing the national wealth'. In
curriculum terms, this meant that pupils should be
taught to 'appreciate how the nation earns and maintains its standard of living and properly to esteem
the essential role of industry and commerce in this
process'. Although subsequent documents emanating
from the D.E.S. and the Inspectorate showed that
there was far from total agreement about how far
such a process should go, there was a general
acceptance that there should be a greater degree of
standardisation in the school curriculum and that it
should be given a greater degree of relevance to
adult and working life than had hitherto apparently
been the case.

Interestingly, a number of neo-Marxist writers,
often drawing upon the work of Holloway and
Picciotto (1977), have made not dissimilar statements about the underlying pressures upon
contemporary educational policy in general and
examination reform in particular. Donald (1978),
for example, has suggested that, as part of a
functionalisation of the state for the accumulation
of capital, one would expect to find 'examinations
being made more "efficient" in terms of what they
test, how the testing is done, and how the system
is controlled'. Another writer, discussing the 16
plus proposals in a radical teachers' journal,
argues that they:

> represent a way in which the 'space' that
> education once had within society is being
> eroded, as the ruling class seeks a more
> direct and effective control over education
> than can be achieved through the Teacher
> Establishment....
> The CSE Boards have not been as dominated
> by the higher education interests as the GCE
> and have therefore been a less effective
> means of curriculum control. The new GCE
> (sic) Boards will correct this and ensure
> more proper representation from 'industry'.
> Put in these terms it is easier to see how
> the 16+ will fit the new scenario where on
> the one hand education is more clearly seen
> to serve the interests of the nation/industry
> and on the other appear to give equality of
> opportunity in the shrinking job market..
> (Hurford, 1979)

Such analyses correctly identify some of the
influences which underlie and affect contemporary

173

state policies for education and school examinations. However, they tend to assume that particular
pressures are the only ones operating and that, by
and large, the needs of capital feed through to and
have effects in the educational arena in relatively
straightforward and unproblematic ways. In doing
so, they are particularly susceptible to Nowell-
Smith's charge of 'falling back into the usual
banalities of British leftism of the "well-it's-all-
capitalism-isn't-it?" variety', and thus invite a
premature rejection of neo-Marxist perspectives as
irrelevant to an understanding of contemporary
educational struggles. In its crudest forms, this
sort of analysis permits critics such as Lawton
(1980) to claim that neo-Marxist theories 'would
have us believe that the control of the curriculum
is simply a question of bourgeois hegemony' and that
the 'whole of the cultural superstructure is a
reflection of the values of the dominant group -
i.e. the bourgeoisie or the capitalist ruling class'.
Although Lawton is certainly correct to claim that
'the question of the control of education and the
content of education is much more complicated than
that', he is not necessarily justified in implying
that neo-Marxist scholarship is thus rendered
entirely irrelevant to an understanding of those
complications. Nowell-Smith is much nearer the
mark when he writes:

> A full analysis of, say, the changes in the
> examination system must take into account
> the way the requirements of capital
> accumulation make themselves felt in the
> education sector....But the ideology of
> examinations cannot be 'derived' in any
> adequate way from the logic of capital and
> the capitalist state. (Nowell-Smith, 1979)

As he goes on to say, the steps from 'a general
analysis of the capital form to a particular analysis of ideologies in conjuncture are many and
slippery' and the arguments that are often employed
in the literature are 'at best devious, at worst
metaphysical'.
    Arguments based upon the progress of a logic of
capitalism tend to obscure the historically
contingent nature of the outcomes of the various
policy initiatives mounted on behalf of capital. To
put it another way, they tend to ignore what, in a
recent article on unemployment and training
initiatives in Australia, Freeland (1980) terms the

'refractions' which the imperatives of capital accumulation and the demands incorporated into state policy discourse undergo in the process of implementation. My own earlier work (Whitty, 1977) perhaps failed to give adequate recognition to this. It ignored the extent to which industrial and governmental initiatives in the field of education have actually been resisted within the dominant order and might potentially have been resisted by more oppositional groupings in and around the educational arena. In what follows, I shall attempt to offer what I consider to be a more adequate account of some of these matters, based upon an analysis of the data generated from the research that was carried out between 1976 and 1982.

A CLOSER LOOK

It is often claimed that industrial and commercial employers of school leavers will not accept the currency of Mode 3 passes as equivalent to the more usual Mode 1s. Certainly some of the examination board officials that we interviewed gave this as one justification for tightening control over teacher-assessed schemes. However, research amongst industrialists did not present quite such a clear picture and, although our interviews with employers did produce various generalised criticisms of schools and their curricula which echoed some of those being voiced in the Great Debate, they also pointed to a rather more ambivalent orientation towards Mode 3 examinations than we had anticipated from our interviews with board officials. In fact, there was a considerable degree of ignorance amongst employers about the nature of Mode 3 schemes but, where they were reasonably well understood, concern about the difficulties of maintaining standards was often balanced with more favourable comments about the ways in which Mode 3s were sometimes of greater industrial and vocational relevance than the typical range of Mode 1 syllabuses offered by many boards. In this connection it is interesting to note that the Rubber and Plastics Industry Training Board was making some very favourable public comments about Mode 3 schemes at the very time that the Confederation of British Industry was joining in the general criticism of teacher-assessed work in the context of the proposed new system of examining at 16 plus (Jackson, 1986). Thus, although it was certainly possible to identify an

industrial lobby in the examinations controversy as
well as in the Great Debate, its position on the
requirements that industry had of schools was
expressed in very general terms and its view of the
best way to meet them was often confused. In
particular, there was an unresolved tension in its
contributions between a demand for a return to
traditional standards in education and a demand that
curricula should be modernised to make education
more directly relevant to working life. A similar
set of tensions could be detected within the
contributions of politicians to the controversy.

Although there were also tensions of this sort
within education itself, the most coherent and well-
orchestrated set of voices in the campaign against
the spread of teacher-assessed work in public
examinations came, in a sense, from within the
system - from the universities and the more
traditional university-based GCE examining boards
(Cameron, 1976). Thus, as the general climate moved
against the concept of teacher autonomy that had
developed during the 1960s, the universities were
quick to re-assert their traditional role as
definers of school knowledge and external arbiters
of standards, even though the universities' own
internal examination arrangements were themselves an
extreme example of Mode 3-type procedures. This reassertion of the role of the universities and their
associated examining boards, which was reflected in
the tightening of procedures for the approval and
moderation of Mode 3 schemes and in the movement
towards the concept of a 'core' externally-examined
paper for all candidates in a particular subject,
has to be seen in the light of other proposals for
the limitation of teachers' freedom that were in
evidence during the later 1970s. The Secretary of
one of the University boards justified the role of
the board - a 'completely independent and impartial'
agency - in a way that suggested that its own
changes in procedures were actually designed to
defend a degree of teacher autonomy against more
sinister threats from outside the system:

> something we've always cherished in this
> country is the freedom of the teacher. Now
> you can't give teachers complete, absolute
> freedom, and in this country we've restricted
> teachers' freedom by making the examination
> system the controlling element in the end...I
> think our system...is infinitely preferable
> to some dictation from on high of some

content, even if it's only part of syllabuses.
In the wrong person's hands this could be
dangerous. (Interview with Board Secretary,
20 January 1977)

Other boards argued the case in more positive terms,
with the Cambridge Board leading the ideological
onslaught in favour of traditional Mode 1 type
examinations and the limitation of teacher-assessed
work within public examinations (U.C.L.E.S., 1976)
Even boards that had previously encouraged Mode
3 submissions declared temporary moratoria on new
schemes, recalled existing schemes for reconsidera-
tion, set up working parties to consider common core
elements and introduced a wide range of procedural
mechanisms which effectively tightened their control
over teacher-assessed work. Teachers interviewed at
the time noted the effects of this and felt that at
least some of the boards were deliberately seeking
to dissuade them from proceeding with Mode 3
schemes. Although the university-based boards were
the quickest to respond to the changing climate in
this way, despite the fact that they had generally
made least progress in devolving powers to teachers
in the preceding period, the non-university GCE
board and the majority of the formally teacher-
controlled CSE boards were quick to follow suit. In
a situation where the various boards were competing
for DES favour in the arrangements for the possible
new system of examining, the CSE boards seemed as
keen to place restrictions on teacher-assessed work
even though they lacked the formal powers of the
GCE boards to reject Mode 3 submissions out of hand.
Particularly significant in the discussions amongst
the CSE boards outside the Midlands region was a
fear that high-status schools would defect to any
new examining group that included the Oxbridge
boards and thus create a hierarchy within the new
system. This fear was exacerbated by the formation
of a strong traditionalist GCE pressure group,
C.O.S.S.E.C., consisting of the three Oxbridge
boards and the SUJB, and was only partially
alleviated by the eventual withdrawal of the Oxford
Local Delegacy from this grouping. In the crucial
period, the activities and pronouncements of
C.O.S.S.E.C. severely restricted the willingness of
other boards and groupings of boards to consider a
large-scale devolution of assessment powers to
teachers under the new system. Even though the more
liberal GCE boards sometimes modified the more
extreme demands of the Cambridge Syndicate and

177

C.O.S.S.E.C., the debate was effectively shifted
firmly onto terrain defined by the GCE rather than
the CSE boards (Doe, 1982).

Despite the fact that in the early stages of
the Great Debate the universities were deemed almost
as culpable as schoolteachers for the decline of the
nation through their maintenance of 'irrelevant and
elitist curricula', as Shirley Williams put it in
the BBC's major contribution to the debate, this
reassertion of the role of universities and the GCE
examining boards was given an increasing amount of
official encouragement as the 16 plus proposals went
through their successive modifications. The Waddell
proposals (D.E.S., 1978a), in granting the
universities a status different from mere 'users' of
examination certificates (such as employers and non-
university further and higher education) in its
proposed regional supervisory bodies, seemed to
legitimate their traditional role in defining
knowledge for schools. Similarly, when the various
boards came together to plan the details of
examining in the new regional consortia that were
eventually formed, single GCE boards were often
given equal representation to as many as three
different CSE boards on their committees even though
the CSE boards have the larger share of subject
entries amongst 16 year olds. When the Conservative
party returned to power, the role of the GCE boards
was further strengthened by giving them a continuing
responsibility for defining standards for the top
three grades of the new system (Fairhall, 1980),
while Sir Keith Joseph has recently been reported to
be considering confining non-traditional modes of
examining practice, such as teacher assessment,
practical work and project work to the lower grades
(Stevens, 1982).

The consequences of the tightening of
procedures by the boards and the increasing
official encouragement for the traditions and
position of the universities and their examining
boards are of considerable interest in view of the
sorts of criticisms being made of schools during the
Great Debate. Both within the existing school
leaving examinations and within the proposals for
the new system that have recently been produced,
there has been something of a resurgence of
traditional O-level styles of examining at the
expense of some of the innovations developed within
the CSE system during the 1960s and early 1970s
(Doe, 1981b). These conventional modes of assessment are associated with the traditional high-status

curriculum, characterised by Young (1971) as
embodying literate, abstract, differentiated and
uncommonsense knowledge. In some respects at least,
this is not the knowledge demanded by corporate
industry, but rather that very knowledge of the
liberal academy that industrialists such as
Weinstock (1976) and politicians such as Callaghan
(1976) have argued is less than appropriate to contemporary needs. That this irony within the outcome
of the 16 plus controversy is something of an
embarrassment in official circles is hinted at in
the following report that appeared in the Times
Educational Supplement in July 1981:

> Lady Young refuses to be drawn on whether the
> commitment to maintain "standards" rules out
> the opportunities to change the exams to fit
> what some see as the real demands of adult
> and working life. But DES officials make it
> clear that the priority is to get the new
> exam off the ground rather than introduce all
> the reforms that might be considerable
> desirable. (Doe, 1981a)

It seems, then, that the universities and the GCE
examining boards have been able to take advantage of
broader attacks on teacher autonomy to regain some
of the influence over the school curriculum that
they ceded to the teaching profession during the
1960s. They have been able to do this via a
selective utilisation of the rhetoric of the Great
Debate, in which they benefited from a tension
between the notion of 'standards' and the notion of
'relevance'. The universities and the GCE boards
have been able to re-assert their role as the up-
holders of standards and, in doing so, they have re-
imposed conformity to conceptions of school
knowledge that had come increasingly under
challenge during the preceding period. In
responding to demands for greater standardisation
which have been the order of the day, this lobby
seems to have granted part of what was demanded by
the broader but unco-ordinated attack on teachers
and, in doing so, to have stolen something of a
march on their early allies in that attack. Not
only has the growth of Mode 3 assessment been
halted, and indeed reversed, but it now looks
certain that the GCE boards will continue to
dominate any new system of examining that takes us
into the 1990s and, in some senses, with increased
rather than diminished power. This is not to say

179

that the university lobby has entirely ignored the
demands for greater industrial relevance, but its
moves in this direction such as the co-option of
five industrialists on to the governing body of one
GCE board, seem often to have been largely cosmetic
in nature. The overall pattern of changes in 16
plus examinations that seems to be emerging is
likely to produce changes in practice at school
level that are considerably at variance with those
initially demanded of the school system in industrial and governmental pronouncements.

ANALYSIS AND DISCUSSION

If we were to concentrate merely on the evidence of
a systematic tightening of control over teachers via
changes in technical procedures within the
examination boards, then it might be possible to
regard the developments described above as a clear
example of what Apple (1980) sees as the extension
of increasingly dominant technical modes of control
from the capitalist labour process into the schools.
This could certainly be argued, for instance, in the
case of those examining boards that have
introduced tight statistical moderation procedures
to counter charges of a lack of reliability in the
assessment of Mode 3 components. As these changes
are partly a response to DES pressures for greater
standardisation and accountability, they would thus
seem to offer some support for the notion of the
state functionalising education for capital. Yet it
seems clear that it is not always the boards that
are most advanced in developing the examining and
moderation techniques associated with this conception of technical control that have been in the
forefront of the attack on teacher autonomy.
Indeed, the very efficacy of the traditional Mode 1
GCE styles of examining which are experiencing something of a resurgence at the present time is highly
questionable in relation to some of the newer styles
of assessment developed by the CSE boards. When we
look at the syllabus content of existing courses and
the draft subject criteria for the new system, the
degree to which education is being functionalised
for capital is even less clear. In order to understand more fully the nature of the settlement that
is now emerging, it may therefore be important to
examine not only the fact of the subjection of
teachers to greater control, but also the struggles
over the exercise of that control and the nature of
the various parties to those struggles.

One way of viewing the whole saga is to regard it as yet another stage in the series of compromises between industrial trainers, old humanists and public educators, which Williams (1961) has argued has provided the basis of the English school curriculum. In broad terms, the contemporary industrial lobby corresponds to Williams' industrial trainers, the universities and their examining boards to his old humanists and the teaching profession and the labour movement to the public educators. The first of these groups is centrally concerned that schools should teach knowledge, skills and particularly attitudes that are relevant to industry and promote a positive image of industry. The second group supports a broader liberal education based upon the traditional disciplines and is particularly concerned with the maintenance of standards amongst that section of the population deemed capable of undertaking academic studies. The third group's main concern has been to extend the right to education to all groups within society, but its curricular pronouncements have often been merely negative expressions of a suspicion of too narrow a curriculum or anything that would place restrictions upon the professional judgement of teachers. In arguing that, despite the obvious oversimplifications, it may be helpful to regard the universities and their associated examining boards as having something in common with Williams' old humanists, I am adopting what Esland and Cathcart (1981) characterise as a pluralist view of the universities. In this view, they cannot be seen as straightforward agencies of corporate capitalism, but rather as 'a site of struggle between two competing forces, the needs of industry and the defenders of liberal culture' (Esland and Cathcart, 1981). This is, of course to recognise that the universities cannot be treated as a mono-lithic 'old humanist' lobby but at the same time to argue that, even today, the activities of the British universities remain far less fully integra-ted with those of corporate capitalism than, say, their American counterparts. The "respectable" version of the anti-industry bias identified by Weinstock (1976) has remained strong and, for reasons discussed by Wiener (1981), this apparently 'residual' set of cultural values has remained remarkably resilient within British universities well into the late twentieth century. It has even been strengthened by those on the left who, while critical of its elitism, have found its model of

supposedly disinterested learning a useful buffer in
the face of corporate encroachments. This has
produced some distinct differences of emphasis
between the position of the university lobby and the
industrial one on the nature of an appropriate
school education. Thus, whatever imperatives may be
identified as emanating from corporate capitalism
via the state, the peculiar cultural ethos of the
English academic world has produced refractions
whose effects must be taken into account in any
adequate analysis. In some ways, the developments
that have been occurring within the school examinations system are paralleled by the recent
restructuring exercise undertaken by the University
Grants Committee, which has been seen by some
commentators as a further example of the frustration
by the 'liberal arts academic establishment' of
industrial and governmental efforts to make the
universities more relevant to the needs of
contemporary industry.

The university and GCE-board initiatives have,
then, ensured the maintenance of a more significant
place for old humanist conceptions of a liberal
secondary education than might have been predicted
from the sorts of attacks on the traditional school
curriculum that emanated from the representatives of
government and industry in the opening stages of the
Great Debate. The old humanist lobby has reasserted
its position in terms of the content and control of
an examination system that will influence the
education of at least sixty percent of school pupils
even if the industrial trainers are ultimately
granted more influence over the remainder. At the
same time the public educators have once again,
through their obsession to secure a common system of
examinations, permitted key questions about the
content and control of that system to be contested
between the other parties to the compromise. Indeed, with the relative decline of the CSE model of
school examining, the teaching profession has
effectively lost some of the control over the system
and its content which it has been exercising in
recent years. Meanwhile the teaching profession's
major allies in the public education lobby - the
left and the labour movement - have developed no
distinctive position about issues of content and
control, since at least until very recently they
have tended to defend the traditional position of
the period of social democratic consensus, which
treated the nature of the school curriculum as an
issue legitimately left to the professional judge-

ment of teachers (Finn, Grant and Johnson, 1977).
This has meant that, with the exception of the
initial contributions by senior ministers who anyway
seemed to be backing the industrial lobby, the overt
interventions of the labour movement in the 16 plus
debate have paralleled its involvement in the
development of comprehensive secondary education itself. In both cases, the major emphasis has been
placed upon achieving an apparently more
egalitarian organisational structure (in this case a
common examinations system), while leaving issues of
the content and control of that system to be contested between groups whose involvement with the
issue has been, in neither case, primarily
egalitarian in intent or effect. Beyond the
remnants of a common shell to the new system, the
substance of the emerging settlement reveals
remarkably little evidence of the presence of the
public education lobby in the debate at all.
Certainly the left and the labour movement has
developed no coherent alternative position of its
own to insert into the debate, even when it has
become clear that the approach based on the
professional judgement of teachers will have to be
modified.

It is clear that the old humanist lobby had
already won some significant victories in the 16
plus controversy well before the Conservative Party
returned to power in May 1979. Yet its preference
for external modes of assessment resonated
particularly strongly with the views of leading
Conservative politicians and it is therefore
scarcely surprising that, when Mark Carlisle
eventually announced his decision to proceed with a
modified version of the common examination system,
it was one in which the GCE boards were to be given
even greater influence particularly over the award
of the higher grades (Fairhall, 1980). Nevertheless, the replacement of Mark Carlisle with Sir
Keith Joseph as Secretary of State has produced
further delays in the detailed planning of the
system and, at the time of writing, he is reported
to be under pressure from some MPs to abandon the
new system and retain O-levels in their present form
(Shaw, 1982). This is ironic given the considerable
concessions that the GCE boards had won from the
government even under the previous Labour administration and might conceivably provide an opportunity
for those groups who were relatively poorly served
by the provisional settlement to launch a counter-
offensive. There is some evidence in the Schools

Council's alternatives to the examining bodies own
draft subject criteria and in the negative response
of many teachers to the latter (Doe, 1981b) that the
professional wing of the public education lobby is
making a belated attempt to regain the initiative.
Yet, in the absence of broader political support, it
seems highly unlikely that the teaching profession
will be able to reverse the gains won by the
universities and the GCE boards much earlier in the
controversy, particularly in view of the likely
demise of the Schools Council. What there is no
evidence of to date is an attempt on the part of the
left and the labour movement to develop and organise
around a distinctive approach to the content and
control of school curricula and examinations which
is in keeping with its broader political objectives
and based upon a tenable redefinition of teacher
professionalism to replace the now outmoded version
that it has hitherto defended. Had such a position
been developed and inserted earlier into the debate,
the emergent settlement might well have been
significantly different from any of the alternatives
with which we now seem to be faced.

While some elements of the left have been
content to achieve organisational reform and
remained unconcerned with other issues, other
sections of the left have become victims of their
own theory and have argued that a socialist policy
on the nature of the curriculum is doomed to failure
in the face of the onslaught of capital's need to
restructure the educational system in its interests.
Yet this study suggests that, even if we are to
understand the genesis of many recent state
initiatives in education as lying in the need to
secure the conditions of existence for a new phase
of capitalism, the outcomes of such attempts are not
in any straightforward sense a determined effect of
capitalist economic imperatives. Outcomes are
achieved via ideological discourse and political
struggle and there is considerable scope for
resisting such imperatives at a political and dis-
cursive level, as the old humanist lobby appears to
have done in this particular instance. For the
left, theories of tendency too often become statements of necessity in ways which effectively obscure
the possibilities for contesting the terrain upon
which tendencies become real outcomes. Thus it need
not be assumed that a more positive intervention in
the examinations controversy by the left, based on a
positive programme distinct from that of either the
old humanists or the industrial trainers, would have

been without significant effects. Even the actual
compromise achieved by the supposedly residual old
humanist elements within the debate seems decidedly
different from that which might have been read off
from the more economistic theories of tendency that
have sometimes been used to account for recent
developments in education.

However, it is obviously possible to argue that
my detailed examination of the debates over the 16
plus proposals reveals merely an indeterminacy of
outcomes in the case of struggles between different
fractions of the dominant order, that is the old
humanists and the industrial trainers. It might
therefore tell us nothing about the real possibilities for oppositional ideological interventions in
the present conjuncture and concern only a struggle
between two alternative cultural forms both of which
are entirely compatible with the successful
performance by the state of the functions that it
carries out on behalf of capital (Dale, 1981b).
Indeed, it might be argued that the differences
between the industrial trainers and the old
humanists in terms of the structures of curricula
and assessment that they favour, as opposed to their
overt content, are minimal and that my data does
nothing to call into question even a relatively
simplistic form of neo-Marxist theory such as that
offered by Bowles and Gintis (1976). Alternatively,
it might be suggested that, although the changes are
not entirely in keeping with the demands of
industrial capitalists, they will turn out to be
functionally well-adapted to the needs of a British
economy dominated by finance rather than industrial
capital - though this argument would surely qualify
for Nowell-Smith's category of 'devious' if not
'metaphysical'. Rather more plausibly, it can
certainly be argued that not only does the emergent
compromise between the industrial trainers and the
old humanists lie well within the limits of what
Kellner (1978) terms hegemonic ideology,but so
would any settlement that might have arisen from a
more concerted intervention by the public educators
into the debate. However, it seems implausible
that all settlements within the ideological and
political spheres are somehow equally functional for
capital and that the differences between the
possible settlements are totally irrelevant to the
capacity of the state to carry out its long-term
functions on behalf of capital. This would
presumably depend upon the relationship of any
particular settlement to the outcomes of other

struggles within the apparatuses of the state.
Indeed, if the various possible settlements that do
fall within the limits of what is appropriate for
the performance of the functions of the state are
the product of concrete historical struggles, so
arguably is the securing of those limits. There is
therefore no compelling reason to preclude the
possibility that oppositional interventions in and
around education might make important contributions
to the nature of the settlements achieved therein
and perhaps even to broader oppositional struggles
in society.

IMPLICATIONS

This study suggests that it is vital, in analysing
the character and dynamics of ideological struggles
within and around education, to move beyond any
notion that the educational apparatuses of the state
respond in a mechanistic manner to the imperatives
of capital accumulation or even that they operate
clearly in the interests of a ruling class dominated
by the leading fractions of capital. It is clear
that an understanding of the developments discussed
here cannot be encompassed by a mode of analysis
that fails to give adequate attention to the
specificities and relative autonomy of political and
ideological/cultural practice or that refuses to
recognise the possibility that their autonomy may
not function merely as a means of masking their
contribution to the reproduction of capitalist
production relations. This is not to deny that
there have been some remarkable similarities between
the state initiatives that have been directed
towards the educational apparatuses of a number of
advanced capitalist societies in recent years
(Apple, 1982), but it is to counsel against
neglecting to account for the differences in the
form that they have taken and assuming that they
will result in similar outcomes. At a theoretical
and empirical level, there is clearly a need to
undertake considerably more work on the concept of
relative autonomy which is increasingly used in
contemporary neo-Marxist writing to signal a recognition of an unspecified degree of complexity whilst
not abandoning a commitment to the notion of
economic determination in the last instance. It
might be that the neo-Weberian forms of analysis
advocated by Collins (1977), which are not
constrained by this rubric, would contribute to our
understanding of the continuing strength of old

humanist cultural values despite their apparent lack
of fit with the demands of contemporary capitalism.

The rejection of those approaches to the
sociology of education that tend to treat
ideological/cultural practices as essentially
epiphenomenal or of purely marginal significance
also has implications for policy interventions. It
argues against the sort of left abstentionism that
derived from those perspectives that made it difficult to see any possibilities for significant
changes in or through the school curriculum in the
absence of a prior transformation of the relations
of production. In the current conjuncture,
curricula and examinations have clearly become an
important site of ideological struggle, even though
they almost certainly lack the overwhelming
significance that the 'new sociology of education'
of the early 1970s sometimes seemed to attribute to
them. The study does not justify a reversion to the
naive possibilitarianism of the early 1970s, which
may well have acted as a justification for some of
the more individualistic Mode 3 innovations, since
it recognises that ideological practice within
education takes place within historically specific
economic, political and ideological conditions of
existence. In view of the disposition of political
and ideological forces in and around education in
the current conjuncture, individualistic acts of
defiance would seem to be an inappropriate means of
contesting the examination terrain. But the failure
of the organised left and the labour movement to
develop a distinctive and coherent position to
contribute to the examinations controversy was an
error that should not be repeated, even if the
consequences of that failure did not in practice
produce the unequivocal functionalisation of
education for capital that some forms of neo-
Marxist theory might have led us to expect. It may
even be that the continuing prevarications of Sir
Keith Joseph (Geddes, 1982), in conjunction with a
mounting tide of opinion that the whole question of
assessment at 16 plus requires a radical rethink
(Janes and others, 1982), will provide the left and
the labour movement with an opportunity to remedy
this political failure even before the emergent
settlement discussed in this paper has finally been
confirmed.

REFERENCES

Apple, M.W. (1980) 'Curricular form and the logic of technical control' in L.Barton, R.Meighan and S.Walker (eds), Schooling, Ideology and the Curriculum, The Falmer Press, Lewes

Apple, M.W. (1982) 'Common Curriculum and State Control', Discourse, 2(2)

Bowles, S. and Gintis, H. (1976) Schooling in Capitalist America, Routledge and Kegan Paul, London

Callaghan, J. (1976) 'Towards a national debate', Education, 22 October

Cameron, S. (1976) 'Oxbridge and London come out against 16+ Report', Times Educational Supplement, 19 March

Collins, R. (1977) 'Some comparative principles of educational stratification', Harvard Educational Review, 47(1)

Cox, B. (1980) 'How education fails Britain's children', Now!, 52

Dale, R. (1981a) 'Control, Accountability and William Tyndale' in R.Dale, G.Esland, R. Ferguson and M.Macdonald (eds), Schooling and the National Interest, The Falmer Press, Lewes

Dale, R. (1981b) 'The state and education: some theoretical approaches' in The Open University, The State and the Politics of Education, Part 2, Open University Press, Milton Keynes

D.E.S. (1977) Education in Schools: a consultative document, H.M.S.O., London

D.E.S., (1978a) School Examinations, Parts 1 & 2, H.M.S.O., London

D.E.S. (1978b) Secondary School Examinations: a single system at 16 plus, H.M.S.O., London

Doe, B. (1981a) 'Fears grow on eve of 16-plus exam preview', Times Educational Supplement, 3 July

Doe, B. (1981b) 'Alarm spreads over proposals for new 16+ exams', Times Educational Supplement, 20 November

Doe, B. (1982) 'Cambridge plan for 16 plus rejected by GCE boards', Times Educational Supplement, 5 March

Donald, J. (1978) 'Examinations and strategies', Screen Education, 26

Eggleston, S.J. (1975) 'Conflicting curriculum decisions', Educational Studies, 1(1)

Esland, G. and Cathcart, H. (1981) 'Education and the corporate economy' in The Open University, The State and the Politics of Education', Part 1, Open University Press, Milton Keynes

Fairhall, J. (1980) 'Single exam system to replace O-level, CSE', Guardian, 20 February

Finn, D., Grant, N. and Johnson, R. (1977) 'Social democracy, education and the crisis', Working Papers in Cultural Studies, 10

Freeland, J. (1980) 'Where do they go after school: youth unemployment, legitimation and schooling', unpublished mimeo

Geddes, D. (1982) 'Joseph adds to doubts over single 16-plus exam', The Times, 30 March

Holloway, J. and Picciotto, S. (1977) 'Capital, crisis and the state', Capital and Class, 2

Hopkins, A. (1978) The School Debate, Penguin Books, Harmondsworth

Hurford, J. (1979) 'Testing Times', Rank and File Teacher, 64

Jackson, M. (1976) 'Sniped at now from all sides', Times Educational Supplement, 3 December

Janes, F. and others (1982) 'Sir Keith's cart before horse', letter in Times Educational Supplement, 7 May

J.E.S.C. (1975) Examinations at 16+: proposals for the future, Schools Council, London

Kellner, D. (1978) 'Ideology, Marxism and advanced capitalism', Socialist Review, 42

Lawton, D. (1980) The Politics of the School Curriculum, Routledge and Kegan Paul, London

Maclure, S. (1975) 'The Schools Council and Examinations' in R.Bell and W.Prescott (eds), The Schools Council: a second look?, Ward Lock, London

Murdock, G. (1974) 'The Politics of Culture' in D.Holly (ed), Education or Domination?, Arrow Books, London

Nowell-Smith, G. (1979) 'In a State', Screen Education, 30

Rowlands, C. (1977) 'How the teaching cheats brand our children', Daily Mail, 5 April

Sharp, R. and Green, A. (1975) Education and Social Control, Routledge and Kegan Paul, London

Shaw, D. (1982) 'Forget single 16-plus exam, says MP', The Standard, 4 February

Stevens, A. (1982) 'O Levels face a test', Observer, 14 February

T.E.S. (1977) 'Blunt call to bring back hard work', Times Educational Supplement, 20 May

U.C.L.E.S. (1976) School Examinations and their Function, University of Cambridge Local Examinations Syndicate, Cambridge

Weinstock, A. (1976) 'I blame the teachers', Times Educational Supplement, 23 January

Wiener, M.J. (1981) English Culture and the Decline of the Industrial Spirit 1850-1980, Cambridge University Press, Cambridge

Whitty, G. (1976) 'Teachers and Examiners' in G.Whitty and M.Young (eds), Explorations in the Politics of School Knowledge, Nafferton Books, Driffield

Whitty, G. (1977) School Knowledge and Social Control, Open University Press, Milton Keynes

Williams, R. (1961) The Long Revolution, Chatto and Windus, London

Young, M. (1971) Knowledge and Control, Collier-Macmillan, London

Young, M. (1977) 'Curriculum Change - limits and possibilities' in M.Young and G.Whitty (eds), Society, State and Schooling, The Falmer Press, Lewes

8. SCHOOLS FOR DEMOCRACY?[1]

A. H. Halsey

INTRODUCTION

The reproduction of generations is everybody's business. If Everyman is a democrat, does it not follow
that, for the upbringing of his children, he must
provide schools for democracy? I have argued elsewhere the general thesis that Britain has democracy
as its most valuable political inheritance[2] (its
'radical tradition') and that the further development of social democracy is an alternative future to
the conventionally hackneyed forecasting of Britain
in economic decline. If we see democratic reform as
unfinished business, then schools come into view as
a problem of government as well as of finance in
educational policies for the nineteen eighties. The
question can be put sociologically rather than politically. Sociologists of education influenced by
Marx have, more or less crudely, argued a correspondence between the structure of the school and the
structure of society (or at least capitalist society).[3] Provided that the functionalism of this
notion is not so rigid as to conceive societies as
internal combustion engines, and provided that
causal directions are not locked into the straight-
jacket of orthodox Marxism, correspondence is to be
expected. If so, a democratic society may in turn
be expected both to practise democratic school
government and to teach democracy to its children.
But what kind of democracy? Direct or indirect?
These questions can be raised in the form of a
possible translation of Yugoslavian socialist self-
management[4] into British social democracy.

SCHOOLS FOR DEMOCRACY?

The Government of Expanding Education

Traditionally the government of child rearing was
largely left to the family. But in societies with a
more complex division of labour, or in groups with
specialised functions like priests, or social strata
with special powers like aristocrats or warriors,
quasi-familial or 'public' arrangements evolved: and
in modern societies the development of vast state
bureaucracies has become normal and dominant. The
expansion of educational provision in first- and
second-world countries, from roughly 1870 to 1970,
was remarkable. It has been overwhelmingly a state
enterprise, the conspicuously successful nationalised industry. Religious and private organisation of
schools and colleges survives with varying degrees
of social significance in most first-world countries.
Indeed, in some a privileged private sector may be
of re-emerging importance, and in the U.S.S.R.
private tuition is among the more flourishing seg-
ments of the underground economy.[5] Nor was marketed
education ever totally absent from the working-class
districts in the factory towns of industrialising
Britain in the nineteenth century. But the dominant
influence from Victorian times, and the major source
of financial support, has been the state. Educational systems everywhere are formidably bureaucratic, combining professional and administrative experts in hierarchical formations to link government
at one end with students and pupils at the other.

Looking back from a British or first-world
vantage point, it all appears as a hugely successful
feature of the development of the welfare state.
Industrialisation pulled and democratised politics
pushed education into providing opportunities for
entry into an increasingly skilled and 'non-manual'
structure of occupations. The proletariat was being
slowly but steadily abolished by cultural incorporation in schools to match political incorporation in
democracy, and economic incorporation in a modernised industry. Education was widely seen as both
the source of wealth (human capital) and the means
of freedom: it was accordingly an important plank
in the platform of liberal and progressive reform
from the middle of the nineteenth to the middle of
the twentieth century. First, universal primary
education was the typical goal of the nineteenth
century. Then, in the early part of the twentieth
century, came the drive to expand secondary schooling. In a third stage it became universal, and
fourth, in what now looks like the final flourish of

educational enthusiasm, there was a massive development of higher education in the 1950s and 1960s.

Some countries, like the United States, Canada,
and Sweden, travelled farther and faster along this
path than did others: but the direction of the jour-
ney was everywhere the same, and progress along it
defined modernity, even if in the later stages the
policy of educational expansion had to be defended
more as an adornment to economic growth than as a
means to its achievement. Meantime, universal
primary and secondary education - a ten-year period
of compulsory freedom to learn - has become the norm
with at least one-quarter, or in some cases more
than one half, of secondary school graduates going
on to some form of post-secondary education.

Yet this Western European and North American
picture has been viewed from a different angle since
the early 1970s - that is since Jencks' Inequality
(Basic Books, 1972), the OPEC intrusions, the welfare state backlash, and finally the rise of such
political figures as Thatcher, Reagan and Frazer.
There is now widespread scepticism with respect to
the wealth-creating capacity of education, and widespread resistance to its further financial support.
Pessimism abounds concerning the power of education
to equalise life-chances, between classes, regions,
ethnic groups, or sexes - at least as a policy isolated from other egalitarian policies. The efficacy
of bureaucratised schooling is challenged. Still
more important, the whole historically-determined
relation of education to work is contested. Marxists
like Bowles and Gintis are able to produce a plaus-
ible caricature of the American school as a state
apparatus selecting and training children for the
class positions which await them in the factory or
the office. Optimists, meanwhile, turn their attention to experiment and debate on the various forms
of continuing education, or l'education permanente.
They do so in uneasy awareness that the record of
liberal expansion (with respect to its three avowed
aims of individual opportunity, effective workers
and a principled social distribution of resources)
is painfully vulnerable to criticism from the left
and the right.

Alternative Forms of Educational Organisation

So the traditional centrist reformers may well put
to themselves the Leninist question: 'What is to be
done?' The answer they seek will be one which best
accommodates the three requisites of individual

193

choice, economic effectiveness and social justice.
Four main answers seem to be on offer.

The first answer, which an unbridled contemporary Toryism would instate, is the market solution.
Its appeal is strong. It belongs to liberal tradition. It promises individual liberty. It reflects
the moral maxim that all decent parents will do
their best for their own children. It tames the
bureaucrat, and keeps the teacher on his toes,
eliminating the one, and paying the other what he
deserves. It makes the family responsible for its
young. It rewards thrift and rational investment.
It motivates people to learn because they pay, and
they pay the penalty for ignorance. This is the
case for the commercial schools: (we should stop
calling them 'public' which is an archaic term per-
petuating the outlook of Victorian upper class
parents who sought alternatives to the private
family nursery): and it is a powerful one.

Why, then, is it unacceptable? The reason is
that it ignores the third requisite of social justice, substituting parental purse for filial wit as
the determinant of educational outcomes. It would
become socially acceptable only by educational
voucher schemes which are too socialistic to be conceivable Tory policy, and which would in any case
restore the bureaucracy. And even then it would be
a dubious servant of the second requisite - that
schools produce an effective work force.

The second answer, urged on by evidence of low
worker-productivity, youth unemployment, and mis-
match of labour supply to labour demand, is to
fashion the schools and colleges in direct response
to analysis of industrial needs. This, not too
unfairly, can be called the Russian solution, for
that country is the outstanding case of resolve and
perhaps success in treating educational development
as an inference from manpower planning. It need not
detain us despite its utility in respect of the
second, economic, requisite. For it rides roughly
over the first value of individual choice, and
yields a social distribution of educational opportunity which is no more acceptable than that of the
western capitalist countries.

The third answer is to do nothing - to accept
that it is the state bureaucratic system which history has bequeathed to us. This solution can be
even more briefly dismissed, for the point is that
we can do better.

The fourth solution is democracy. This principle of human association, extended to schools and

colleges, could, it is argued, optimally balance the claims of the individual, the economy and society. It must be said at once that, universal adult franchise, locally-elected County Councils, the N.U.T., and amateur School Governors notwithstanding, democracy in school government has yet to be tried. But democracy, skeptics may immediately object, is too vague and easy a slogan. Democracy of whom? Are infants to be enfranchised? Are producer co-operatives envisaged, and if so, who are the producers?; teachers?; students?; parents?; administrators? Democracy for what? Who is to decide the curriculum? HMI?; CEO?; Headteacher?; the Socialist Workers' Association? Clearly democracy is an ambiguous principle, and not an absolute one.

Yet a catalogue of advocacy can be compiled for democratically-governed schools which is at least as compelling as that given above on behalf of the market. It gives individuals a fair say in decisions taken about their lives. It is the proudest boast of the British political tradition. Unless subverted by the tenuous chain of parliamentary government and administrative hierarchy which is the present system, it makes a much reduced number of bureaucrats into public servants. It accords to the teacher the dignity of professional service to his or her community. It makes people collectively and equally responsible for the rational use of scarce resources.

A YUGOSLAVIAN ALTERNATIVE

Almost all history is against this solution and in favour of the nationalised industry: almost but not quite all. Yugoslavia offers an exception. In the peculiar context of escape from the Russian empire and a vigorous tradition of ethnic pluralism and intense local loyalties, Yoguslavia has developed a form of market socialism which flourishes as much in schools as in factories. There is no federal budget and no commercial schooling. The standard Western pattern, and indeed even more that of the Russian communist block, is of a system initiated, funded, administered, and controlled by the state. In the early years after the War, Yugoslavia followed the same path, and still today one can identify some of the same traditional features. There remains a federal system of law and administration, the former laying down a constitutional framework for schools, and universities, the latter monitoring and encouraging the realisation of nationally-agreed program-

mes for reform. But, in an important sense the 22
million inhabitants of Yugoslavia see themselves as
having been collectively reborn in 1947 when the
travail of early post-war reconstruction was ended
and the first five-year development plan was adopted.
A qualitative shift in the nature of Yugoslav society has taken place in the thirty-five subsequent
years.

Much of what went before has been forgotten.
Before the Second World War Yugoslavia was an underdeveloped country towards the top of the bottom
quarter of the world in terms of GNP per capita.
Over half of the Yugoslav people were illiterate.
Three-quarters of them worked in agriculture. The
average life expectancy was forty-five years. The
republics and regions were politically fragmented
and economically largely stagnant. But old battles,
movements and emnities are as obscure now as the
names of their proponents. Turkish and Austrian
imperialism, Venetian dominance, Serbian hegemony,
Radic's Croatian Peasant Party, pre-War politicians
like Pasic, Masec, Kovosec, Davidovic, or Cverkovic,
even King Alexander, Prince Paul and Mihailovic,
have been over-shadowed by the immense figure of
Josep Broz Tito, whose image appears everywhere in
school classrooms, public buildings and popular
books, marking the identity of a new Yugoslavia.

What is remembered is the liberation struggle
of World War II, the formation of a socialist federal republic, the break with Stalin, the pursuit of
non-alignment abroad and, above all, of rapid economic and social development at home towards a distinctive form of democratic and decentralised
Communism. A transition towards socialist democracy
on the principle of self-management has involved a
series of reforms in the government of territories,
enterprises, schools and public services. The
result of numerous changes - culminating most recently in the Constitution of 1974 - is an elaborate
complex of governing bodies at the local, provincial,
republican, and Federal levels. To the newcomer, as
no doubt to the indigenous child, they are at first
baffling in their variety. But they are informed
by concepts which, though unlikely to be found in an
anthology of elegant phrases from modern literature,
do have their place in any serious grammar of modern
politics.

Socialist Self-Management

No discussion of society, the economy, government, or the schools in Yugoslavia proceeds without repeated references to the concept of "self-management". It is the most ubiquitous term in the Yugoslav political lexicon. It appeared on banners and flags to rally the partisans in World War II. It so permeates the society that understanding the idea and learning the skills to practise it are essential for any citizen. It is the fundamental notion which epitomises the independence and the self-directed nature of the Yugoslavian people. The essence of self-management is that all those who work in a factory, a business or a school share as equals in the running of it. Participatory decision-making includes determining what to produce or what services to offer, pricing those goods or services, setting wages, and selecting managers. Not every worker is fully incorporated into the self-managing economy for there remains a non-socialised sector, notably in small-scale farming. Nevertheless, the principle of self-management is intended - in theory at least - to be carried out at every level and in every operating unit of the society.

In the smallest and economically simplest unit, the concept of self-management translates into straightforward practice. The self-managing group of workers who run, for example, a restaurant, meet to decide the menu, the prices, the opening hours, and the division of labour between them. If people patronize the restaurant and the enterprise is successful, there will be a surplus of income over expenses which is then distributed to the workers as wages.

Organisation on such a small scale permits direct democracy. Operations of larger scale complicate self-management because every worker cannot in practice be consulted about all policies. Representative democracy must be built on direct democracy. If hierarchies are unavoidable, mechanisms must be devised to make them the servants rather than the masters of the workers in the enterprise. Complications also ensue as in the case of education, in which the relationship of the enterprise to the 'market place' is neither direct nor immediate. Prices in such sectors of the economy must emerge not from economic supply and demand but from a process of social persuasion and agreement.

The smallest self-managing institution, or
basic organisation of associated labour (BOAL), is
an elementary or secondary school. All the staff,
whether teachers or ancillaries, form a Workers'
Council. Then there is also a Governing Council
which includes not only representatives of the
school staff but also of local citizens and parents
in the case of an elementary school or of local work
organisations and of students in the case of a secondary school.

The university presents a more complex arrangement of self-management. It could be argued that
self-management in European universities generally
has a long history. At Bologna in medieval Italy
it took the form of defining the constituency as the
students. In Paris it was the teachers. However,
the modern western university has typically evolved
into a hierarchical structure of departments and
faculties, bureaucratically administered, though
with considerable power over internal affairs in the
hands of the academics. Only Oxford in modern times
approximates to the model of a self-governing
democracy of dons. On a modern Yugoslavian view, an
Oxford college would be a BOAL. The Governing Body
or 'Workers' Council' of the college is where all
decisions are made by an assembly following the
principle of one don one vote. A difference is
immediately apparent in that students are excluded
from this franchise, and their interests are incorporated by a system of consultative committees.
Nevertheless, the English 'medieval survival' and
the Yugoslavian 'socialist experiment' have a further parallel in the high degree of autonomy of
their colleges and faculties respectively. The
university at Oxford, like any of the 19 universities in Yugoslavia, has been, at least until recently, a loose federation of physically and constitu-
tionally separate colleges in the one case, and
faculties in the other.

But here again, the parallel stops. Certainly
the dons in their University Congregation can collectively and democratically decide Non Placet in
the face of proposals from the Vice-Chancellor
(Rector) whom they have elected from among themselves for a four-year term of office. But though
dons fully and democratically control their several
college properties and their administrative offices,
the overwhelming fact of the environment of Oxford
University is its 85% income dependence on the
state, whereas Belgrade University, besides having
an internal democracy of teachers and students, is

now firmly set in the environment of a free exchange of labour between itself and the users of its products of knowledge and knowledgeable people - the 'self-managing communities of interest' and the relevant organisations of associated labour.

The Federal state was eliminated from control of education by the Yugoslav revisions of the Constitution in 1974. The further drive towards establishing self management, which began in the factories in the 1950s, has now spread throughout the social fabric and both reflects and propels current developments in higher education. The consequence is that the BOALS and working organisations of the faculties and schools, linked together to form universities, are vitally dependent on the proposals ana proddings of a large number of social, political and professional bodies, inside and outside their gates. They depend, in other words, not only on the state but on a large number of groups with a producer or user interest in the higher studies and in the supply of scientific ana technological manpower.

The University of Ljubljana as an Example

The self-management system may be exemplified from the presentation of self which is published by the University of Ljubljana. Lubljana is neither the biggest nor the smallest, nor the oldest nor the youngest, nor the most nor the least famous of Yugoslav universities. A proud possession of Slovenia, it has late sixteenth-century antecedents in a Jesuit School and an eighteenth century Lyceum. But the establishment of the university proper had to await the fall of the Habsburg monarchy. It dates from 1919 when 5 faculties were set up (of Law, Philosophy, Technology, Theology and Medicine). It flickered and almost died during the years of Italian and German occupation from 1941-45, but then sprang again into life and vigorous growth to become, by the mid-1970s, an association of ten faculties joined by ten other higher schools and academies. The university now boasts over 1,000 professors and other teachers and researchers, and it contains more than 13,000 students.

Over the past twenty years Ljubljana, like all other Yugoslav institutes of higher education, has been learning self-management and unlearning the traditional 'administrative manner of decision-making'. The present arrangements were introduced by the Republic of Slovenia's University Act of

1975; but these also are undergoing further modifi-
cation as the universities are drawn further into
the developing system of vocationally-directed
education. Again, like all other Yugoslav universities, Ljubljana is a community of working organisations including faculties, academies of art,
vise skole (two-year advanced vocational colleges),
four-year colleges and teacher training colleges.
Twenty such working organisations make up the
University of Ljubljana: three of the faculties are
in fact sub-divided into BOALS (which were formally
departments of a faculty). BOALS and other working
organisations are the primary self-governing units
of the university. But there are also groupings of
students in each year of study which are similarly
self-governing.

Each of these primary units, in addition to its
assembly, has a Council to manage its affairs, composed of delegates of students, teachers and non-
teaching staff, as well as of users. The users are
other working organisations or BOALS, socio-political
organisations and communities with interests in
higher education. The worker, student, and user
delegates each make up one-third of the total
Council membership. All three groups are on an
equal footing. A decision of the Council is not
valid if a majority of any of the three groups does
not agree with it. Each group, in other words,
decides separately on such matters as the draft of
a statute, the curriculum, the election of teachers,
or the budget before the Council as a whole makes
its decision. Further, the teachers and the non-
teaching staff by constitutional right negotiate
separately their own working conditions and personal
incomes.

These governmental arrangements at the primary
level are repeated at the level of the university
where the essential organ of government is the
University Council. It is composed of one delegate
from among the workers, students, and users of
every working organisation. It thus has 60 members,
20 from the staff, 20 from the students, and 20 from
the users. Decisions of the University Council are
carried out through various committees, commissions
and professional enterprises. The Rector is the
central coordinating administrator of the University. He serves for two years and can only be
nominated once again for a further two-year period.
The central administrative functions (professional,
financial and technical) are in the hands of a
Secretariat in the university led by a Secretary

General who is nominated by the University Council for a period of four years, and is eligible for re-nomination without limit.

To deal with the essential issue of academic appointments, there is a 'habilitation commission' of 21 members, 7 of whom are nominated by the Executive Council of the Assembly of the Republic of Slovenia, and 14 are elected by the University Council on the recommendation of the Socialist Alliance of Working People from among the teachers, researchers, students and prominent professionals. The habilitation commission puts forward proposals for the election of professors, lecturers and their assistants. It is only from the Commission's lists that the Council of one of the relevant BOALs or working organisations makes its final decision on the appointment of a member of staff.

The income of each of the primary units is secured by a direct free exchange of labour with other organisations of associated labour, or through the self-managing communities of interest for education. Similarly income for research activity is acquired through the corresponding self-managing communities of interest for research. In cases where there is no community of interest the negotia-tion has to be made through the self-managing com-munity of education for the Republic. Assemblies of such communities of interest have two chambers - the chamber of producers and the chamber of users. The first is composed of delegates from the facul-ties or other working organisations in higher education: the second is composed of the delegates of the relevant outside organisations of associated labour, mainly business enterprises. The chambers work on an equal footing to fix prices for educa-tional activity which in turn determine the income of each of the educational units. Research is directly financed by contracts between the education organisations on the one hand and enterprises or communities of interest on the other. In short, self-management and free exchange of labour link workers and students, producers and users.

Internally BOALS are democratically self-governing in higher education as in the economy at large. Externally these social markets yield a bar-gain between the educational organisations and society as a whole where the latter is represented either by working organisations or by communities of interest. The state in such a system has retreated into what traditional liberals would have called the night-watchman role. In Marxist terminology, it is withering away.

Self-Management and Continuing Education

Continuing education is the much discussed system which is advocated, nowhere more passionately than in Yugoslavia, as the next phase of development of a fully democratic arrangement for the education of a modern citizen. It is usually discussed in the context of social equality echoing a widespread concern in the failure, or at any rate limited success, of prevailing policies. Nevertheless, this is by no means the whole story, whether in OECD countries in general, or in Yugoslavia in particular. Another approach is to be had by first noticing that a worker in industrial society will commonly spend at least 100,000 hours of his life at work. The question of how to arrange the life cycle of education, work, leisure, and retirement is accordingly an intriguing calculation-cum-gamble for the free man or woman. The allocation of 100,000 hours is, to be sure, a vital question for egalitarian policy: but it can claim attention also from the point of view of individual liberty. Industrial men and women are doubtless freer from toil than their grandparents. Nevertheless, these libertarian trends cannot be presumed fully to have taken even the rich countries out of the world of unremitting toil or to have placed them satisfactorily in the world of social complexity which calls for maximum flexibility in the arrangement of their affairs.

The idea of a flexible contract between citizen and society, covering education, work, leisure and social security is now much discussed in western countries.[6] In Yugoslavia it is taken for granted that responsible government on behalf of individual liberty has to go beyond the enforcement of contracts voluntarily entered and the natural tendencies of men to conspire against the rigours of the free market. Nevertheless, Yugoslavian socialism claims to seek ways to increase freedom of choice for the individual in modern society. And, like any other modern society, capitalist or communist, Yugoslavia is committed to the efficient production of abundance, the maintenance of full employment, and the abolition of all unnecessary labour.

On these assumptions, if behind a different political rhetoric, Yugoslavia, like Sweden, seeks deliberately greater variation and diversity in the life patterns of education, work, leisure and retirement, in such a way as to transfer decisions as far as possible from the bureaucracy to the individual. The underlying conception is of a new social contract. The individual has a lifelong bargain with society to work in exchange for material rewards. In such a society the individual, within a broad framework of agreed rules, would determine the phasing and pacing of the exchange, week by week, year by year and over the course of his whole lifetime. The sharp divisions of the life-cycle, bequeathed by the harsh necessities of pre-industrial society and entrenched in the rigid formulae of statutory school leaving ages, weekly hours, annual holidays and compulsory retirement ages, would go. Instead there would be 'flexi-time', study rights at personal discretion, vacation rights not tied to calendar years, sabbaticals and temporary retirements not tied to old age.

In order to effect these new freedoms, which are in any case gradually and patchily appearing in the rich countries, it is desirable (though not absolutely necessary) to systematise the piecemeal arrangements we already have for providing income to those who are not in paid employment because they are young and in school or unemployed or pregnant or sick or old and therefore retired. Collectively, a country has to decide on the generalised drawing rights to be allocated to each citizen. Of course, in a developed social contract, safeguards would have to be built in against those with undue preferences for 'a short life but a gay one' and not all state or community payments to individuals need be, or could be, included. But the general idea stands as a proposal for the reduction of bureaucracy and the enlargement of personal choice. As such it describes a major component of the Yugoslav intent.

The Yugoslavs see themselves now at the beginning of a third developmental stage where the first was statist, and the second was self-managing. In this third stage the distinguishing concept is that of continuing education. The radical character of the new concept is fully appreciated by the Yugoslavs. They are aware of both its libertarian and egalitarian implications. They understand, in other words, that their plans and hopes are both to maximise and to harmonise the free choice of individuals and the occupational and cultural needs of society. They see the future structure of education not as hitherto in four phases, but in two. The first phase of pre-schooling and elementary schooling is of a larger and common syllabus, followed by a second phase of vocationally-oriented secondary

and higher education integrated with work and life
to form a diversity of opportunities which are never
final because they are life-long. They understand,
too, that the concept goes beyond schooling to
involve the family, the work place, the political
and social organisations, and the mass media as
partners in a total scheme of learning. And they
believe that the multiple partnership entailed requires and can be delivered only in an environment
of democratic participation by both the producers
and the users of knowledge.

EDUCATION, PROSPERITY AND FREEDOM: THE WESTERN
REACTION

Reactions to all this in other countries will vary
widely between the exhilaration of perennially
optimistic educational progressives, and the dis-
belief of disillusioned educational pessimists. The
principle of recurrent education has had widespread
acceptance in the western countries. But practice
dawdles behind principle. In 1979 an OECD report
assessed events in recent years, using the phrase
'progress and stagnation', and concluding that:

> it is therefore not unduly cynical to pose
> the question whether recurrent education,
> originally conceived during the period of
> educational expansion, will face the fate
> of being one of those educational ideas
> that are verbally and policy-wise accepted
> and supported but with very little impact
> on educational practice. Such a scenario
> can certainly not be excluded as we are
> approaching the 1980s with serious uncert-
> ainties concerning the economy, employment
> and public expenditures. However, it might
> also be that this new and emerging socio-
> economic situation will accelerate the
> development of recurrent education. [7]

Is Yugoslavia on the way to a continuous education
system irrespective of fashion or economic growth?
Of course, in Yugoslavia, as elsewhere, we are discussing principles and plans more than history and
establishment. Yet the Yugoslav version of linking
reform in education, work and social management
certainly appeals as a coherent intellectual construction. On the other hand, even about the general conception there can be legitimate doubt. From
the vantage point of individual choice, caution

suggests that the underlying assumptions are somewhat flattering to ordinary mortals. They postulate
a world of individuals who are not only intelligent
and calculating marginalists, but also people who
would have the strength of their libertarian convic-
tions and would thus be willing to accept the
cruelties of life's uncertainty as well as the
tragedies of youthful folly.

Such general theoretical caution is well taken.
Nevertheless, at the level of practice the reality
of individual choice is already an improvement over
what Yugoslavia inherited from before the Second
World War - a set of institutions like that all over
traditional Europe which condemned the majority to
an elementary education which was terminal, and a
brief prelude to a life of manual work. The further
plans in Yugoslavia can, at the very least, be
expected to yield some further loosening of the traditional ties between social origin and occupational
destination, even if they do not result in a maxim-
ally open society as defined by the most rigid
theoretical conception.

Similarly, egalitarian critics may entertain
their theoretical doubts. They are of two basic
kinds. First, it may be questioned whether, notwithstanding the emancipation of learning opportunities from the strict confines of the formal school
system, any social or political plans can encompass
and discipline to the principle of equality all
influence on learning. At some point equality of
educational opportunity can only be obtained at the
cost of freedom. This is true even where, as in
Yugoslavia, formal private education is forbidden.
It is massively and endemically true when it comes
to parental teaching 'in the kitchen'. Second,
even the most determined programme of 'positive
discrimination', multiple and repeated educational
opportunities, alternative routes or other devices,
must find its limits in practicability and in the
limitations of social and psychological science.
After all, we simply do not know what is the optimal
learning environment of individual A compared with
individual B; yet that knowledge is a precondition
of establishing full equality of opportunity between
them. But again, the reply is similar. Both current practice and future plans in Yugoslavia are an
improvement on the inequalities of the past. Though
we must note the limitations of solidarity funding,
the reply cannot be gainsaid. The argument is one
of more or less. Experience, not theory, will be
the ultimate test of the idea of continuing educa-

tion in its Yugoslav version.

It may well be argued that there is a general logic of continuous education in which all social organisations,informal as well as formal, are drawn into, or at least heavily influenced by, a conscious pedagogical policy. There are, to be sure, obvious dangers here of a new tyranny. It is always a basic problem of any revolutionary regime that it must ensure the allegiance of its citizens. Indeed, as the self-management movement amply demonstrates, a fundamental task of the revolution is to create social conditions which encourage people to develop those qualities of social personality on which the success of revolution depends. The Yugoslavs have recognised this in their provision for self-management courses in schools, and their arrangements for recruitment of the League of Communists of Yugoslavia by selection rather than election.

Yet prosperity and freedom also create space for other influences. In one sense the increase of money in private pockets, television in every household, shorter hours of work, etc., represent achievements of the revolutionary aims. But in another sense they change the conditions of freedom and control. Social and political consciousness become amenable to new forces. Consequently, either tacitly by inaction or purposefully by exercising some kind of political control, Yugoslavia or any other country, has a policy. It can be a policy of laissez-faire or, to put it pejoratively, of rampant individualism. Or it can be a policy of tight control or, to put it equally pejoratively, of political tyranny. No western country has placed itself at either of these extremes. But the exact position taken is everywhere subject to continual debate.

To illustrate from another country, there has never ceased to be contention in Britain as to how far the government should control the content of B.B.C. broadcasting. The dominant doctrine of the B.B.C.'s first and powerful director, Lord Reith, was that the cultural level of programmes should, as opportunity and response allowed, be tilted slightly in the direction of 'high' rather than 'popular' culture. The perennial criticism has been that this Reithian doctrine offends the principle of democracy. The defence has been that minority tastes need protection and that, since the demos has decreed educational expansion, the mass media must support by staying somewhat ahead of today's educational level in anticipation of tomorrow's tastes.

Taking a second example from Yugoslavia itself,
I was struck by the absence of the pornography which
is ubiquitous in western cities. The use of sexual
titillation on advertisement hoardings and the display of pornographic magazines is not a feature of
Zagreb or Novi Sad. And I was impressed in observ-
ing young people on the evening streets of Belgrade
by a sense of relative innocence and decorum more
reminiscent of inter-war Paris or London than
present-day Hamburg or Amsterdam. These phenomena
are not accidental. Our hosts reminded me that I
was visiting at a time of international mourning for
the death of Tito. Yet I would still insist on the
contrast and, in any event, the example of public
sexual mores serves to illustrate the point that,
in a country which takes continuous education seriously, a very wide range of difficult decisions have
to be taken about the scope and the method of educational intrusion into the totality of social life.
The question is whether the Yugoslavs are thinking,
or intend to think, systematically through the
policy issues involved.

What they clearly are doing is to analyse the
implied relation between continuous education and
working life with its serious potential problem of
finance. Self-management involves dependence on
solidarity funds for equality of distribution, and
on BOALS for linking education to work. Neither of
these features is beyond question in the search for
a financial underpinning of the idea of free individual choice and social equality. Both of these
problems seem to us to be likely to persist even
supposing that the general shortage of funds for
educational activity is overcome. The problem is,
in a sense, circular. It will require enlightened
self-sacrifice on the part of BOALs and communities
to freeze personal income and consumption to ensure
both adequate investment in a changing technology
and adequate funding of work-training. This itself
challenges the educational sympathies of the parti-
cipating workers. It puts democracy to a severe
test. Moreover, beyond the direct interest of
workers, continuing education makes large claims for
the unemployed and the retired. The bonds of solidarity and fraternity will also be severely tested if
the needs of these groups are to be satisfied. The
observer, however well disposed, is bound to wonder
whether a fully-developed continuing education can
be supported by a financial system so heavily dependent on decisions in the workplace.

Yugoslavia has espoused a Communism which takes seriously the original Marxist idea of the withering away of the state and eventually even of the Party, leaving economic organisations and social activities to evolve and survive by free exchange of labour between groups which afford full participation in decisions to their members who elect delegates to represent them in negotiations with other groups.

A BRITISH TRANSLATION?

Can Britain learn from the Yugoslav experience? Obviously there could be no question of mechanical translation, and one lesson is entirely repugnant - the fact that 'propaganda against the regime' has led, and continues to lead, to imprisonment of some dissidents. A policy which does not guarantee freedom of speech and association to its citizens has no serious claim to be called a democracy. Nevertheless, imaginative translation of the idea of self-management in Yugoslavia to local democracy in Britain is an attractive possibility.

Without abrupt departure from the custom of mixed central and local taxation, we could, in British terminology, begin by making every school a direct grant school. School government could be simultaneously reformed along the lines recommended in the Taylor Report. A central national administration, but a slimmer one, would remain with three main tasks: to administer the direct grant formula, to collect and disseminate information on the performance of the educational system, and to inspect. The L.E.A.s and their apparatus of administration, advice, and control over finance and appointments, would go. School governing bodies would govern, and be answerable to their electorate in the local community and the school itself.

Native tradition, the warning of American school boards, and lack of confidence in the translation of Yugoslav solidarity funding all point to the retention of national financial support. But the direct grant formula, though based on a simple head-counting, could and should include a strong positively discriminatory element to ensure equal educational opportunity as between rich and poor school districts. Local variety also occasionally implies local disaster, and therefore implies provision for national rescue where minimum national standards are not met. Hence, the inspectorate would need an ambulance brigade in reserve to be deployed by the Secretary of State where local democracy was failing its children to a point of scandal closely defined by Parliament.

Local school democracy, moreover, would not have a simple structure. It would live within geographical boundaries set by catchment areas, but would include parents, teachers, and the older pupils and students who would be progressively enfranchised as apprenticed democrats. In each school the staff would be a democratic group electing its own head teachers (not for life), and its own representatives on the school governing body. A corollary would be that democracy, as the art of collective self-management, would occupy an indispensable place in the curriculum of every school. Any candid observer of a typical once-a-term school governors' meeting as hitherto constituted has to dismiss it as a ritual farce of democratic gossip about a trivial agenda. All serious matters of finance and curriculum are decided elsewhere. My colleague, Andy Hargreaves, is producing research evidence of admittedly more subtle processes of control over staff discussion within schools as they are presently run. The proposed changes in the internal life of schools would help to free them from the inhibitions of conventionally-received opinion - which Marxists call hegemony - and so encourage that more substantial democracy which is thwarted by present tacit understandings as to what is a possible agenda in a meeting of the governors or of the staff.

Reform in the direction of local democracy would produce local variety of response and therefore new inequalities of opportunity. But these would be more than compensated by the release and creation of new energies for education from parents, teachers, and children: and the antidotes in reserve are national minima, the discriminatory element in the direct grant formula, the inspectorate, and the educational ambulance service. Defenders of the status quo will appeal to our exhaustion from past upheaval. They will say that other problems of democracy, whether those of Margaret Thatcher or Michael Foot, must take precedence over worries about educational democracy. The answer is where I started. The reproduction of generations is everybody's business.

NOTES

1. This chapter is a much expanded version of my article on 'Democracy for Education' in New Society (March 1981) which in turn was based on a talk given to the North of England Education Conference in January 1981. I owe to OECD the opportunity of visiting Yugoslavia in 1980 as an Examiner of Yugoslav education. The full account is OECD, Review of National Policies for Yugoslavia, (OECD, Paris, 1981), and I have drawn heavily here on what I wrote for the OECD monograph.

2. See Halsey, A.H. (1981) Change in British Society, 2nd edn, Oxford University Press, especially chapter 7.

3. E.g. Bowles, S. and Gintis, H. (1976) Schooling in Capitalist America, Basic Books Inc., New York.

4. For a general discussion of industrial democracy see Hirszowicz, M. (1981) Industrial Sociology, Martin Robertson, Oxford, chapter 10 and the works therein cited.

5. See Dobson, R.B., 'Social Status and Inequality of Access to Higher Education in the USSR'., in Karabel, J. and Halsey, A.H. (eds) (1976) Power and Ideology in Education, Oxford University Press, New York.

6. The prophet of flexibility in this context is Gosta Rehn, the Swedish labour economist. See Rehn, G. 'Flexibility in Working Life', in Mushkin, S. (ed) (1973), Recurrent Education (National Institute of Education, Washington.

7. OECD, CERI/CD(79)12. FD(79)16. p.5.

9. ACCOUNTABILITY, INDUSTRY AND EDUCATION -
Reflections on Some Aspects of the Educational
and Industrial Policies of the Labour
Administrations of 1974-79

John Beck

INTRODUCTION

Writing in the CBI Review in June 1971, Sir John
Partridge, the then President of the CBI, offered
the following description of the role and responsibilities of employers:

> Every employer worthy of the name knows that
> the effective conduct of a business depends
> on the continuous observance of four sets of
> interests - the interests of investors, of
> employees, of customers, ...and the general
> interests of the community at large, both
> local and national. The whole art-cum-science
> of industrial and commercial management lies
> in a concern to balance these interests in
> such a way that a business remains viable and
> onward-going...Management stands for employee
> interests, even though it also has to stand
> for other essential interests (Sir John
> Partridge, 1971, pp.8-9).

A remarkably similar analysis of the employer's role
was presented in a talk given in 1980 by a director
of a multi-national oil corporation to an audience
of student teachers who were taking a course on
school-industry relationships as part of their professional training programme:

> What you aim to do is meet the needs of four
> important interest groups: the first one is
> the customer; you must also meet the needs of
> your employees; you must also satisfy the
> needs of the wider community; and finally, you
> must be able to meet the needs of your share-

holders. And if you only satisfy three out of
four of them, then however good you are, you
are destroyed. So it's a balance and a
desperately important one: for example, if
you don't meet the aspirations of your
employees, you're eventually on a hiding to
nothing because the whole thing is totally
interdependent on the contribution of everyone
in the firm.

Several of the student teachers present on this
occasion later indicated that they thought that
there was something a little idealised about this
CBI-preferred image of the responsible employer,
conscientiously balancing the legitimate interests
of these four constituencies. One student commented:
'the speaker talked about concern for employees -
but there evidently are employees in this and other
countries who are in such a weak economic position
that they are grossly exploited in pursuit of
profit'. Instead of dwelling on this point, however, I want in this paper to draw attention to
another characteristic of such self-portraits by
employers: their paternalistic presumption that the
task of adjudicating between these four sets of
interests legitimately rests exclusively with senior
management, even though such management is in
English law directly accountable to only one of
these constituencies - the shareholders. Of course,
organizations like the CBI are at pains to stress
that responsible and successful managements should
and do consult widely - with trade unions, with
representatives of the local community, etc. However, as Peter Scrimshaw a philosopher of education
has noted in another context, consultation is in no
sense an adequate substitute for a right to parti-
cipate in decision-making: 'to consult a person
before deciding what he is to do is not to recognise
his right to be treated as a free agent; it is in
fact to make explicit your belief that he is not
entitled to such recognition' (Scrimshaw, 1975, p.
64).

THE LABOUR PARTY'S INDUSTRIAL STRATEGY, 1973-75

A concern to make employers more accountable - both
to employees and to the wider community - was an
important element in the Labour Party's Industrial
Strategy which was first publicly set out in
'Labour's Programme for Britain' (The Labour Party,
1973) and subsequently incorporated into the Labour

Manifesto of February, 1974. The overall aim of this new industrial policy was to reverse the long term decline of British manufacturing industry through a programme of greatly increased state intervention. It was not, however, simply an attempt to reinstate old-style nationalization as a central element in Labour's programme. The Industrial Strategy proposals included several novel and progressive elements, progressive that is, from the standpoint of a commitment to democratic socialism. The proposed strategy involved first, the creation of a National Enterprise Board which would, by selective nationalization and by channeling public finance into private industry, boost investment in profitable manufacturing concerns. Secondly, it proposed the introduction of 'planning agreements' which would involve the workforce in the planning of company policy at all levels. As Prior has pointed out, the degeneration of this strategy following 1974 'should not obscure just how ambitious was the original concept: it proposed the admission of the workforce into areas of company planning never open to them before, backed by the authority of a state agency, the NEB, able to intervene directly in any industry that did not follow particular patterns' (Prior, 1980, p.3).

The proposals sought to increase the accountability of employers in two main ways. First, it was argued that government financial assistance to private industry should only be given in return for an extension of public control. As Sir Harold Wilson succinctly put it: 'where public money goes, there must go corresponding public control through public ownership' (Wilson, 1973). Such public subsidies to industry had in fact increased massively during the years of the previous Conservative administration. Tony Benn, who in February 1974 became Labour's Secretary of State for Industry, published figures based on the DI's own statistics which showed that up to March 1974, government had paid out more than £3 billion to 'private' industry in various subsidy programmes. And in relation to this disclosure, even Mr. Benn's political adversaries have conceded that 'Benn's criticisms of industry having half what it paid in taxes back in grants did have a certain point when firms were shouting about free enterprise while in partnership with Heath they were conniving at the destruction of free enterprise' (Lewis, 1978, p.135). The second main way in which the Industrial Strategy sought to make employers more accountable was through the planning agreements proposals which involved a very signifi-

213

cant extension of industrial democracy. The case
for giving employees a greater role in company planning and decision-making was cogently presented by
David Basnett in an article published in The Times
in March 1975:

> We need to end the system where decisions about
> millions of pounds worth of investment are made
> behind closed doors and without reference to
> the interests of the work people they directly
> affect nor the interests of society as a whole.
> Funds should only be provided in return for a
> share in the real control of industry. If
> responsibility is to be shared, power must be
> shared too. This sharing of power applies
> even more to the planning process: this plan-
> ning process cannot be carried through without
> the involvement and ultimately the consent of
> those who any major planning decision affects
> most directly - the workers whose jobs are
> involved. It is for this reason that the
> argument about planning is also an argument
> about industrial democracy (Basnett, 1975, p.
> 14).

The actual proposals for planning agreements which
were contained in the White Paper 'The Regeneration
of British Industry' (DI, 1974) were somewhat weaker
than those which had been set out in Labour's 1973
proposals - most significantly planning agreements
were to be voluntary. Even so, the White Paper did
propose a major role for trade union representatives
in company planning and it announced that companies
would be required to disclose to such union representatives 'all the necessary information relevant
to the contents of Planning Agreements' (DI, 1974,
p.5).
Industrialists and employers' organizations
responded to the White Paper and to the subsequent
Industry Bill of 1975 with a sustained campaign of
resistance. 'Aims of Industry, a business-sponsored
organization, launched a £100,000 campaign against
nationalization, or, as it was more and more coming
to be called, 'Bennery'' (Lewis, 1978, p.138). CBI
spokesmen repeatedly attacked all those elements of
the proposals which were of a democratic socialist
character and which proposed a transfer of effective
power from management to employees' representatives.
Such proposals were dismissed as 'politically inspired' or as 'proposals deriving from ideological
desires to extend state control over the private

sector' (Campbell Adamson, 1975, p.40) - as if the
defence of private enterprise and managerial prero-
gatives was somehow not 'political' or 'ideological'.'
Lord Watkinson, chairman of the CBI Companies
Committee and clearly speaking with the approval and
backing of the confederation, gave notice (in a
speech in the House of Lords) that the private sector of industry could soon be driven into a policy
of confrontation with the government in which its
'muscle-power' would be used in the same way as
trade unions were now using their power to achieve
their aims' (The Times, 13th May, 1975, p.1).
    Before considering the fate of the Industrial
Strategy during and after 1975, it is relevant at
this point to briefly examine the second attempt
which was made during the period 1974-79 to give
employees a greater share of control over industrial
decision-making - The Report of the Committee of
Inquiry on Industrial Democracy (Bullock, 1977).
The majority report of the Bullock Committee, which
'incorporated the thinking of advanced socialist
trade unionists' (Hirst, 1981, p.59) proposed the
establishment in industry of unitary management
boards 'consisting of an equal number of directors
elected by shareholders and by employees with the
balance held by a smaller third force of directors
co-opted by agreement between the two main interest
groups' (The Times, 27th January, 1977). Representation of employees was to be through a 'single
channel of representation based on the trade unions'
rather than from a constituency of individual members of the firm acting as 'representatives of labour by reason of being workers themselves' (Hirst,
1981, p.60). The latter system of representation
is ostensibly more democratic than the former - as
employers' representatives on the Bullock Committee
were not slow to point out. However, as Paul Hirst
has persuasively argued, 'industrial democracy cannot be even handed; it either extends the unions'
powers or it confers a 'new legitimacy' on the
management as it does in the Federal Republic of
Germany'. The merit of the single channel of representation in Hirst's opinion is that it 'draws
representatives from organized workers experienced
in dealing with management; ...it means that representatives have access to national union structures
for information about policies in other companies,
advice, and so on' (Hirst, 1981, pp.60-62). The
three employers' representatives who signed the
Bullock minority report expressed their support precisely for the West German system which, as has

been argued, fails to make employers effectively
more accountable to employees' representatives and
leaves managerial autonomy very largely unimpaired.

Reaction by organized management to the Bullock
majority report was just as hostile, just as intran-
sigent as their response to the Industrial Strategy
proposals had been. Hirst speaks of 'an unprecedented campaign against the Report'. Len Murray,
speaking on behalf of the TUC, commented: 'I have
been astonished at the synthetic hysteria that the
CBI has been whipping up in recent weeks. I am sur-
prised that they should have put themselves into a
position of defending out-dated concepts of managerial authority' (The Times, 27th January, 1977,
p.1). Once again the CBI used the threat of non-
cooperation - this time non-cooperation with the
Callaghan government's revised Industrial Strategy -
as a means of defeating the Bullock recommendations:
'Employers are now replacing the threat of pulling
out of the strategy altogether with a more subtle
approach. They are indicating that in the absence
of flexibility on worker directors, the strategy
will simply peter out for want of enthusiasm by the
industrialists' (The Times, 2nd February, 1977, p.1).

A short paper such as this is not the place to
attempt a measured assessment of the many and complex reasons why both the 1973-4 Industrial Strategy
proposals and the majority recommendations of the
Bullock Committee were not implemented. Resolute
opposition from the leaders of private industry and
their allies within the civil service was obviously
a very important factor. Sir Anthony Part, who was
permanent secretary at the Department of Industry
during Tony Benn's period of office as secretary of
state, has been described as 'fundamentally opposed'
to the new industrial policy and has been credited
with orchestrating opposition to it within Whitehall.
'He was repeatedly seen at the Treasury and certainly kept in close touch with them and other departments to try and circumvent Tony Benn' (Prior, 1980,
p.10). It is also quite clear that a significant
fraction of the Labour Party's leadership never
really supported the proposals and was more than
willing to emasculate the strategy when an opportunity occurred. Nevertheless, this scenario of civil
service conspiracy and betrayal by a right wing
leadership is manifestly overdrawn and oversimpli-
fied. Between 1974 and 1977, the economic and the
political context was highly inimical to the pursuit
of socialist policies. The rapidly worsening economic situation during 1975, with rising inflation,

the PSBR growing, the exchange rate falling, severely circumscribed the government's freedom of action.
Politically, it should not be forgotten that from
February to November 1974 Labour functioned as a
minority government, and that even after the election of 10th November Labour's overall majority was
only 3, this being subsequently eroded in by-election
defeats in 1976-7 with the result that, in Michael
Foot's words, 'a majority of three or two or one or
even less was all we had at our disposal' (Foot,
1982, p.13). It is very doubtful if any government
in such a precarious situation and needing to stimulate new industrial investment, could have successfully pursued a strategy which leaders of private
industry defined as one of 'confrontation'. Certainly no Labour government could have done so without strong and united support from the trade unions
and the Parliamentary Labour Party. Such unity was,
however, conspicuously absent. Even those most
closely identified with the 1973 proposals, for
example Michael Meacher who was a junior minister at
the DI under Tony Benn, have recognized that 'there
was a lack of awareness in the labour movement of
what the policy was and why it was worth having' and
that 'the trade union leaders at their level didn't
understand it either, or were not particularly committed' (Prior, 1980, p.9). And within the PLP
there was, of course, a considerable body of social
democratically inclined M.P.s who were just as
determined as some right wingers within the Cabinet
that the socialist elements of the strategy should
be neutralised. For example, on 1st May, 1975, ten
Labour M.P.s voted with the Conservatives to defeat
a left-wing amendment to the Industry Bill which
would have made planning agreements compulsory 'if
in the opinion of the Secretary of State for
Industry they affected or were likely to affect
national needs' (The Times, 2nd May, 1975). There
can be little doubt either that the failure of the
Callaghan government to implement the proposals of
the Bullock Report was due in no small measure to
ambivalence and even hostility from both left and
right within the labour movement - ambivalence
resulting from fears that 'traditional trade union
forms and issues of struggle (would) be confused,
displaced and subverted by formal participation in
management' (Hirst, 1980, p.56).

THE 'REVISED VERSION' OF THE INDUSTRIAL STRATEGY,
1975-79

Following the EEC Referendum - which had itself been
a factor further polarizing the debates around the
Industrial Strategy - Harold Wilson removed Tony
Benn from the DI and replaced him with Mr. Eric
Varley. This signalled the beginning of a gradual
metamorphosis in which the radical and controversial
elements in the original proposals were allowed to
atrophy and a new 'non-partisan strategy for reforming manufacturing industry' took shape (The Times,
29th January, 1977). An Industry Act was passed in
November, 1975 but its provisions differed considerably from the original NEB/planning agreements strategy. 'Planning agreements were now entirely
voluntary. The government hadn't even taken powers
to ensure compliance after default and cash hand-
outs to companies were not tied to planning agreements' (Forester, 1978, p.8). More important still,
the government - faced with continuing threats from
the CBI - made no attempt to implement any of the
more controversial measures which had been left in
the Act. 'While we got an Industry Act in November
1975 on the statute book, absolutely nothing was
done to implement it; it was just left dormant'
(Prior, 1980, p.8). In point of fact, the Act was
not a complete dead letter. The creation of the
NEB for example, was significant, even if its
functions were circumscribed by stringent restrictions on its powers and by shortage of finance.
Nevertheless, it is difficult to disagree with
Prior's judgement that after 1975 the policy degen-
erated.
     The revised version of the strategy was un-
veiled following a meeting of the National Economic
Development Council at Chequers on 5th November
1975. It was presented as a significant new departure - a basis for industrial regeneration founded
upon agreement and cooperation between government,
industry and the trade unions. 'The Prime Minister
said it was the first time a common approach to
tackling Britain's flagging industrial performance
had been agreed...The Government believed that a
successful approach to industrial strategy...would
have to satisfy two conditions. It must be realistic and flexible and it must get away from policies
of confrontation' (The Times, 6th November, 1975,
p.1). The proclaimed objective of the new approach
was the same as that of the 1973-4 proposals:
industrial regeneration. The means available,

however, were necessarily limited to what could be
agreed between the three partners in the new Tripartite approach - which, in effect, meant that they
were limited to policies which were acceptable to
employers. It was scarcely surprising therefore,
that the main innovations in the area of economic
policies turned out to be precisely those which the
CBI had suggested in its own 'constructive response'
to the industrial strategy debate: 'we have argued
for a more effective system of setting out coherent
industrial strategy on a voluntary basis at sectoral level within the structure of the NEDC...'
(Campbell Adamson, 1975, p.39). Forty of these
sectoral working parties were eventually established
but there is little evidence that they made significant contributions to improving industrial performance in any sector of the economy. Even supporters of the new approach recognized that it was
having a negligible impact. Sir Charles Villiers,
chairman of the British Steel Corporation, warned in
1977 that 'the 15 month old industrial strategy
could remain a paper chase for far too long' (The
Times, 3rd February, 1977, p.20). And Mr. Geoffrey
Chandler, the Director General of the National
Economic Development Office, reviewing the effectiveness of the industrial strategy in October 1978,
admitted that 'if one expects statistical improvement too soon this can lead to disappointment' and
that 'import penetration of many sectors is still
unacceptably high' (The Times, 10th October, 1978,
p.17). Apart from the sectoral working parties,
initiatives in the area of economic policy were
limited to a series of 'pious declarations such as
the NEDC's 'Improved Industrial Performance Scenario' of August, 1976, which provided for a return
to full employment, higher investment and productivity, and a remarkable 5.5 per cent growth rate
in 1977 and 1978' (Forester, 1978, p.9). Meanwhile,
the NEB's main role became increasingly that of a
rescuer of 'lame ducks' and only one voluntary planning agreement was concluded by the end of 1978 -
with Chrysler UK.
    Economic policy was not, however, the only ele-
ment in the new-style Industrial Strategy. The
government came increasingly to stress that industrial regeneration would require changes in other
areas of policy making too. Preliminary indications
that the strategy was to be broadened in this way
were given in the document which the Department of
Industry prepared as a basis for the discussions at
the 5th November Chequer's meeting. This paper

announced that 'an agreed strategy for industry...
must involve the better coordination of policies
affecting the efficiency of industry. This will require us to identify the industrial implications of
the whole range of government policies' (DI, 1975,
p.6). Interestingly enough, the introduction to
this paper also contained a list of putative 'reasons for our poor performance by international
standards'. These were said to include:

Investment

(i) a low rate of investment
(ii) inefficient use of capital, which has resulted
in a relatively poor return on new investment
(iii) poor choice of investment.

Labour

(iv) inadequate development of a manpower policy and
the consequent regional and sectoral shortages
of skilled labour
(v) low labour productivity reflecting poor management, inadequate consultation, restrictive
practices, overmanning and disruption by
industrial action
(vi) attitudes to productivity and labour mobility
based on views about appropriate pay and tax
structures which reflect long-standing attitudes
to relative pay in industry.

Government

(vii) sharp and frequent changes of economic regulators
to meet the conflicting needs of economic and
social priorities, which make it difficult for
companies to plan ahead
(viii) pre-emption of resources by the public sector
and by personal consumption to the detriment of
industry's investment and export performance
(ix) Government intervention in the pricing, investment and employment policies of the nationalised
industries.

Finance

(x) a declining rate of industrial profitability
(xi) imperfections in the capital markets mainly at
the medium- and longer-term ends
(xii) a capital market which does not give priority to
the needs of industry.

                                    (DI, 1975, p.5)

Given this analysis, the strategy which emerged after November 1975 might have been expected to have included measures aimed at, for example, redirection of investment through the NEB, or establishing a stronger state presence in the financial sector of the economy. What in fact was presented, however, was a different diagnosis which claimed that these economic weaknesses were themselves symptoms of an even more intractable underlying malaise - inappropriate and economically harmful attitudes. From 1975 onwards, increasing prominence was given to assertions by industrialists and by government spokesmen that industrial regeneration depended first and foremost upon changing attitudes. 'The first and overiding priority...is that we change our whole attitude to economic growth and the creation of wealth...The second and complementary change is our whole attitude to change itself' (Campbell Adamson, 1975, pp.36-38). 'Our industrial sector does not enjoy the same esteem and goodwill as in other countries'; this situation, 'if allowed to continue, can only have a devastating effect on an economy whose survival depends so much on the efforts of productive industry' (Sir John Methven, 1976). It was acknowledged that such attitudes had been shaped over a long period and that a variety of influences had contributed to their formation. Nevertheless, within the framework of the new 'broadened' Industrial Strategy, it was Britain's educational system which was increasingly made to bear the main burden of responsibility for the country's relative economic decline.

Several writers have described the intensive campaign of criticism which companies, employers' organizations and certain government departments directed against the education system from late 1975 onwards (Beck, 1981, pp.92-101; CCCS, 1981, pp. 191-227; Donald, 1979, pp.13-49; Esland and Cathcart, 1981, pp.68-74; Whitty, 1981, pp.32-33). Two rather separate educational causes of British industrial decline were identified - though both had to do with the formation of attitudes. First, it was asserted that the longstanding 'academic bias of much of the educational system' (DI, 1977, p.2) had played a major part in creating and maintaining the situation described by Sir John Methven in which wealth creation, the profit motive and engineering were accorded less status in Britain than in most other manufacturing countries. One important consequence of this was said to be that teachers, consciously and unconsciously, discouraged their most

gifted pupils from aspiring to careers in industry.
The second area of criticism concerned the alleged
effects of more recent educational developments -
notably, the growth in progressive teaching methods,
the increased autonomy of the teaching profession,
and certain unintended consequences of comprehensive
reorganization. These developments, it was claimed,
had resulted in falling standards of attainment in
basic subjects, a growth in negative attitudes to
work and to authority especially among school-
leavers, and a curriculum which was teacher-
dominated and increasingly irrelevant to the
nation's economic needs. In short, too many of the
nation's schools were making pupils unemployable at
the very time when youth unemployment was rising at
an alarming rate. Criticisms of the first type were
expressed mainly by employers and by the Department
of Industry whereas it was the new Conservative
'right' - the authors of the Black Papers on education and certain sections of the press, particularly
the Daily Mail and the Daily Mirror - which led the
offensive on 'standards' and 'discipline' (CCCS,
1981, pp.221-225).

One of the main concerns of the writers of the
Black Papers on education (Cox and Dyson, 1969;
Cox and Dyson 1970a and 1970b; Cox and Boyson, 1975)
had been the issue of teacher accountability. And
it is significant that this quickly became a central theme of the employers' critique. In an
article published in the Times Educational Supplement early in 1976, Sir Arnold Weinstock, managing
director of GEC Ltd., argued that the current
'malaise in British education' made it imperative
for employers to raise 'the whole thorny question
of accountability of teachers and educationalists
to the community' (Sir Arnold Weinstock, 1976).
Throughout 1976 and 1977, employers continued to
press this claim that educationalists should be more
accountable and in particular, that they should be
more accountable to those who had responsibility for
the nation's economic well-being. By mid-1977,
following Prime Minister Callaghan's Great Debate
on education and the publication of Shirley Williams'
Green Paper 'Education in Schools - A Consultative
Document' (DES, 1977b), the CBI was able to report
with some satisfaction that 'it can be said to have
been a salutary exercise for the school system to
be subjected for the first time to this kind of
public scrutiny, which has, amongst other things,
served to emphasise that accountability for what
takes place in the classroom cannot be divorced from

responsibilities that lie beyond the school' (CBI, 1977, p.1). It is important to note here that the employers did not seek direct control over educational institutions, either at national or at local level. David Bridges' work for the Cambridge Accountability Project illustrates the stance of one group of <u>local</u> employers on this issue: 'in my own interviews with employers...I collected a mixture of hesitant responses which levelled some criticism at what went on in schools (in general) but stopped short of seeking control' (Bridges, 1981a, p.143). Significantly, one of the employers interviewed by Bridges is quoted as saying: 'We don't want control. That smacks of Eastern Europe to me' (Bridges, 1981b, p.89). This revealing comment perhaps makes it easier to appreciate why the strategy which employers' organizations pursued at a <u>national</u> level was one which sought a strengthening of <u>central government</u> control over the education system – on the basis of a tacit understanding that government would continue to be especially receptive to the employers' point of view. Working in this way, industrialists were able to extend their influence over educational policy-making without exposing themselves to the damaging criticism that they were disregarding the legitimate rights of the teaching profession. The point is nicely illustrated by the following extract from a CBI report on the speech which James Callaghan delivered at Ruskin College, Oxford, in October 1976 – the speech which launched the Great Debate:

> On the issue of the school curriculum, one of the most sensitive touched on by the Prime Minister, employers are firmly against any idea of State control, but believe that there is room for a stronger central influence. They would therefore welcome an exploratory approach by the DES and the Inspectorate into the desirability and feasibility of a common core curriculum, as well as into means of ensuring minimum acceptable standards for all school leavers in subjects such as mathematics and English. It would, however, be essential to ensure the acceptability of such measures by the teaching profession by respecting the legitimate claims of teachers as to the exercise of their professional judgement. A greater vocational influence on the curriculum could well improve both pupils' communication skills (sic) and their

motivation (CBI, 1976b, p.1).

One important reason why the employers could be confident that government would continue to prove responsive to their educational proposals was the fact that education had come to assume such a salient role in the government's much publicised new approach to industrial strategy. As early as March 1976, Mr. Fred Mulley, who was briefly Secretary of State for Education, made a speech in which he identified education as 'a key to our industrial regeneration':

> I am concerned that young people appear to attach little esteem to careers in the wealth generating industries and in commerce upon which the country's economic future depends. The problem goes far beyond my ministerial sphere of responsibility but I believe it provides a key to our industrial regeneration. A start could be made by an attempt to change the attitudes of our ablest students...If the country does not concentrate more of its talents on the basic necessity of earning its own living, our present problems are almost certain to multiply (CBI, 1976a, p.27).

Both the content and the timing of this statement are significant. In its content, it faithfully prefigures themes which were to be developed more fully in the succession of heavily publicised speeches and documents which appeared from October 1976 onwards: Sir John Methven's speech and the Ruskin College speech - both delivered in Oxford in October 1976; the background paper to the Great Debate (DES, 1977a, January); the 1977 Green Paper itself (DES, 1977b, July) and the so-called Mueller Report on Industry, Education and Management (DI, 1977, June). (These last two documents contain many references to the government's Industrial Strategy and education's role within it.) The timing of Mr. Mulley's speech - the fact that a minister of education delivered such a speech within four months of the unveiling of the new Industrial Strategy proposals - strongly suggests that government, in consultation with employers' organizations, had decided at a very early stage that education should play a more prominent role in the revised version of the strategy. This interpretation is corroborated by reports that the Department of Industry's discussion paper Industry, Education and

Management, which was not actually published until June 1977 so as to coincide with the appearance of the Green Paper, 'had its origin in an informal meeting of representatives of industrial management, education and government as early as 1975' (Fowler, 1979, p.79).

It seems clear from this and other evidence that the government's actions in this area of policy formation were not simply a series of hastily improvised responses to a rising tide of criticism of the education system. Certainly they were influenced by considerations of expediency but they were also adroit and calculated. From the government's point of view, effecting a closer linkage between educational and industrial policy had several advantages - mainly of a tactical nature. First, it enabled Labour to present its response to the politically damaging Conservative critique of the education system as a positive initiative - an element in an over-arching strategy to reverse industrial decline - rather than as a humiliating capitulation to right wing pressure. Secondly, it did something to bolster the fading credibility of the Industrial Strategy itself - at least among moderate members of the Labour party and among labour supporters in the trade union movement. There was, after all, some real validity in the claim that the cultural ethos of Britain's schools and universities had contributed to 'the decline of the industrial spirit' (Wiener, 1981), and many trade unionists shared the doubts of those who argued that progressive education was not necessarily in the best interests of working-class children. A third advantage which the government gained from the decision to incorporate education within the Industrial Strategy was that this provided a new sphere for tripartite cooperation. Although the tangible outcomes of such collaboration were hardly spectacular, the creation of the Schools' Council Industry Project being one of the most worthwhile, the mere existence of such cooperation was probably of some symbolic value to a government whose political life was coming to depend more and more on its ability to maintain tripartite agreement in the politically much more important and contentious area of prices and incomes policy.

The educational costs of this policy, however, may prove to have been considerable. The incorporation of education within the Industrial Strategy had the effect of conferring an unprecedented degree of educational legitimacy on industrialists - as those best qualified to determine the educational changes

225

needed to reverse the country's economic decline.
And ironically, the more vigorously the government
promoted educational initiatives (as a surrogate for
economic proposals) within the revised strategy, the
more vulnerable it became to the employers' criticisms of the education system. This increasing vul-
nerability led to tensions even among right-wing
members of the Cabinet. The 1977 Green Paper had to
be repeatedly re-drafted to satisfy the conflicting
demands of those like the Prime Minister who 'took
an active part in getting the Green Paper shortened
and toughened up' (TES, 8th July, 1977, p.1) as
against those like Mr. Hattersley and Mrs Williams
herself, who apparently feared that the government
would be presenting educational reactionaries 'with
a whole new arsenal of anti-comprehensive weapons'
(TES, 24th June, 1977, p.80). In its final form,
of course, the Green Paper had implications which
went far wider than the debate about comprehensive
schools. It systematically endorsed a clearly
instrumental view of education as a means of engen-
dering the transformation of attitudes which employers had been demanding, and it called for appropriate changes both in the school curriculum and in
the training of teachers.

It was followed up by a series of policy initiatives (in which the DES and HMI played a much more
prominent role than hitherto), for example, the
Curriculum Review initiated by circular 14/77 (DES,
1978); the expansion of the role of the Assessment
of Performance Unit; the restructuring of the
Schools' Council in such a way as to reduce the
influence of teachers' representatives; the establishment of the Department of Industry's Industry/
Education Unit in 1978 and of the associated
Industry/Education Advisory Committee in 1979 (CBI,
1979, p.19).

It is still too soon to attempt any overall
assessment of the effects of these developments; as
Esland and Cathcart have noted, 'there are few
studies of the actual influence of industry within
educational policy making' (Esland & Cathcart, 1981,
p.93). Preliminary indications, however, suggest
that the impact of these attempts to change the content of education in schools and in teacher training
institutions has been uneven. Whitty's research on
school examinations indicates that as far as the
curriculum of those pupils who take GCE examinations
is concerned, the university-dominated GCE examination boards have successfuly resisted the industrial
lobby and have 'ensured the maintenance of a more

significant place for old humanist conceptions of a
liberal secondary education than might have been
predicted from the sorts of attacks on the traditional school curriculum that emanated from the
representatives of government and industry in the
opening stages of the Great Debate' (Whitty, in this
volume, p. 181). For the non-elite, the situation
appears to be rather different. Here, concern
about chronic and large-scale youth unemployment has
helped to produce a situation in which a substantial
number of teachers appear to have been persuaded,
at least to some extent, that the kinds of curriculum change called for in the Green Paper and subsequent documents are necessary and should be introduced. Such sentiments have been reinforced by the
fact that school examination certificates, particularly CSEs, now have little currency on the labour
market and are therefore less effective as a source
of extrinsic motivation. For these reasons, it has
been claimed that the traditional curriculum has
failed the 'average 16 year old' largely because it
is too academic and irrelevant to the real world
which such pupils will now have to face when they
leave school.

A crucial question which arises from all this
concerns the character of the more 'relevant' education which is being called for. There is obviously considerable justification for the view that the
traditional curriculum of most schools in Britain
has indeed failed to provide pupils with even a
rudimentary political or economic education.
Stradling's research testifies to the depressingly
high level of political ignorance among school-
leavers (Stradling, 1977) and there can be little
doubt that ignorance of economic matters is equally
profound. However, it does not follow from this
state of affairs that the appropriate educational
remedy is that schools should indoctrinate their
pupils in favour of 'a particular view of the
socially and politically desirable' (Bailey, 1978,
p.4). Yet, as Bailey, Donald and others have
pointed out, this is what the Green Paper consistently urged schools to do, as did some employers
(Bailey, 1978; Beck, 1979; Donald, 1979). It is in
fact rather unlikely that overt indoctrination
would be tolerated in schools: teachers and pupils
are far too sensitive to bias. There is, nevertheless, a real danger that the kinds of social,
economic and political education which may be
offered to 'average and below average' pupils may
result in covert forms of indoctrination. The kind

of social education which has been strongly supported by governments, the DES and industrialists, is
one which sets up a separation between the so-called
'academic' curriculum and a more practical, experiential approach which is said to be appropriate to
prepare 'ordinary' pupils for 'the world of work' or
for unemployment. Such preparation tends to be
defined in terms of increasing the 'employability'
of these pupils by providing them with the 'social
skills', 'life skills' and relevant first-hand
experience which they are said to lack. Consider
for example, the following extracts from the CBI
Education and Training Committee's reply to the
Green Paper:

> The Green Paper is weak on the need for an
> alternative to subject teaching through
> greater use of practical and relevant
> material...The development of general voca-
> tional preparation courses with the emphasis
> on improving general employability in terms
> of basic communication and social skills,
> has taken place largely in the post-school
> situation. However, much of the form and
> content of these courses is clearly relevant
> to school education (CBI, 1977b).

Once this kind of separation between 'academic' and
'practical' courses is set up, it threatens to become a means of denying 'ordinary pupils' access to
the concepts and forms of understanding (developed
within the Social Sciences and the Humanities)
which alone would enable them to develop an autonomous understanding of the social, economic and
political structure of their own society. An
intellectually serious form of social education does
not have to be academic in the 'ivory tower' sense;
there is no reason at all why it should not involve
a great deal of out-of-school work or participation
by 'outsiders' from industry and elsewhere. But if
it is to be educationally defensible, it must draw
attention to the fact that many matters concerning
industry and the economy are controversial - there
was no recognition of this in the Green Paper -
and it must involve what Bailey calls 'evidential'
teaching:

> To be sure that a student's...autonomy is
> developed he must be taught evidentially.
> That is to say he must not only be made able
> to know things, understand things and do

things, but he must become able to see on
what grounds certain beliefs, procedures and
actions can be held to be justifiable (Bailey,
1980, p.16).

Perhaps the most damaging educational legacy of
the Callaghan government's policy of linking education to industrial regeneration was the legitimacy
it gave to forms of educational practice which substitute political socialization for evidential
education. Critical and assumption-testing education about the 'world of work' was correspondingly
delegitimised; for example, there was no suggestion
in the Green Paper that pupils should be encouraged
to discuss arguments for and against industrial
democracy! Indeed, it is particularly ironic that
while employers were successfully resisting attempts
to make them more democratically accountable in
their own sphere, they were enabled to extend their
influence over education in the name of 'greater
accountability'. However, the labour movement and
particularly the left cannot escape some responsibility for this state of affairs. Their neglect of
the content of education, which Whitty has criticised in relation to the debates about comprehensive
reorganization and the sixteen-plus examinations,
was no less evident in relation to this area of
industrial and economic education. (Whitty, in this
volume, p. 183). Democratic socialists failed to
formulate any alternative to the employers' proposals which might have commanded widespread support.
Such an alternative could probably only have been
developed on the basis of arguments for forms of
accountability which were more democratic than
those proposed by the employers, combined with the
defence of a degree of professional autonomy for the
teaching profession. But given the implicit and
explicit anti-professionalism of so much of the
radical sociology current at the time (Ahier, in
this volume, p.18-19), support for an alliance of
this kind was never a real possibility.

REFERENCES

Ahier, J. (in this volume) Histories and Sociologies
      of Educational Policies.
Adamson, C. (1975) 'The CBI View', in CBI Review,
      No. 18, Autumn, pp.34-42.
Bailey, C. (1978) 'A Strange Debate: Some Comments
      on the Green Paper', Cambridge Journal of

Education, Vol. 8, No. 1.

Bailey, C. (1980) 'Teacher Role and Function as an Aspect of Teacher Education', unpublished MS, Homerton College, Cambridge.

Basnett, D. (1975) 'Why Industry Bill Points Us in the Right Direction', The Times, 3rd March.

Beck, J. (1979) 'Education, Industry and the Needs of the Economy', Cambridge Journal of Education, Vol. 11, No. 2.

Bridges, D. (1981a) 'Teachers and the World of Work' in J. Elliott, D. Bridges, D. Ebbutt, R. Gibson and J. Nias (eds) School Accountability, Grant McIntyre, London.

Bridges, D. (1981b) Case Studies in School Accountability, Vol. 2, SSRC Cambridge Accountability Project Monograph, Cambridge Institute of Education, Cambridge.

Bullock, Lord (1977) Report of the Committee of Inquiry on Industrial Democracy, Cmnd. 6706, HMSO.

CCCS (Centre for Contemporary Cultural Studies), (1981) Unpopular Education, Hutchinson, London.

CBI (Confederation of British Industry), (1976a) CBI Education and Training Bulletin, Vol. 6, No. 2, May.

CBI (1976b) CBI Education and Training Bulletin, Vol. 6, No. 4, November.

CBI (1977a) 'Great Debate - Stage Three', CBI Education and Training Bulletin, Vol. 7, No. 2, July.

CBI (1977b) 'Green Paper on Education in Schools - Report by CBI Education and Training Committee, v270.77.

CBI (1979) CBI Education and Training Bulletin, Vol. 9, No. 3.

Cox, C.B. and Dyson, A.E. (eds) (1969) Fight for Education: A Black Paper, Critical Quarterly Society.

Cox, C.B. and Dyson, A.E. (eds) (1970a) Black Paper 2: The Crisis in Education, Critical Quarterly Society.

Cox, C.B. and Dyson, A.E. (eds) (1970b) Black Paper 3: Goodbye Mr. Short, Critical Quarterly Society.

Cox, C.B. and Boyson, R. (eds) (1975) Black Paper 5: The Fight for Education, Dent, London.

Cox, C.B. and Boyson, R. (eds) (1977) Black Paper 1977, Temple Smith, London.

DES (Department of Education and Science) (1977a) Educating our Children - Four Subjects for Debate, DES, London, January.

DES (1977b) Education in Schools - A Consultative Document, Cmnd. 6869, HMSO, London.
DES (1978) Annual Report, HMSO, London.
DI (Department of Industry) (1974) The Regeneration of British Industry, Cmnd. 5710, August, HMSO, London.
DI (1975) An Approach to Industrial Strategy, Cmnd. 6315, November, HMSO, London.
DI (1977) Industry, Education and Management: A Discussion Paper, DI, June.
Donald, J. (1979) 'Green Paper: Noise of Crisis', Screen Education No. 30.
Esland, G.M. and Cathcart, H. (1981) Education and the Corporate Economy, Open University E353, Society, Education and the State, Block 1, Unit 2, The Open University Press.
Foot, M. (1982) 'My Kind of Party' in The Observer, 17th January.
Forester, T. (1978) 'How Labour's Industrial Strategy Got the Chop', New Society, 6th July, pp.7-10.
Fowler, G. (1979) 'The Politics of Education' in G. Bernbaum (ed) Schooling in Decline, Macmillan, London.
Hirst, P.Q. (1981) 'On Struggle in the Enterprise' in M. Prior (ed) The Popular and the Political: essays on socialism in the 1980's, Routledge and Kegan Paul, London.
Labour Party, The (1973) Labour's Programme for Britain.
Lewis, R. (1978) 'Tony Benn - A Critical Biography' Associated Business Press, London.
Methven, Sir John (1976) 'What Industry Wants', Times Educational Supplement, 29th October.
Partridge, Sir John (1971) 'The Role of the CBI', CBI Review, December, pp.8-9.
Prior, M. (1980) 'Problems in Labour Politics: Interviews with Stuart Holland, Frank Field and Michael Meacher' in Politics and Power 2, Routledge and Kegan Paul, London.
Scrimshaw, P. (1975) 'Should Schools Be Participant Democracies?' in D. Bridges and P. Scrimshaw (eds) Values and Authority in Schools, Hodder and Stoughton, London.
Stradling, R. (1977) The Political Awareness of the School Leaver, Hansard Society, London.
Weinstock, Sir Arnold (1976) 'I blame the teachers', Times Educational Supplement, 23rd January.
Wiener, M.J. (1981) English Culture and the Decline of the Industrial Spirit 1850-1980, Cambridge University Press.

231

Whitty, G.J. (1981) Ideology, Politics and the
    Curriculum, Open University E353, Society,
    Education and the State, Block 3, Unit 8, The
    Open University Press.
Whitty, G.J. (in this volume) 'State Policy and
    School Examinations 1976-82: An exploration
    of some implications of the sixteen plus
    controversy'.
Wilson, H. (1973) 1973 Labour Party Conference
    Report.

10. THATCHERISM AND EDUCATION

Roger Dale

In a relatively brief period, 'Thatcherism' has become an essential part of the vocabulary of British politics. It is used on both the left and the right of the political spectrum. However, its exact meaning, and what it implies in any given context, remain rather imprecise; it is connotative rather than denotative. It is, though, clearly distinguishable from other forms of conservatism, if only in its relative readiness to own up to being 'ideological', while it is possible to identify intellectual guiding lights in Friedman and Hayek, though neither of these is followed slavishly. It is further characterised by what Stuart Hall (1979, 1980) has very aptly called 'authoritarian populism', which both draws on selectively, and recombines, existing strands of conservatism (particularly those which appeal to the grass roots rather than the hierarchy of the Conservative Party), and it loosely knits these together with opportunistic reactions to contemporary problems.

In examining the impact of Thatcherism on education policy, I shall be seeking both to define it rather more precisely and to question the assumption of its unequivocal dominance in all areas of Mrs Thatcher's government policy. Education policy is, in fact, a particularly useful area to carry out this kind of examination given its control for the second part of Mrs Thatcher's 1979-84 government by the chief ideologue of Thatcherism, Sir Keith Joseph, backed up by its chief propagandist, Dr Rhodes Boyson. The opportunity and the desire to implement key percepts of Thatcherism can rarely have combined more favourably than they did in education at the beginning of the 1980s.

233

The opportunity was provided by the education-
political situation that was crystallizing towards
the end of the 1970s, whose chief characteristics
(described at greater length in a number of contributions to this book) may be very broadly listed as:
the withering of the Welfare State consensus: growing unemployment, especially of youth: the failure
of social democratic policies, not only in not producing greater equality and social justice, but in
the production of casualties in the form of the
neglected and those who felt themselves 'levelled-
down' (a key constituency of Thatcherism): and associated with these things, the decline of faith in
the state education system. This situation was one
to which the educational traditions of conservatism,
especially as felt at the grass roots and under Mrs
Thatcher, were far better able to react than those
of the Labour Party. However, before moving on to
discuss Tory education policy under Mrs Thatcher, it
will be necessary to make a very brief diversion to
consider the kinds of education policies which previous post-war Tory governments had followed.
Certainly from 1955, when Sir David Eccles was
appointed Minister of Education, until the 1964
election, Tory education policy was essentially non-
partisan and even, when Sir Edward Boyle was Minister of Education, almost bipartisan; following the
precepts of R.A. Butler's 1944 Act, the education
service expanded greatly, in the number of schools,
teachers, and students in higher education, and so
on. Under Boyle, commitment to selection for
secondary education and automatic opposition to comprehensive education ceased to be central parts of
official Tory education policy, while the value of
education in producing the kinds of people and
skills necessary to ensure continued economic growth
was very much taken for granted.
　　This approach was not, however, without its
critics, particularly after the election defeats of
1964 and 1966. It was in this period that the first
Black Papers were published, with their emphasis on
standards, excellence, authority and the other traditional virtues held to be at the core of the
grammar school. In this period, too, suggestions
based in anti-statist, economic liberal thought, and
the airing of ideas for educational voucher schemes
began to appear (see Corbett, 1969). Most of this
opposition came from the grass roots of the
Conservative Party, rather than from its parliamentary representatives or from those with responsibilities for the party's education policy. For

instance, an analysis of motions on education submitted between 1965 and 1970 to the Conservative
Party conference shows that around 55% of them emanated from what the author calls the libertarian
right and which has a number of features in common
with Thatcherism (Wilson, 1977). The two commonest
topics were tax relief on private education fees,
and opposition to comprehensive schools. The
strength of this opposition is clear from the fact
that at the 1968 party conference the official
motion on education was defeated, with Sir Edward
Boyle stating that he would not fight Socialist
dogma with Conservative dogma.

So, by the time Margaret Thatcher was appointed
Minister of Education in 1970, to the delight of the
Party's right wing (Russell, 1978), there were clear
cracks under the surface of the non-partisan approach of Eccles and Boyle. There is insufficient
space to go into Mrs Thatcher's period at Education
in any detail, but it is certainly important to try
to draw out some general impression of it (see
Woods, 1981). Such a task is not, in fact, very
easy. True, within three days of taking office she
issued circular 10/70, which removed the obligation
on LEA's to submit plans for comprehensive reorganisation and before much longer, she was, notoriously,
'snatching milk', but at the same time she did
implement the Raising of the School Leaving Age
(which the previous Labour government had postponed)
and she did increase spending on primary education.
The powerful advice from a number of quarters of her
party to smother the new born Open University was
rejected. And while 'she wasn't disposed to listen
to the unalloyed liberalism of the education
service' (Kogan, 1975, p.44) she did not, at a time
when the belief in the value of education was beginning to be seriously questioned, and when sceptical
eyes were being cast on human capital theories, cut
back overall spending on education or introduce
policies which very obviously prefigured Thatcherism.
However, if the contents of her policies were pre-
Thatcherite, it is possible to read more proto-
Thatcherite leanings in her style. On comprehensive
schools, for instance, she not only legislated
against their compulsory spread, but she also deliberately slowed down even those schemes for comprehensive reorganization submitted by conservative
local authorities, often by going out of her way to
encourage pro-grammar school groups of parents
(Woods, 1981).

In fact, many of the roots of Thatcherism were contained within the so-called Selsdon philosophy, which the Party adopted under Edward Heath and to which it was committed when it won the 1970 general election. This philosophy represented an attempt to break the neo-social democratic, state intervention-ist consensus through which the country had been governed for almost two decades. State intervention in industry was to be severely curtailed, lame ducks were (in a mixed metaphor) to be allowed to go to the wall, market forces were to be unshackled. The reversal of this policy and a return to Keynesian strategies, and in spite of that, the defeat in the 1974 election held on the issue 'Who Governs Britain', restoked the fires of ideological conflict within the Conservative Party and forged the alli-ance within the Party which brought Mrs Thatcher to the leadership. The hope was that she would both demonstrate who governed Britain and, with her greater personal commitment to Selsdon-type policies than her predecessor, refuse to be deflected from that course when the going got tough. The mood was certainly right for radical change within the Tory Party. Objectively, the oil price rises of the early 1970s had accelerated and highlighted Britain's long-term economic decline. Subjectively, the 1974 defeat was the more humiliating not just because it showed a loss of national confidence in the Party and because it had been received at the hands of militant trade unionism, but also because it could be seen to be in an important sense self-inflicted, the result of the desertion of some basic principles of conservatism. The neo-social demo-cratic Welfare State policies for which they had abandoned those principles had been a mistake - the price that had been paid was too high, the pay-off too low. Not only was such a level of state inter-vention against their deepest instincts, it proved what they had always felt about its ineffectiveness. The Welfare State had provided not so much security as featherbedding, weakening the moral fibre and the incentive to work and be responsible for self, without succeeding in eliminating anti-social beha-viour, for instance, or even illiteracy. This is most graphically illustrated in Sir Keith Joseph's initial embrace, and subsequent rejection of, the idea of a cycle of deprivation (Joseph, 1979).

Quite crucially, however, this reaction, which formed the basis of Thatcherism, was not homogenous, but brought together a number of strands of old as well as new conservative thought into a far from

easy, and frequently shifting, alliance. And in
order to understand Thatcherism we have to begin to
separate out some of these contributing strands, and
to locate their history and the nature of their
support.

THE INDUSTRIAL TRAINERS

This strand of thought is part of the 'pragmatic'
(as opposed to 'principled') reaction to the Welfare
State. The label comes from Raymond Williams (1962)
well-known tripartite division of educational ideologies (though I am no more happy with its exact
appropriateness than I am with that of the labels
I will suggest for other groups).
  Though the ideology of the bipartisan policy
may come largely from those I will call the Old
Tories, what might very loosely be called its
'material base' was located in those sections of
(large) industry which had a great deal to gain from
an expanded and improved state provision of qualified manpower. Their interest was in maximising the
benefit they could draw from the education system,
through exercising direct and indirect pressure to
deflect it in directions amenable to them. Ralph
Miliband defined this group's position very neatly;

> the people who run the most important and
> powerful sectors of British capitalist
> enterprise are by no means unequivocally in
> favour of 'free enterprise'. On the contrary,
> they very much want the state to help them,
> in a permanent and extensive system of inter-
> vention which would yet leave them free from
> state control; and the same people have long
> found that this could be got from a Labour
> Government, as well as from a Conservative
> one...They may, on the whole, prefer a
> Conservative Government, to a Labour one;
> but unlike many Conservatives at the grass-
> roots and in the political leadership, they
> are not at this point bent on 'counter
> revolution' (Miliband 1978, p.406).

It is from this position that arguments about education, like those put forward by Arnold Weinstock
(1976) of G.E.C. and John Methven (1976), then
Director-General of the CBI, emerge. There is a
clear, if implicit, acceptance that the state is
the appropriate provider and controller of education. It must, though, recognise how those who

provide its revenue and the country's wealth, generate that wealth, and attempt to make sure that the education system is at the very least not counter productive - which is what Weinstock claims many teachers are - and at best productive, which is what Methven's programme is designed to ensure.

Industry does though suffer from policies designed to cut public spending and state intervention in industry. Especially in periods of economic slump, large scale industry has become more dependent on Keynesian counter-cyclical state initiated projects for support. These Thatcherism was resolutely opposed to, with consequent complaints and requests for better treatment from the CBI. As I shall detail below, this shift from neo-Keynesian to neo-Friedmanite strategies on public spending seriously affects both the place and the funding of state education, having little appeal for those who have until now received major benefits from the state education system, in both the provision of variously skilled labour, and of research and development. However, as will again be elaborated below, one thrust of Thatcherite education policy may welcome the administrative separation of 'training' from 'education'. This is already beginning to happen, with the increasing scope and responsibility, especially in the 16+ age range of such para-educational institutions as the Manpower-Services Commission. The MSC has already had a tremendous effect on the structure and practice of further education and training, putting in question the effectiveness of the formal control of these institutions. At the government level, the DES's relatively slow and 'educationist' response to problems posed by widespread youth unemployment has led to its losing ground in the provision for this group to the relatively more open and pragmatically attuned MSC/DoI/DoE. And while the MSC was originally inspired by a human capital rationale, it seems clear that the purposes of current programmes are becoming less to fit young people for jobs, and more, because the jobs aren't there, to perform a kind of social holding operation.

The industrial trainers do, though, continue to be one of the legs propping up the key themes of accountability and standards. Though the precise meaning to be attached to these terms is elusive, the need for education to be broadly responsive to the demands of the economy remains a central component of Conservative (and, it should be said, Labour) education policy. The question of whether

that accountability and those standards are best
brought about through market mechanisms or by the
state appears not to be a crucial issue for this
group.

THE OLD TORIES

It is in this group that traditional conservative
values are still dominant. Their essence is that
kind of benevolent paternalism which Robert
Eccleshall takes to characterize English conservatism. As he puts it 'During the nineteenth century,
the idea of paternal guardianship was deployed by
many Tories in order to condemn the effects of growing industrialization upon traditional bonds of
social dependence.' More significantly in a period
when the working class was becoming enfranchised,
the persistent appeal of a stable, intimate social
hierarchy enabled Disraeli to devise a formula for
the leadership of propertied groups around the theme
of one nation. The effect, by furnishing a set of
potent cultural symbols around which to marshal
attitudes of social deference was to bequeath the
legacy of protective elitism to the twentieth
century (1980, p.4). The relative decline of influence of this strand of conservative thought can
be recognised in the use of Disraeli's name and
authority as a 'code' to attack Thatherite policies;
at one point Edward Heath hardly seemed to make a
speech which did not contain Disraeli's famous
statement that 'it is upon the education of the
people of this country that the future of this
country depends'. And as a member of the Tory
Reform Group, Trevor Russell, points out, the social
order which Disraeli is said to have brought to
Victorian England, and which Mrs Thatcher and Dr
Boyson like to recall as a 'golden age', was, in
fact, based not on Thatcherite policies, but on a
considerable level of state intervention (Russell,
1978).
    Another of the principles of 'Old Toryism' is
the belief that political wisdom resides in a dominant minority. This was perhaps most clearly expressed by the then Quintin Hogg, in the aftermath of
the 1944 Education Act. 'Precisely because it
arouses fierce religious differences and social
resentments education is a matter which must be han-
dled by statesmen on pragmatical and objective lines
in a country of many religious differences and
social distinctions', while 'not the least valuable
feature of (Mr. Butler's Act) is that it has placed

the general framework of our educational system beyond the range of party politics' (1947, pp.143-144). This contrasts rather with the kind of populism and the emphasis on parental choice in education, which is much more characteristic of Thatcherism.

A further contrast is found in the interpretation of the idea of self-help. Eccleshall brings this out well. He contrasts the 'paternal guardianship' and 'one nation' themes of Disraeli, with what we would see as a much more Thatcherite, bourgeois rhetoric in which

> society appears...as a collection of independent individuals each intent on pursuing self-interest...(it is) a fluid structure in which individuals rise to the social level concomitant with their natural abilities. Riches are seen as the due reward of those who have expanded maximum energy, intelligence and agility in making material provision for themselves. Conversely, poverty is taken as a sign of some innate deficiency, the failure of individuals to exercise sufficient skill to secure comfortable existence; those who prove themselves incapable of seizing opportunities that are equally available to everyone must expect to pay the penalty of a lower standard of living (1980, p.4).

The distinction between these very different notions of self-interest, individualism and a kind of commonality, albeit one which 'contrives a cosy image of an affective community where all may be brothers but never equals' (Eccleshall, 1977, p.68) emerged very clearly in the House of Lords rejection of that part of the 1980 Education Act dealing with the proposed introduction of the possibility of charging for school transport, where a coalition of Old Tories, Roman Catholics and Socialists successfully fought against the measure (see Bull, 1980). This was then denounced by Ralph Harris, writing in the Spectator, as 'a triumph for false compassion, sectarian interest, timidity, nostalgia, political paternalism and economic irresponsibility (as)... complacency, conformity, old fashioned conservatism and cheap compassion - at other people's expense' (1980, pp.12-13).

The continuing strength, but novel defensiveness, of this traditionally dominant strand of conservative educational ideology (best epitomized in Butler's Act and above all in Sir Edward Boyle's

tenure of the DES) is seen in the frequency and tone
of the objections to its supercession by a much more
abrasive and divisive approach. Not only conservative politicians like Mr. Heath and Sir William van
Strabenzee, (see TES, 16/10/81) but other such bul-
warks of Old Toryism as the chairman of the Head-
master's conference, (Thorn, 1981) spoke out against
the nature and the extent of the cuts imposed on
education by the Thatcher government. There is a
consistent theme running through all of them, that
of betrayal of the duty to succour the less well off,
and of the failure to mitigate the price the many
have to pay for the success of the few.

The differences between this previously dominant
approach and key stands of Thatcherism may be best
gleaned from a consideration of the differences between two views of educational vouchers, published
in The Times Educational Supplement in 1975. The
one, in a paper prepared for the Conservative
Political Centre by Vernon Bogdanor, may be taken as
broadly representative of what is called here 'Old
Toryism'. The other is a response to it by Rhodes
Boyson, a major power in Thatcherite education
policy. For Bogdanor, 'there is a necessary tension
between the freedom of the market and the demand for
equal rights in a democracy' and believers in parental rights must strike the balance between these.
'What is at issue' Bogdanor concludes, 'is whether
the commercial principle should be brought into the
state sector of education so as to override the
equal rights established by modern legislation and
in particular by the Butler Education Act of 1944'.
Boyson's response focusses very much on individual
parents' freedom. He claims that educational voucher schemes are weapons against socialist excess
since they 'move power from the state to the family'.
He argues, too, that the Government 'can never maximise the potential of each individual child...Only
the parent can know his own child sufficiently well
to fit his individual talents'. There is much more
to this significant and interesting debate than
space permits me to include here; it not only
catches very well the distinction between 'Old
Tories' and 'Populists' but also indicates something
of the nature and the extent of the departure from
traditional conservative thought which Thatcherism
represents.

THE POPULISTS

So far populism has been examined as it contrasts with 'Old Toryism' but I want now to consider it in slightly more detail. Populism in the broad sense of appeal to the 'national instincts' of the people and to unifying factors like nationality above 'divisive' factors like class, race and gender has been identified by a number of writers (e.g. Hall, 1979, 1980) as a key strand of Thatcherism. One of its most explicit adherents and propagators, generally, and particularly with respect to education is Rhodes Boyson. I wish here merely to identify what seems to me some salient points of Boyson's educational philosophy, which contribute powerfully to the structure of Thatcherism (see e.g. Boyson, 1975b, and numerous speeches reported in the educational press; see also Wright, 1977). Basically Boyson is set upon promoting common sense above theory, and the people (together with 'natural' social units, like the family) above the experts. His attacks are aimed at the betrayal of the people by experts, social engineers who claim to know best what's good for people, but whose half-baked theories have led only to drastic decline in standards and discipline, and to a collapse of confidence in education. It is this strand of conservative educational thought to which the Black Papers have most contributed, with their revelation of the consequences of half-baked progressive ideas and of the follow of assuming that all children can be equal.

Four points need to be noted about this kind of populism to enable us to make some evaluation of its contribution to Thatcherite education policy. First, we should recognize that 'the people' appealed to and allegedly represented in this populist strand, by no means includes 'everyone'. Effectively it means the deserving, those able and willing to make the most of opportunities offered them, and those most stifled by Welfare State nannying. It does not include the improvident or those unwilling to help themselves. The second point to bear in mind is that this kind of populism is not so much anti-statist as anti-social democratic. The objection to the social democratic state is that it tries to bring about 'unnatural' things, like social justice. This involves upsetting the natural hierarchy - or even meritocracy - which it is the legitimate task of the state to maintain, along with the family and other 'natural' social units. It may even be a part of the state's job to make sure that the natural

hierarchy of talent is properly attuned to national
economic needs through the education system. Indeed,
it is in this way that the state education system
can be most effective, both for the individual and
the nation. Third, we should note that it is not
only through the Black Papers that this strand of
thought has been publicised. It is also the educational theme, most commonly represented in the
conservative popular press, especially perhaps the
Daily Mail (see School Without Walls, 1978). This
press support has proved a very potent factor and
undoubtedly contributed greatly to the shifting of
the whole ground of educational debate which took
place in the middle 70s and which culminated in a
Labour government donning at least some of the populist's clothes in the creation and agenda of the
Great Debate on education (see Donald, 1981). This
link with the popular press suggests a fourth distinguishing feature of the populist approach. It
tends to replace the pragmatism of traditional
Toryism with a much more abrasive opportunism; having
inherited neither the feeling of a natural right to
rule, nor the benevolent paternalism which the Old
Tories insist should be the corollary of such an
inheritance, and hence lacking, too, a stablising
belief in the ability of the basic social hierarchy
inevitably to adapt to superficial change, the
populists are squeezed towards creating and seizing
short term political advantages which their 'grand-
er' colleagues would disdain and find distasteful.
Hence a certain volatility, and unpredictable interpretation of its basic themes, might be expected
from adherents to the populist approach.

THE MORAL ENTREPRENEURS

Once again this label is used in a rather different
way here from its original use by Howard Becker.
What I have in mind is in fact not too distant from
what Alan Wolfe, in his analysis of Reaganism, calls
'conformist individualism'. He writes

> There is apparently a distinction made in
> right wing thought between individualism and
> self-indulgence. Hence discipline is as
> vital as freedom. An inability of the nation
> to control its libidinal impulses - in short,
> sin - is responsible for inflation (too many
> people consuming instead of saving); crime
> (too many people accumulating the easy way,
> without working); urban decline (too many

> governments spending too carelessly);
> national weakness (too much pleasure seeking
> at the expense of sacrificing to meet the
> external challenge); and dissent (women
> wanting to avoid housework - gays having too
> much fun.) (1981, p.26)

In respect of contemporary education policy, however, it does seem important to identify a crusading
group rather than an orientation which would be
common to several of the stands I am discussing.
Those I am calling the moral entrepreneurs see
education at the heart of a fight for a particular
morality and against (im)moralities which would
undermine it. This group is inevitably associated
with the name of Mary Whitehouse, who when she was
a teacher, became concerned that certain TV programmes were seducing children into sub-christian life
styles (see Tracey and Morrison, 1979). This led to
the 'clean-up TV' campaigns, and hence to the
Festival of Light and other campaigns against sexual
permissiveness. This kind of moral entrepreneurship
is curiously poised between authoritarianism and
privatism. On the one hand, it argues that things
like sex education are essentially private matters
and are the concern of the family rather than of the
state or school. On the other hand, the whole
point of the moral entrepreneurs is that social behaviour should be controlled by a set of rules and
moral imperatives, and that it is an area which
laissez-faire had no place. It is not state intervention but unrestrained market forces which produce pornography. Hence, both legislation and some
kind of moral lead from the state are called for by
the moral entrepreneurs - which puts them in the
difficult and paradoxical position of asking that
institutions like schools must give a moral lead on
matters which are simultaneously held to be properly
none of their concern.
    Nevertheless, in spite of these paradoxes, and
irrespective of whether such groups as Mrs
Whitehouse's have any links with the Conservative
Party, the moral entrepreneurs do seem to be an
important influence on current education policy in
at least four ways. First, they have a clear influence on some well-known Conservative Politicians
(for instance, Mrs Jill Knight), whereby their views
are both publicly amplified and inserted into intra-
Party debates. While their direct influence is more
clearly evident at the grass roots of the Party and
at Party conferences, there seems little doubt that

Mrs Thatcher herself is in much greater sympathy with such sectors of the Party than any of her predecessors, and hence the fact that that particular set of views is not adopted by the traditional Party hierarchy is less important now than it has been previously.

Second, the moral entrepreneurs pick up and reinforce themes prominent in other strands of conservative ideology. The clearest examples here are the need for self-discipline and a national moral regeneration. Third, and closely associated with this, is the encouragement of, and conviction of the importance of, the traditional family as the basis of social harmony and healthy personal development, which begins to identify working mothers, and feminism generally, as key causes of many of the evils it sees. That women's place is not predominantly at work has been an implicit theme of British post-war education policy (see Wolpe, 1976; Deem, 1981).

Recently though, Miriam David (1982) has argued that the emphasis on preparation for sex differentiated roles in adulthood is becoming established in official curricular advice. She argues that the DES now clearly acknowledges that family life is not entirely a private matter but is circumscribed by public laws and state policies. 'It accepts its own duty to clarify to children what the state believes is entailed in being a parent' (p.33). These beliefs, David argues, draw on particular fundamental values, which are to be achieved 'both by means of moral exhortation and special teaching or moral or religious education'. Matters may not yet have reached this stage, but the pressure on parents to be responsible for their children and not 'leave everything to the state' is clearly mounting, reaching a peak with captions to front page photos of children involved in the 1982 summer disturbances which asked boldly what their parents were doing to allow this, and comments in the same papers that it was not a social breakdown which produced the disturbances, but the breakdown of the traditional family and parental authority.

The final form of the influence of the moral entrepreneurs may have the most immediate and effective impact upon educational practice. It results from the climate of caution and circumspection created by the tactics typically adopted by the moral entrepreneurs, of public exposure of what they classify as immorality. This can easily lead to mild self-censorship, and soft-pedalling, even avoiding, potentially contentious issues. Though it

is most difficult to prove, impressionistic evidence
suggests that the threat of public exposure, even
when one believes totally in the rightness of what
one is doing, is a very effective way of ensuring
schools' conformity.

THE PRIVATISERS

It is this group which provides the intellectual and
economic case for the move away from the Welfare
State and for the return of the services it provides
to the market. (The recently formed Social Affairs
Unit takes up these themes: see Anderson, Lait and
Marsland, 1981). There are a number of interesting
similarities between this group and those dubbed the
neo-conservatives in the United States, but space
precludes examining those similarities in any depth.
Indeed, for our immediate purposes the appointment
of the Conservative Party's chief ideologue, Sir
Keith Joseph, to head the DES in 1981, makes it particularly appropriate largely to confine this analysis to a brief consideration of his relevant
statements.
    An article by Nick Bosanquet (1981) outlines
Sir Keith's view of conservatism. It is composed,
he argues, of elements of thesis and antithesis.
'The thesis - the integrating force in society - is
the underlying process of economic growth. The
antithesis is the impact of 'Politicization' set up
by the short-term stresses of 'creative destruction'
and the nature of the political process itself'
(p.326). The elements of the thesis are briefly
summarised as (a) Society has inherent tendencies
towards order and justice. This role of government
should be restricted to that played by the maintenance department of a factory; citizens are able to
act in their own best interest. (b) 'Inequality is
the inevitable and tolerable result of social freedom and personal initiative'...('it arises from the
operations of innumerable individual preferences
and so cannot be evil unless those preferences are
themselves evil'). (c) 'Capitalism is a system
which has ensured growth and improved standards in
the long run'. (d) 'The entrepreneur is the key
figure in ensuring for all the gains to be had from
economic growth'. (e) 'Economic growth will first
reduce their eliminate poverty in absolute terms'.
    The elements of antithesis picked out by
Bosanquet are (a) origins of politicization - which
leads to the despotism of the majority, centraliza-
tion and statisms (which will almost always produce

bad results, while individual action will nearly
always serve the interests of the 'spontaneous
order'). (b) A more intense class conflict. (c)
The fallacy of social cost - i.e., the market does
not necessarily ignore social needs. (d) The short-
comings of the Galbraith thesis; giant corporations
do not control the state. (e) Rising public expenditure; brought about by self serving bureaucracy,
and political 'vote buying'. (f) Industrial subsidies. Government intervention in industry will
always find, and generate, problems of efficiency,
productivity etc., in subsidized forms. (g) The
failure of the Welfare State. The wealthy benefit
most from it, while strong vested interests support
it in spite of its failures. The poor would generally benefit from a market orientated system. (h)
The pressure from bureaucracy. Bureaucracy also
works both independently and under pressure from
political democracy to raise public spending. (i)
The fall of the trade unions.

Some idea of Joseph's views on education may be
gained from consideration of speeches reported by,
and articles written for, The Times Educational
Supplements in late 1974. The initial Birmingham
speech, which became so notorious for its apparently
eugenicist arguments attacked the education system
largely for its part in the decline of civilised
values. Indeed, with its references to the danger
of left-wing ideology both in higher education and
among teachers it has a lot in common with the moral
entrepreneurs. But Sir Keith's chief concern was
that the demand for absolute equality had turned
into a new inequality, with the universities, he
claimed, having been constrained to lower their
entry standards for entrants from comprehensive
schools. He summed up his beliefs as follows: 'I
remain a passionate advocate of education; but blind
partisanship is the worst enemy of a cause. If
equality in education is sought at the expense of
quality, how then can the poisons created help but
filter down' (TES 25.10.74). In his reply to criticisms made by the TES of his Birmingham speech, Sir
Keith acknowledged the Tories 'had been remiss in
neglecting our own instincts for those of self-styled
progressives' and reiterated the need to 'stop the
rot', again emphasising the importance of the traditional family and authority, and the dangers of
the few percent of radicals (in the teaching profession) 'who reject as bourgeois what we should call
professional conduct and fair play' (Joseph, 1974a).

His rejection of the post war progressive consensus, which 'has not furthered the greatest good
of the greatest number' (ibid) is fairly comprehensive. Its essence seems to be, for him, the project
of social engineering and it is this which he finds
both distasteful and unsuccessful. First, as we
have seen, he considered its major goal - equality -
inherently unattainable as well as undesirable; its
pursuit has been responsible for the difficulties of
the education system. Second, these difficulties
were compounded by the increased power of the teachers entailed by the progressive consensus. This
enabled a minority of them to disrupt the whole
process and purpose of education. And third, Sir
Keith has doubts about one of the central aims of
the progressive consensus, 'human capital theory'.
He does not, for instance, accept arguments for university expansion which are premissed on it (though
it should be noted that he does see a place - the
proper place - for vocationally relevant courses, in
the polytechnics). University expansion has been
'encouraged by fallacious views of the economic
benefits to be gained and by slovenly thinking regarding the moral and social justification for
providing benefits on such a scale for a minority
at the expense of a majority, which is not nearly
such a cut and dried question as expansionists take
for granted' (Joseph, 1974b). And the earlier
themes are tied in when he writes 'the worship of
vocational relevance owes everything to an overgrown
and grotesquely status conscious academic profession
which has argued that the quality of the work force
would be improved by the fastest possible expansion
of universities of the traditional type' (ibid).

THATCHERISM IN EDUCATION

So what distillate of these five ingredients constitutes Thatcherism in education? I want to argue
that the crucial factor uniting the various strands
into a coherent philosophy and policy (insofar as
these exist) is Mrs Thatcher's own personal political stand. She has seen herself as representing the
greatest casualties (though she might want to call
them victims) of the social democratic Welfare State
and the inflation that is held to be its automatic
companion, who are also those least deserving to
suffer as a result of its policies. This is the
group whose embrace of the traditional virtues of
thrift, hard work, self restraint, responsibility
and respectability has been set at nought (often

literally) by the Welfare State's pursuit of the
illusory goals of equality and social justice. 'Deservingness' is the inevitable victim of egalitarianism and universalism, and it is this quality
which Thatcherism defines, identifies and seeks to
reward above all, in education as in other sectors.
It entails accepting selectivity and unequal treatment, with a full awareness of the consequences for
those who show themselves undeserving. It accepts,
and wittingly reinforces, social stratification and
social inequality, purposely and explicitly doing
more for some than for others.

This philosophy appears to be directly rooted
in Mrs Thatcher's own personal experience, and, we
might add, in those of Rhodes Boyson and Norman
Tebbitt, too. There is little respect here for
those Tory grandees and paternalists who preach a
form of universalism without ever having to experience its dirty end. There is little readiness to
dole out equal benefits to those who are going to
make good use of them and those who will just
squander them. There is a distinct reluctance to
support those unwilling or unable to support themselves, especially if it means that there is less
for the deserving. And so, Thatcherite education
policy might be seen as not so much anti-statist as
anti-universalist and anti-social democratic. While
the state is to be rolled back - or at least cut
back - that is to be done selectively. Thatcherism
is very much in favour of selectiveness, of allowing
the natural differences between people to grow, both
as a reward to the talented and successful, the
intellectually and morally deserving, and as a spur
to the less well-endowed, successful or responsible,
to make the most of what they have. This spur is
signally absent from a universalistic, social democratic Welfare State.

This does not mean that the approach is not
anti-statist. Far from it. The market is to be
preferred to the state at all points because the
desired stratifying power and mechanism are intrin-
sic to its operations. The market ensures that the
best is available to those, and only those, who
deserve or can afford it, and that those who neither
deserve nor can afford anything else end up with the
worst, or nothing, or what is left. But while there
is a consequent pressure to return many state provided services to the market, there is also a recognition of both the practical and the political difficulties associated with such a project. One
further, crucial, point must be made before we go on

to look at the outcomes of education policy under
Mrs Thatcher's government. This is that Thatcherism
cannot be assumed to have been the only, or the
overwhelmingly dominant, force creating that policy.
It is clear from the contributions made to Thatcherism by the various strands of conservative educational thought I have briefly outlined that there are
major differences of approach and emphasis, goals
and assumptions between Thatcherism and especially
what I called Old Toryism. It is also clear - from
the House of Lords' decision on school transport
finance, for instance, and from the serious reser-
vations about the drift of education policy expressed by senior and influential figures at the 1981
Conservative Party Conference - that Thatcherism by
no means has things all its own way as far as
education strategy and programmes are concerned.
Indeed, Mr. Heath threatened, proposals for a massive shift of expenditure from the state to the
private sector of education would split the Conservative Party from top to bottom, split the country,
and alienate the teaching profession (Guardian,
15.10.81). And so we have to recognize that the
government's education programmes do not represent
undiluted Thatcherism, not because of its ineffectiveness or incoherence, or because it is demonstra-
bly unsuitable or irrelevant but because it is not
overwhelmingly pre-eminent in the Conservative Party
itself.

OUTCOMES AND EFFECTS

This is, of course, a very long way from saying
that Thatcherism is an irrelevance, at least as far
as education is concerned, or that it has had
negligible impact. It undoubtedly has had major
and perhaps lasting effects on the state education
system. The most important of these is its confirm-
ation of the gradual removal of education from the
place in the public expenditure sun it had enjoyed
for the previous 20 years or more. Crudely put,
the replacement of Keynes by Friedman as the guiding
light of the government's political economic strategy entails both quantitative and qualitative
changes for education. Not only is it, along with
all other items of public expenditure, to be severely cut back, but also both what is, and can reasonably be expected of it, is altered. Albeit more
gradually, a shift from state to private provision
is to be encouraged and implemented. So for example, the appeal of human capital theories declines,

with a concomitant pressure towards the separation of education and training, which is, of course, most visible in the debates and discussion about the appropriate educational provision for 16-19 year olds.

However, there are distinct limits to the extent and direction of any changes in education policy, to how far and how easily desired outcomes can be achieved through the formal political process - and the nature of these limitations itself deflects political activity into particular demands. It is, for instance, interesting to speculate how far it would have been possible to introduce even those changes that have been brought in without the 'slack' created by falling rolls. A former DES minister, for instance, has estimated that 98% of the budget of the education service is consumed in the execution of its basic statutory duties (Fowler, 1981). An analysis of the government's education record in its first year in office (Williams, 1981) suggests that if we are looking for education policy initiatives that are worthy of all three labels (i.e. genuine reflections of policy preference rather than tactical reactions), Mrs Thatcher's government could claim little more than the Assisted Places Schemes.

Williams' paper is confined to legislation, but we should not assume that this is either the only or the most effective way to implement party preferences in education. The cumbersomeness of legislation and its relative ineffectiveness in some areas has had a number of effects on both the strategy and the target of Tory education policy. It tends to lead to change efforts being directed at targets outside the statutory (5-16) system. At a time when pre-school provision is already rather sparse, and the further education sector under great pressure as a result of youth unemployment, this has contributed to the higher education system becoming the most prominent victim of the cuts in education spending. Such cuts also fit in well with the Thatcherite emphasis on deservingness and with Sir Keith Joseph's views of the proper roles of higher education.

However, an equally important consequence of Thatcherism's less than total dominance of the Conservative Party, and the difficulties associated with introducing education policy initiatives, has been the continuing centrality of its ideological barrage. This becomes increasingly important as it serves not just to refine ideological purity, but as

251

the means through which its impact on actual educational practice is most direct. I have already
argued that the moral entrepreneurs have a particularly direct impact through their implicit threat of
exposure, and it seems likely that well publicised
aims and preferences, likes and dislikes, through
letting it be known clearly which way the wind is
blowing, suggest what kinds of practices, policies
etc., will be rewarded and which penalised.

One clear example of this is the continuing
emphasis on the role of the school in the moral
regeneration of a nation whose morale, motivation,
self respect and self responsibility are seen as
seriously damaged by prolonged exposure to a nannying and intrusive Welfare State. The Welfare State
has removed the incentive to do a fair day's work
for a fair day's pay and to behave in decent, up-
right ways. The education system, it is held, cannot escape blame for this, taken over as it has been
by alien, progressive, morally relative and socialistic doctrines, and it bears a major responsibility
for rectifying this state of affairs. It is difficult to see how changes of this kind could be
brought about effectively through legislation, and
which puts added emphasis on forms of direct intervention. It is too early yet to isolate any effect
of this trust towards moral regeneration, but it is
difficult to ignore its palpable targetting.

The clearest examples of the effects of this
Thatcherite ideological barrage are seen in the hostility towards both social science in general and
the 'progressive consensus' among educators. This
hostility has certainly been expressed quite directly in the very close attention paid to the SSRC and
the withdrawal of the Schools Council's life support
system (for which the legendary CIA phrase 'termi-
nation with extreme prejudice' seems not inappropriate). This hostility is able to draw on the deep
rooted opposition within many sectors of conservative ideology towards the intrusion of 'experts'
into areas of social life which, if left alone,
naturally achieve a kind of organic harmony. The
intrusion of experts undermines the sense of community which means so much to the Old Tories. The
professionalization of teaching under a progressive
banner has turned children against industry and
wealth production. It has led to teachers dictating
to parents what can happen to their children. It
has led to the questioning and undermining of
Christian morality, by people who live off the state
and use it to destroy society.

252

This hostility extends particularly to sociology. Not only is the very idea that a thing as
naturally and organically self regulating as society
might be subject to analysis and deliberate change
offensive to many conservatives, but it is taken as
demonstrated (especially in the influential writings
of the American neo-conservatives) that 'expert'
tampering with social institutions only makes them
worse.

Underlying much of this hostility towards both
sociologists and progressive teachers is the fear
that they may be politically motivated, that they
are using the state education system to destroy not
only (or not even preeminently) capitalism, but the
sets of values on which conservative conceptions of
the order of things are based. This is clear, for
instance, in many of Sir Keith Joseph's speeches
quoted above. It reached its apogee in a pamphlet
by C.B. Cox, one of the original Black Paper authors,
published by the Conservative Political Centre,
which appears to see reds under, in, and making, the
bed. Cox's theme is that education policy has been
dominated since the 1960s by left-wing educationalists 'whose aim is revolution, not by armed over-
throw of the government, but by transformation of
institutions from within' (Cox, 1981, p.5).

In a very brief summary, then, its own ideology,
its strength within the Conservative Party, and the
relative difficulty of directly implementing policy
initiatives mean that the main consequences of
Thatcherism for education are likely to be (1) its
further displacement from its previous uncritically
accepted place of honour (2) increasingly lower
levels of funding especially in the non-compulsory
sectors (3) a gradual separation of responsibilities
for education and training (4) further encouragement
of private education (5) pressure towards using the
school as an agent of moral regeneration (6) continuing attacks on, maybe culminating in action
against, radical teachers (7) further moves aimed
at restratifying especially secondary education.

This is an edited version of a talk given to the
Politics, Education and Society Group in November
1980. My thanks are due to those present for their
helpful comments and particularly to Madeleine Arnot
and Rosemary Deem for a number of valuable suggestions.

BIBLIOGRAPHY

Anderson, Digby; Lait, June and Marsland, David
(1981) Breaking the Spell of the Welfare State
Social Affairs Unit, London.
Bogdanor, Vernon (1975) Defending Equal Rights
Times Educational Supplement, 28th May.
Bosanquet, Nick (1981) Sir Keith's Reading List
Political Quarterly 52, 3, July-September,
324-41.
Boyson, Rhodes (1975a) More Power to Parents
Times Educational Supplement.
Boyson, Rhodes (1975b) The Crisis in Education
Woburn Press, London.
Bull, David (1980) Time to Reform School Transport
Where 159, July 8-11.
Corbett, Ann (1969) The Tory Educators New Society
22nd May, 785-7.
Cox, C.B. (1981) Education: the Next Decade
Conservative Political Centre, London.
David, Miriam (1982) Sex, Education and Social
Policy: Towards a New Moral Economy. Paper
presented to Westhill Sociology of Education
Conference, Birmingham, January.
Deem, Rosemary (1981) State Policy and Ideology in
the Education of Women, 1944-80 British Journal
of Sociology of Education, 2, 2, 131-44.
Donald, James (1981) Green Paper: Noise of Crisis,
in Dale, Roger; Esland, Geoff; Fergusson, Ross
and Macdonald, Madeleine (eds) Education and
the State, Volume 1: Schooling and the National
Interest Hossacks: Falmer Press, 99-113.
Eccleshall, Robert (1977) English Conservatism as
Ideology Political Studies 25, 1, 62-83.
Eccleshall, Robert (1980) Ideology as Commonsense;
the Case of British Conservatism Radical
Philosophy 25, Summer, 2-8.
Fowler, Gerry (1981) The Changing Nature of Educa-
tional Politics in the 1970s in Broadfoot,
Patricia; Brock, Colin and Tulasiewicz, Witold
(eds) Politics and Educational Change 13-28
Croom Helm, London.
Hall, Stuart (1979) The Great Moving Right Show
Marxism Today January, 14-20.
Hall, Stuart (1980) Thatcherism - a new stage
Marxism Today February 26-8.
Harris, Ralph (1980) The Revolt of the Lords
Spectator 22nd March, 12-13.
Hogg, Quintin (1947) The Case for Conservatism
Penguin, West Drayton.

Joseph (Sir) Keith (1974a) Time to Stop the Rot
    Times Educational Supplement, 1st November.
Joseph (Sir) Keith (1974b) The Pursuit of Truth or
    Relevance? Times Higher Educational Supplement
    15th November.
Joseph (Sir) Keith (1979) The Class War, Guardian.
Kogan, Maurice (1975) Educational Policy Making
    Alan and Unwin, London.
Methven (Sir) John (1976) What Industry Wants
    Times Educational Supplement 24th October.
Miliband, Ralph (1978) A State of Desubordination
    British Journal of Sociology, 29, 4, 399-412.
Russell, Trevor (1978) The Tory Party, Penguin,
    Harmondsworth.
School Without Walls (1978) Lunatic Ideas, School
    Without Walls and Corner House Bookshops,
    London.
Thorn, John (1981) Enemies on Left and Right
    Times Educational Supplement 25 September, 4.
Tracey, Michael and Morrison, David (1979)
    Whitehouse, Macmillan, London.
Weinstock (Sir) Arnold (1976) I Blame the Teachers.
    Times Educational Supplement, 23rd January.
Williams, Gareth (1981) The Government's Educational
    Policy during the First Parliamentary Session
    1979-80. Education Policy Bulletin 8, 2,
    Autumn, 127-44.
Williams, Raymond (1962) The Long Revolution Penguin
    Harmondsworth.
Wilson, M. (1977) Grass Roots Conservatism: motions
    to the Party Conference, in Nugent, Neill and
    King, Roger (eds) The British Right, 64-89,
    Saxon House, Farnborough.
Wolfe, Alan (1981) The Ideology of US Conservatism
    New Left Review 128, 3-27.
Woods, Roger (1981) Margaret Thatcher and Secondary
    Reorganization Journal of Educational
    Administration and History, 13, 2, July, 51-61.
Wolpe, Anne-Marie (1976) The Official Ideology of
    Education for Girls, in Flude, Michael and
    Ahier; John (eds) Educability, Schools and
    Ideology, Croom Helm, London.
Wright, Nigel (1977) Progress in Education, Croom
    Helm, London.

INTRODUCTION

Contemporary work in the sociology of education has
been marked by the re-emergence of questions concerning the political determination of educational
provision. This development serves as an important
corrective to the recent and pervasive tendency to
reduce the political to the economic in Marxist-
inspired theories of social reproduction, or the
claim that the political is determined by the economic in the last instance. The opportunity of
breaking out of the constraints of such theorizing,
provided, for example, by the work of Demaine (1981)
and Salter & Tapper (1981) enables the problematic
nature of the formulation of educational policies,
as well as their implementation and outcomes, to be
restored to the agenda of the discipline. This
development in the sociology of education has been
reinforced by the intervention of central and local
state agencies in managing the contraction of the
education system in the context of falling school
rolls, pressures to redefine educational priorities
and attempts to reduce public expenditure. In a
situation where the future of the education system
is uncertain and where political interventions in
the management of the education system have quite
clearly overriden the professional's claims to autonomy, the educational policies of the major political parties are crucial as they set out in more or
less coherent form the educational priorities to be
persued in government.
     This paper will examine and attempt some assess-
ment of the educational policies that seem likely
to be adopted by the Social Democratic Party, and
analyze these policies in relation to other aspects

257

of the Party's social, economic and political programme. The intention is to delineate how the emergent and adopted policies of the S.D.P. are likely
to influence the kinds of intervention that will be
made in the education system either at local level,
or nationally in the event of the Social Democratic-
Liberal Alliance either forming a government after
the next election, or holding the balance of power
in a 'hung' parliament. In considering this it is
instructive to compare the character and implications of these policies, and the electoral strategy
which underlies them, with the revisionist or social
democratic perspective developed within the Labour
Party and articulated in the writings of Anthony
Crosland.
    Although the British Social Democratic tradi-
tion has been formed out of an amalgam of different,
although overlapping political traditions, it has
been given its most coherent and decisive expression within the Labour Party. It is possible to
identify certain recurrent themes and political
objectives that make up the social democratic or
revisionist tradition within the Labour Party. There
has been the use of state power to effect some
degree of control on the operations and outcomes
of the market economy. There have been efforts to
establish a comprehensive range of state-financed
and administered services, taking a predominantly
non-commodity form, to secure minimum welfare provision and living standards. Such provisions, in
conjunction with fiscal policy, have sought to
achieve some redistribution of income, wealth and
opportunity as a means of redressing some of the
arbitrary effects and social inequalities arising
from the market economy and its distributive mechanisms. This has been combined with a broader
strategy of breaking down those social, political
and economic barriers that sustain inequalities of
power and opportunity, thereby to secure the necessary preconditions of citizenship within a pluralist
democracy.
    The S.D.P.'s overall political strategy and
programme may be seen to be grounded in part at
least on a displaced or re-formed revisionism. It
is displaced insofar as it crucially seeks to detach the social democratic or revisionist tradition
from its political roots within the Labour Party and
labour movement. It is re-formed by virtue of the
particular interpretation of revisionism that is
advanced, the stress that is placed on certain selected elements to the exclusion of others, and the

way these are combined with other political tendencies, notably those which have their source in
political liberalism. Such developments are celebrated by the S.D.P. as the means of constructing a
new radical left of centre party, of 'breaking the
mould' of conventional class-based party politics,
and of forging a set of economic and social policies
which may be consistently pursued in the 'national
interest'. However by virtue of the electoral alliances and strategy that the Party seems destined to
adopt it seems that this will only lead to an emas-
culated revisionism. As Stuart Hall has argued the
effect of this attempt to re-align British politics
may be seen to involve 'the bending and articulating
of liberalism (and liberal political economy) to a
Conservative rather than radical pole' (1981). It
is this strategy, together with the sectional divisions and conflicts in the Labour Party, that
stands as a major barrier to the formation of a
broad based alliance of progressive political forces
capable of capturing electoral support.

It was during the 1930s that the social democratic tradition was consolidated in the Labour
Party following the electoral setback suffered by
the Party in 1931 (Howell, 1976). Whilst for the
most part a weakened and divided left in the Party
sought to retain their socialist purity, the emerging alliance of the Labour Party and trade unions,
shifted the Party as a whole to a clearer conception
of 'practical socialism' and policies framed in
relation to the economic and social problems of the
day. This involved, as Pimlott (1977) makes clear,
a rejection and shift away from the utopianism and
class based politics of 'direct action' espoused by
sections of the Labour left and other radical political groups. What followed was a period of detailed policy making that was to be significant not only
in terms of Labour's representation in the wartime
coalition government, but for the electoral strategy
and programmes of post-war Labour governments. In
the present political conjuncture the strategy of
the utopian left rests on an attempt to radically
change the political direction of the Party. However in pursuit of this goal it has undermined the
coalition of political groups that made up the
Labour Party and contributed to the emergence of the
S.D.P. Although the Labour Party retained some sem-
blance of unity and collective purpose in the early
1970s, the divisions in the Party that were apparent
then have been deliberately magnified and the achievements of the Party whilst in government denigrated.

In seeking to construct a more radical socialist programme underpinned by popular support the left appears to have foresaken the possibility of short-term electoral gains in return for a dramatic advance at a later date. This rests on a political calculation about the impact of further economic decline and higher levels of unemployment on the presumed latent political radicalism of the working class. Such a notion of some future conversion of the working class to socialism rests on a class essentialism that treats politics as the expression of class interests. This has not only sustained numerous debates about which policies are best able to capture, represent and express the alleged latent socialism of the working class but has tended to cut off policy formation from immediate economic and political conditions. One likely effect of this is the creation of propitious conditions for the emergence and consolidation of political movements and groups that are overtly or manifestly hostile to socialism. The reluctance particularly of the left to unite with other groups within the Party around a common programme capable of attracting electoral support, and based on an assessment of what limited socialist advances are possible in present conditions, seems destined to affect the capacity of the Labour Party to resist the advance of the S.D.P.

I want now to analyze the political programme that is being formulated by the S.D.P. which, I suggest, is a necessary preliminary to understanding the character of the educational policies the Party is likely to pursue. In analyzing the S.D.P.'s political programme I want to point to the relationship between political activity and ideology and the social, economic and institutional conditions to which they are a response. Such responses are actively constructed by political agents within agencies that have a definite constitutional and institutional form, and which in various ways constrain the formulation of political programmes and their implementation. Such constraints are however not to be conceived as determinants; they do not rule out specific courses of action or policy for these ultimately rest on the pursuit of goals formulated with respect to perceptions of present conditions, the opportunities and limitations they present and some desired state of affairs. In this process political ideologies play a crucial role in securing an identity of purpose for the attainment of certain political ends, and in providing a language and conceptual apparatus that moulds conceptions of what is desirable and possible and in winning support for specific courses of action.

The recent emergence of the S.D.P. as an electoral agency has occurred in propitious conditions for a major challenge to the two party system. Some of the most important factors that have contributed to what appears to be a significant restructuring of British politics are discussed in this paper. These include the long term decline in support for the major political parties, the dissolution of the coalition that made up the post-war Labour Party, changes in the composition of the work force, and the failure of successive governments to resolve Britain's economic problems. The formation of the S.D.P. has also been a response to that breakdown of the post-war settlement between the state, capital and labour in the mid-1970s, and the subsequent and divergent reactions to this of the Conservative and Labour Parties. The S.D.P., in both its electoral strategy and the policies it is likely to adopt, may be seen as attempting to re-form this settlement albeit on different terms and in quite different economic and political conditions. Primarily the political strategy of the S.D.P. rests on its capacity to coalesce and capture the support of 'moderate opinion', to take advantage of the present volatile nature of electoral attitudes at a time when both the Conservative and Labour Parties have embraced radical domestic programmes but without clear-cut popular support. The emergent structure of the S.D.P., and the forms by which it seeks to represent and forge an alliance between different social groups and political philosophies are destined to have a major effect on the Party's economic and social programme. Whilst initially the Party adopted a largely 'reactive' stance to policy issues, resting primarily on a critique of 'doctrinaire' political policies and practices of the Labour Party and the incumbent Conservative administration, it is now possible to identify the character and major parameters of the political programme the S.D.P. is attempting to pursue.

I want to suggest that the political programme and strategy of the S.D.P. may be regarded as a displaced or re-formed revisionism. This characterization can be justified on the following grounds. Firstly in terms of its political programme the moral or ethical components of social democratic politics are emphasized at the expense of a hard commitment to egalitarian economic and social policies. Secondly the character of the electoral support the S.D.P. is likely to attract, together with the political alliance that is being forged with the Liberal Party, is likely to compromise the initially dominant presentation and perception of the Party as a radical left of centre party offering a reconstructed social democratic programme. Thirdly the disengagement of at least part of the British Social Democratic tradition from its origins and links with the labour movement is likely to consolidate tendencies which are hostile to a collectivist notion of politics. I will suggest that this is reflected in the economic, industrial and educational policies being formulated by the S.D.P.

THE CHARACTER OF THE S.D.P.'S POLITICAL PROGRAMME

It is possible to detect certain distinctive features of the S.D.P.'s political programme from the writings and recent pronouncements of its leading members, from conference papers and from outline proposals from the various policy groups within the Party. Many of these texts and papers reveal a nostalgic celebration of consensus politics, particularly those of the 1950s and early 1960s. Such politics were seen to rest on a broad communality of purpose and upon acceptance of gradual parliamentary and institutional reform within an expanding economy as the means of constructing a classless society. The present concern to revive the basis of consensus politics is one factor underlying the campaign for proportional representation and the reliance upon techniques of neo-Keynesian economic management, advocacy of the virtues of the mixed economy, the reassertion of traditional social democratic values that underpin the 'welfare society' and the implicit commitment to recreate a new settlement between the state, capital and labour.
The most influential founders of the S.D.P. trace their political and intellectual heritage to post-war Labour Party social democracy and the expression of this in Crosland's writings. Constant reference to this tradition serves two major tasks. It forms part of an appeal to a significant body of Labour supporters who, it is claimed, are no longer adequately represented within a left-inclined Labour Party. It is bound up also with the task of constructing the ideological basis of the S.D.P.'s political programme. This involves an attempt to present the S.D.P. as a party distinguished by its unique commitment to certain ethical or moral principles, decentralized forms of political and insti-

tutional control and its stresses on participatory
democracy. The emphasis placed on what Bradley
(1981) refers to as a 'decentralized social democracy' is associated with an alternative popularist
critique of corporate and bureaucratic politics to
that recently advanced by the Conservative Party.
The combined effect of these elements is the eleva-
tion of the S.D.P.'s 'moral' programme above any
firm commitment to a programme of distributive
socialism.

Anthony Crosland's The Future of Socialism
(1956) was at once a theoretically grounded analysis
of various political, economic, social and institutional changes that had taken place since the 1930s,
and a major contribution to debates in the Labour
Party about its future political programme and electoral strategy. The Future of Socialism may be seen
as a political and theoretical statement of the
post-war 'settlement' between capital, labour and
the state. This settlement grew out of various institutional structures developed particularly during
the war years to enable the state to manage, plan
and regulate the economy, consumption and the labour
force; the participation of trade unionists and
representatives of industrial and finance capital in
various state planning agencies; the commitment of
the coalition government and post-war governments to
maintain high levels of employment by the regulation
of demand and the consolidation and extension of
welfare provisions to secure minimum living standards and the eradication of poverty. Resting on a
critique of Marxism, Crosland sought to show how
following changes in the organization and control of
industrial production, economic growth, the development of liberal democratic structures and major institutional innovations (notably the expansion of
educational opportunities), the class conflict that
was endemic to entrepreneurial capitalism had either
been contained or displaced from the sphere of production to the sphere of consumption.

Crosland's analysis of the emergence of post-
capitalist society, which in a number of respects
parallels Dahrendorf's (1979) influential sociological treatise, gave support to the argument that
the electoral weakness of the Labour Party during
the 1950s could in large measure be attributed to an
outdated programme that retained its traditional
commitment to public ownership as a means of advan-
cing the interests of the working class. The case
was advanced by the social democratic or revisionist
wing of the Party that Labour's electoral prospects

would not be improved until it reduced its dependence on a declining and less cohesive working class,
and broadened its appeal to win the support not only
of blue collar but white collar voters. In calling
for the Party to present itself not as a narrowly
sectional or class party Crosland asserted that 'the
steady upgrading of the working class both occupa-
tionally, and still more in terms of social aspirations, renders Labour's one-class image increasingly
inappropriate', and called for policies that carried
'a wide appeal to broad sections of the population
including the newly emerging social group' (1960).
A broadly based party acting in the national interest, albeit from a base that claimed to be socialist,
was thus regarded as a precondition for reversing
the decline in the Labour Party's electoral fortunes.
What Crosland sought to formulate was a political
programme that would articulate with his analysis of
post-war social, economic and political change. This
involved the calculation that a specific set of
policies would appeal to the marginal voter and win
over a large section of the electorate including the
socially aspiring section of the working class and
the new middle class. Programmatically, as Rose has
pointed out, 'this led to the conclusion that what
was needed was a displacement of the emphasis in
socialist political argument from production to distribution' (1980).

Labour Party revisionism in the 1950s and 1960s
in its contemporary guise as heir to the tradition
of Fabian socialism, sought to redefine the central
core of the Party's policies away from the extension
of public ownership towards policies that would
bring about greater equality in the social distribution of opportunities and living standards. This
involved a much less clear-cut critique of the
operations of the market economy compared, for
example, to that found in the writings of R.H.
Tawney. Whilst Crosland recognized that the market
economy sustained inequalities of wealth and income,
he believed that these could be significantly reduced without transforming the existing economic
structure. Essentially this involved the development of countervailing institutions and controls in
relation to the operations and distributive mechanisms of the market economy in the form of legislation, fiscal measures and the development and extension of a state-financed and administered network
of services and benefits. The primary emphasis of
these policies was on a form of distributive socialism: policies that sought to create greater social

equality through the redistribution of wealth, income and opportunity, and the utilization of public expenditure both as a means of alleviating social inequality and controlling the level of demand within the economy.

Although subject to later modifications Crosland's original formulation of the revisionist case rested on a naive understanding of the economic pre-conditions of an expanded social and educational programme; it grossly over-estimated the claimed egalitarian effects of post-war economic growth, expanded state welfare and educational provision, and it displayed some antipathy to a strong central state. Nevertheless there is a recognition in Crosland's writings of the significance of state action and public services in modifying the distributional networks of society to secure the basis of social integration, full citizenship and a pluralist democracy. This can be contrasted to the major parameters of the S.D.P.'s political programme that is grounded on a predominantly individualist ethos and a muted egalitarianism. Despite the egalitarian sympathies of Owen & Williams, there is little in the initial policy proposals of the S.D.P. to suggest that the party is firmly committed to a major redistribution of wealth, income and opportunity. Indeed references to Crosland's writings involve a significant bending of his political stance, with an emphasis being placed on certain libertarian and moral themes, the development of which is bound up with the S.D.P.'s perception of certain trends in political opinion.

Further support for this line of argument comes from the idealist conception of class found in all of the major S.D.P. texts. There is the claim, for example, that the S.D.P.'s economic, industrial and social policies, together with proposed constitutional reforms, will provide the means of conciliating different class interests. However the concept of class is primarily understood in terms of ideas and attitudes, with polarized class attitudes being regarded as anachronistic and a major barrier to economic recovery and social well-being. Although certain idealist elements are apparent in Crosland's writings, there is nevertheless an important recognition of the part played by the operations of the market economy, different types of property and inequalities of wealth, income and opportunity in sustaining class divisions. It is no accident that the major S.D.P. texts make few references to the class structure of British society given that an essential part of the Party's electoral strategy involves an attempt to establish a new political and social consensus.

Certain parallels may be seen between the calls made by the founding members of the S.D.P. for a new centre party, embracing the ideals of liberty, fraternity and equality, and the recent reflections of Dahrendorf (1979) on the progress of liberty and liberalism in western industrial democracies. A major theme found in Dahrendorf's Life Chances and other publications is the demise of traditional social democratic politics and the modern crisis of political authority. Briefly his argument is that traditional social democratic politics have collapsed in Europe mainly as a result of a crisis of legitimacy. Dahrendorf argues that in pursuing social and economic egalitarianism via state action, traditional social democratic parties have not only created for many an artificial dependence on the state, but in so doing have undercut their own economic conditions of existence by raising general expectations about improved opportunities beyond a point that could be reasonably satisfied. Whilst Dahrendorf acknowledges the part played by traditional social democracy in extending opportunities, or 'horizons of choice', and securing the basis of citizenship rights, he sees the price of further such policies as leading to a 'decreasing intensity of social ligatures' or social bonds. Indeed he suggests that optional life chances, in the narrow meaning of the term, were probably reached by the mid-1970s. Drawing on the Weberian critique of bureaucracy, and reflecting on the form and determinants of social integration in modern society, Dahrendorf sees this now 'false concern with egalitarianism threatening liberty' and the meaningfulness of human action. It is this line of analysis that leads him to call for the reconstitution of liberal politics.

> If it is true that the strain towards equality inherent in modern societies has reached the point at which restrictions on the range of available choices make nonsense of the opportunities opened up by citizenship...then it would follow that an acceptable balance requires concentration on a new theme. We have described this theme in a variety of ways, it has something to do with ligatures, or linkages' (1980a).

Dahrendorf understands life chances in terms of both options and ligatures. It is the relationship between these two elements that provide him with the means of assessing social development. 'Ligatures without options are oppressive, whereas options without bonds are meaningless. Pre-modern societies with their overpowering forces of family, estate or castle, tribe, church, slavery or feudal dependence were in some ways all linkage and no choice' (Dahrendorf, 1979). In contrast modern societies have often created options through the erosion of ligatures. Traditional social democratic politics in particular are seen to have furthered individual opportunities at the expense of a qualitative change in the nature of social relationships, and the meaningfulness of human action.

> Today, social policy has often become a costly instrument of immobility. Worse still the dynamics of equality has increasingly tended to blur the boundary between necessary equality of opportunity and a discouraging equality of actual conditions; extreme forms of progressive taxation and misguided notions of comprehensive schools provide topical examples. Bureaucratization on the one hand, and social levelling on the other, are challenges to the liberal social policy which represents the achievements of the welfare state but never tires in its insistence that these achievements are about giving the individual more life chances, and that means an optimal combination of ligatures or bonds and room for manoeuvre on options. In the secular dialectics of liberty and equality, the hour of liberty has come, because it is threatened by a false egalitarianism. To this extent, the alliance of liberalism and socialism has exhausted its utility (Dahrendorf, 1980a).

Distancing himself from conservative and collectivist politics, Dahrendorf seeks to draw up a new agenda for liberal politics and focusses on the question of 'how to find new ligatures without abandoning the choice of options developed'. Supporting the pursuit of economic growth, maximizing new production technologies, controlling inflation and stabilizing people's expectations, Dahrendorf also calls for constitutional changes and what amounts to a new social ethic. In relation to the former he supports constitutional changes to bring about a devolution of political authority, decentralization and increased participation. Such changes are viewed as the means of opening up space for human action out of which it is thought new ligatures will develop spontaneously as individuals seek to give meaning and purpose to their lives. In his call for a 'distinctive liberalism which combines the common ground of social democratic achievement with the new horizons of the future of liberty' (1980b), Dahrendorf comes close to endorsing the formation of new centre parties in western democracies. Indeed he sees real opportunities for the advance of such political movements in the context of the breakdown of the post-war social democratic consensus, shifts in political loyalties, and the 'massive disorientation of the most numerous stratum of modern societies, the employed middle classes' (Dahrendorf, 1980b).

A number of Dahrendorf's ideas and his analysis of the present social and political situation overlap with or are drawn on directly by the founding members of the S.D.P. There is the case that Marquand makes for 'moral reform from below rather than mechanical reform from above' (1980), and the emphasis that is placed on communality and reciprocity of bonds and relationships. There is Owen's (1981) attempt to formulate an alternative socialist tradition that reasserts the value of fraternity, and calls for the new democratic forms of control and the decentralization of decision making to promote new patterns of social integration. Dahrendorf's 'new romanticism' is also drawn on directly by Shirley Williams: 'One thing the new politics is about is how far socialists can understand the significance of the quality of life, of ligatures and linkages, as well as the significance of wider opportunities and choices often derived from economic growth. They should understand - for ligatures are what fellowship and fraternity are all about' (1981a).

THE S.D.P.'S ELECTORAL CONSTITUENCY

The claim that the S.D.P. is a radical, left of centre party is likely to be severely compromised by the electoral constituency the Party is seeking to form, the different groups and traditions represented within the S.D.P. and the political alliance that is being negotiated with the Liberal Party. In terms of its electoral strategy, the S.D.P. is seeking to coalesce and activate various strands of moderate opinion around what are claimed to be non-doctrinaire policies and political practices. This may be seen as an attempt to realign British politics by forming a political movement capable of occupying the centre ground of British politics vacated by the radicalism of new Conservatism, and the apparent leftward shift of the Labour Party. The electoral prospects of the S.D.P. have been aided, as Husband's analysis of voting trends and party support makes clear, by a significant weakening of the electoral appeal of the two major parties, and a 'corresponding decline in the strength of partisan attachment of these parties' (1982). In a situation where electoral opinion is unstable, the S.D.P. is seeking to construct an electoral base by attracting the non-aligned and floating voter and those who have become disillusioned with or detached from the major political parties. It is a political movement which seeks to provide a platform for the politically suppressed and disillusioned sections of the electorate and to forge a mutuality of the not-so-common people.

There are various sections of the electorate to whom the S.D.P. is seeking to appeal. There is the attempt to detach from the Labour Party a significant part of that broad middle class body of support built up in the post-war period. It is a strategy directed at the substantial new middle class, of those employed in state institutions and service professions, who were attracted to the consumption and welfare politics of the Labour Party and its conception of the opportunity society. Within the S.D.P. Owen & Williams may be seen as attempting to represent this body of opinion. As Owen puts it 'the challenge is to develop a philosophy that will be welcomed by those voters who identify with socialist values, yet are reluctant to see further rationalization or a growth of bureaucracy' (1981). This appeal also extends to those non-politicised members of the new middle class who have become increasingly disillusioned by their lack of political influence. Commenting on this group and their political sympathies Peter Jenkins has suggested that because their material wants are more or less satisfied 'they are in a position to concern themselves with the politics of value-liberty, democracy and the like. Yet at the same time they feel themselves to be excluded in the running of things, denied status and esteem by the ruling elite...' (1981). The S.D.P. provides an opportunity for the new middle class to assume a more coherent and assertative role in political life.

This may be seen as an outcome of the growth of this
class in the past 20 years, the collective experience and involvement in institutional and community
decision-making, their relative insulation from the
harsh realities of economic decline and unemployment,
and as Samuel has argued, their growing cultural
cohesiveness (Samuel, 1982). The S.D.P. may also be
seen as attempting to attract the support of those
from within the skilled and employed working class
who voted for the Conservative Party in 1979 largely
on the basis of pragmatic considerations, thinking
that 'high taxation, high public expenditure and
the welfare state exist for the organized and the
unemployed, not the worthy working class' (Crick,
1981).

The chances of the S.D.P. gaining a substantial
number of seats at the next election will depend on
their capacity to win from the Conservative Party a
considerable number of constituencies in suburban
areas. This will depend in part on the appeal of
the Party's programme in converting what appears to
be a considerable degree of tactical and protest
voting into consolidated support. As such, the
Party will need to gain support from disaffected
Conservative voters anxious about high levels of
unemployment and inflation within a stagnating
economy, and who are reluctant to see further cutbacks in public services. It is to this section of
the electorate that I suspect Roy Jenkins' particular brand of political liberalism is likely to be
attractive. Calling for a 'fresh start in politics'
Jenkins (1979) has made clear his commitment to the
profitability of the market economy and his reluctance to envisage any change in the mix between the
public and the private sector. 'There is no substitute for market forces both in the overall creation
of wealth and in the essentially democratic function
of giving power to the consumer' (R. Jenkins, 1981).
It has been statements such as this about the management of the economy that has attracted to the
S.D.P. some financial backing from industrial, commercial and retail enterprises. Further support
from these sources is likely given the compatibility
between the S.D.P.'s initial economic policy proposals (S.D.P. Conference Paper, 1981) and specific
measures advocated by the C.B.I. for reviving the
economy, and in the event of the Conservative Party
failing to improve its standing with the electorate.

Negotiations between the S.D.P. and the
Liberal Party to form a political alliance involve
an attempt to construct a broad party base from

which to mount a campaign capable of undermining
'adversary politics'. It is the culmination of a
campaign originally mounted in the Liberal Party by
Grimond, and currently pursued by Steel, to bring
about a re-alignment of left of centre politics in
which the Liberal Party would play a leading role
(Ingle, 1982). In forging the S.D.P./Liberal
Alliance both parties are seeking to negotiate a
programme from their stated commitment to the values
of personal freedom and social equality, the maintenance of the mixed economy and the construction of
an open and classless society (Marquand, 1981).

The combination of the S.D.P.'s electoral constituency, and the alliance with the Liberal Party
at both national and local level, will have a decisive impact on the political programme being formed.
Derived from a particular popul... appeal there is
at once a celebration of a more pragmatic response
to various policy issues, an ideological attachment
to notions of the classless society and the formation of an economic and social programme which claims to transcend sectional politics. These stances
constitute some of the broad ideological parameters
in which policy responses are conceived. A further
constraint on these responses stems from a need to
maximize rather than foreclose policy alternatives
and thereby avoid alienating potential supporters.
Pimlott has pointed out that such a 'vote-oriented
party', 'which is based on no region, section,
interest or group...is particularly vulnerable to
the attitudes of its own active supporters and
voters, from wherever they are drawn' (1981).

Further constraints on the political programme
of the S.D.P. stem from the constitution of the
Party itself and its undertaking to introduce electoral reform. Drucker (1981) points to the tension
that exists between the apparent commitment of the
Party to participatory democracy and the diffusion
of political authority, and a party constitution
which assigns to area parties a largely 'confirma-
tory role' in the policy making process. This tension is likely to be exacerbated by the support of
the central party, for policies that are conceived
to be in the 'national interest', like measures to
restrain incomes which are premised on a strong
central state. One might speculate on the impact of
the S.D.P./Liberal Alliance's support for electoral
reform via a system of proportional representation
which, if introduced, would lead to the strong likelihood of successive coalition government, and the
predominance of what Bogdanor has referred to as

271

'negotiation politics' (1981). Support for such constitutional reform is presented on various grounds.
These include a concern to devise a fairer method of
parliamentary representation and the political and
economic need to transcend adversary or class-based
politics. There would also appear to be a strong
possibility of the S.D.P. supporting the state funding of political parties. Rustin has convincingly
argued that such a measure is 'tailor-made for a new
Social Democratic or Centre Party, providing a mechanism for it to reproduce itself...Its introduction
would constitute a Centrist blow to the financial
influence on political life of both organized labour
and capital, and is likely to depend on a party of
the centre first achieving considerable electoral
power' (1981).

    Early indications of the policy preferences and
political attitudes of S.D.P. members were evident
in the findings of various opinion polls. A poll
conducted on behalf of Weekend World (1981) indicated that a clear majority of S.D.P. members saw the
Party as standing for moderate reform and in favour
of Britain's continued membership of the E.E.C. and
opposed to unilateral disarmament. On domestic
issues there was general support for an expansion of
the economy to bring about a substantial fall in
unemployment, higher public spending with a moderate
redistributive effect and the introduction of a
wealth tax. In addition there was support for legislation to reduce trade union immunities and the
ending of closed shop agreements, and opposition to
proposals to curtail tax relief on mortgages and
steps to alter the position of private schools.
Findings such as this suggest that the more egalitarian sympathies of at least sections of the
S.D.P. leadership are not likely to be embraced enthusiastically by the majority of the Party's membership.

ECONOMIC AND INDUSTRIAL POLICY

The 1970s and early 1980s has been marked not only
by a continuous decline in Britain's economic performance and the restructuring of capital, but also
changes both in the composition and collective
forms of representation of labour. With respect to
the latter such changes may be attributed to a number of factors. Firstly the impact of high levels
of unemployment, deskilling and technological change
in conditions of severe economic recession. The
effects of these trends have been most marked in the

manufacturing sector and have been associated with a
marked decline in the proportion of manual workers
within the employed work force. Secondly there has
been an erosion of collective forms of ownership of
labour, and accompanying changes in the patterns of
control and effective bargaining strategies available to trade unions in negotiating conditions and
terms of employment. Such developments have resulted not only from a stagnant demand for labour but
from trade union legislation which has sought to redefine the boundaries of legitimate union action.
Such legislation, together with the Conservative
Government's rejection of corporatism has, as Purdy
points out, sought 'to oust trade unions from any
governmental role and restore them to their proper
place as a minority section group competing against
other groups within the framework of the mixed
economy' (1981a). The combined effect of all of
these changes has led to a growing class of dispossessed labour constituted by a massive increase in
those made redundant, together with the young unemployed who have had no direct experience of work
within capitalist industry. It has released from
the disciplines of work and union representation
growing numbers who are indirectly represented politically and economically. Under these conditions
there has been a marked reduction in trade union
membership and in the strength and influence of the
labour movement, together with a tendency towards
heightened sectional divisions within this movement
and between the employed working class and a class
of dispossessed labour.

It is in response to these changes that the
emergence of the S.D.P. and the policies it will
adopt needs to be seen, for its electoral prospects
depend crucially on the impotence of the labour
movement and the declining electoral appeal of the
Labour Party. What is particularly significant is
the attempt by the S.D.P. to advance its claims to
be the inheritors of a re-formed social democratic
tradition but one which is freed from any political
and institutional links with the labour movement.
In a strategy which involves the reassertion of a
new centrally led political consensus, the S.D.P.
is seeking to make a virtue of its claimed capacity
to act independently from any institutional links
with either labour or capital. This is informed by
a particular assessment of the means of economic and
social recovery. It involves winning broad-based
electoral support for a set of economic, industrial
and social policies in the context where the capa-

city of the labour movement to resist or present politically viable alternatives has been eroded.

I want briefly to discuss the character and question the viability of the S.D.P.'s economic policy and its programme to restore the profitability of a substantial private sector within a mixed economy. Although at the time of writing no detailed economic policies have been formulated, it is possible to identify what are likely to be the major characteristics of its approach. Initially it may be noted that in the context of severe economic recession, high levels of unemployment and inflation and low levels of capital investment, together with the consequences of this in terms of living standards, public services and the social wage, that leading figures in the S.D.P. in various ways celebrate the virtues of the free market economy. There is also a repeated emphasis in all of the major S.D.P. texts on the need for attitudinal and institutional change and consistency of economic policy as the preconditions of sustained economic recovery. As for specific economic measures these are likely to involve job subsidies and some expansion of aggregate demand within the economy in order to generate growth in output and bring about some reduction in the level of unemployment; selective investment of North Sea oil reserves in sectors of private industry with growth potential; some increase in the level of public expenditure and the tempering of monetary discipline; the adoption of an incomes policy and a small devaluation of the pound. Whilst a priority is given to economic recovery, it is not at all clear that such measures will be successful. In view of the strength of the Party's commitment to the Common Market it seems unlikely that the necessary measures would be adopted to contain import-led growth resulting from this reflationary package (Ward, 1981). There are other crucial aspects of the S.D.P.'s approach to economic management which are also problematical. A few examples will suffice. Although there may be a strong case for a range of measures to stimulate economic activity, it is by no means self-evident given the structure and patterns of ownership of capital that any increase in the level of profit will be recycled in the British economy or support improvements in public services. Secondly it is not clear what stance the S.D.P. will take to the Bacon & Eltis thesis (1976) that informs one key element of the economic strategy of the present Conservative administration. This thesis asserts

that the growth of public sector expenditure and
employment has limited the availability of investment capital and skilled manpower to the private
sector with a consequent impact on new investment
and the level of profitability. Owen, it would seem,
subscribes to this thesis when he comments that
socialists who advocate a mixed economy 'risk emas-
culating a private sector by constraining its driv-
ing force, so limiting its scope for initiative
that its strength and economic contribution are
fatally sapped' (1981). Thirdly the arguments presented by the S.D.P. in support of the mixed economy
are quite nebulous when examined closely. Whilst
the S.D.P. is clearly not advocating a new programme
of public ownership, its stance with regard to what
is considered to be its optimal level is quite unclear, especially in view of the extensive programme
of denationalization being implemented by the
Conservative Government.

I have mentioned earlier the efforts being made
by the present Conservative administration to restrict and redefine the activities of trade unions,
and the significance of this within an overall economic and political programme that seeks to recover
the disciplines and competitiveness of the market
economy. A similar emphasis is placed by the
S.D.P. on restoring the efficiency and profitability
of the market economy, encouraging higher levels of
investment and modernization and the rewarding of
initiative and enterprise. In Rodgers' (1982) discussion of economic and fiscal policy he rejects
detailed state planning and emphasizes instead the
part a reformed tax system could play in restoring
initiatives and rewarding enterprise.

Within the approach to economic management that
is being formulated by the S.D.P., new trade union
legislation and an incomes policy play an important
role. Various proposals have been made about the
reform of trade union law, including compulsory
secret ballots for union elections and changes in
the political levy in order to make this more representative of the political sympathies of trade union
members. A clear majority of S.D.P. M.P.s also
voted in support of the Conservative Government's
Employment Bill (January 8th, 1982). The S.D.P.'s
support for new trade union legislation is underpinned by an emphasis placed on the need to promote
greater flexibility in the workings of the labour
market. This involves an attack on what is perceived to be the monopoly power of trade unions in
the disposition and terms of employment of labour.

As far as the S.D.P.'s proposals for some measure of income control is concerned, support for this rests on an analysis of the ways in which the bargaining practices of trade unions fuel inflationary wage settlements. Meade (1981, 1982) in particular has argued that certain trade union practices and immunities have sustained inflation at high levels and operate as a major constraint on both full employment and economic growth. Meade's suggestions for the reform of wage bargaining are essentially designed to encourage a re-orientation of trade unions towards the maintenance of full employment and away from the traditional defence of wage levels and living standards. He has proposed a decentralized system for fixing wage rates and settlements for occupations, industries and regions which promote employment in these sectors (Meade, 1982). Although Meade is opposed to any statutory national incomes policy, he envisages the setting out of national guidelines for wage settlements, and the referring of disputes between trade unions and employers to a 'permanent arbitral body'. Whilst there are marked differences within the Party between those who support a decentralized incomes policy and those in favour of more detailed central control of wage settlements, there seems little possibility of the Party combining this with a formal social contract. The character of any incomes policy the S.D.P. is likely to pursue seems destined to contrast sharply with proposals made on the left for an egalitarian incomes policy with a clear redistributive effect (Purdy, 1981b).

The different elements of the S.D.P.'s economic and industrial programme may be seen as the beginning of an attempt to constitute the basis of a new settlement between the state, capital and labour. Rather than this resting primarily on formal institutional channels of negotiation, it is dependent on the capacity of the S.D.P. to form and capture support for moderate policies that it is claimed will provide the means of conciliating or balancing different class interests. It seeks therefore the restoration of a 'balanced equilibrium' managed by what is presented as the rational and humane centre. In anticipation of increased levels of investment and continued modernization or production, it offers to capital the prospect of a consistently pursued economic strategy within a mixed economy, measures to boost demand, increase efficiency and restrain wages and union militancy. In a context of continued high unemployment, a weakened

labour movement and a divided Labour Party, it seeks
to present to working people the prospect of a less
harsh road to economic recovery and improved standards of living and some recovery at least of public
and welfare services.

EDUCATIONAL POLICY

At the time of writing the S.D.P. has no formally
adopted educational policies. It is possible to
discern the likely character of the policies that
will be pursued from the foregoing analysis of the
political programme, the electoral strategy and constituency of the S.D.P., and from preliminary statements made by some of the Party's leading members
and supportive elements within the liberal intellectual community. Most of the initial statements
about the S.D.P.'s educational priorities have
emerged from what appears destined to become the
radical wing of the Party and display some continuity with traditional Labour themes. Tyrell Burgess
(1981a, b) and Shirley Williams (1981a) were both
prominent in sketching the parameters of the
S.D.P.'s approach to educational policy calling for
reforms in a number of areas. Their policy suggestions included support for a wider degree of parental
choice within secondary education; the restructuring
of public examinations that would involve replacing
'O' Level and C.S.E. examinations by a mixture of
internal examinations, continuous assessment and
pupil profiles and a broader 'A' Level examination;
the phasing out of state support for private schools
and moves towards integrating the private and maintained sectors; the long-term consolidation of academic and training provision within a post-16
tertiary sector; the extension of nursery places,
and the development of community and recurrent
education.
    A concern for equality of educational opport-
unity as a means of promoting social justice and
economic efficiency is one strand within the early
outlines of the Party's educational programme. This
however coexists alongside other themes which attest
to the predominance of the Party's 'moral' programme. There is at once a recognition of the limits
of state intervention in effecting progress to a
more egalitarian society if individual liberty and
freedom of choice are to be preserved and enhanced,
and of the role of state educational provision in
effecting certain sorts of social and cultural
changes. Such arguments are associated with the

demand for a greater degree of parental choice and variety of provision within the maintained sector, and measures to extend community participation in the running of schools. In addition an emphasis is placed on the role of education in moral or social reconstruction, of securing the basis of social or communal integration in an open, classless society. (A sociological analysis of the scope of educational policy in helping to 'equalize the distribution of inherited fortunes', and of establishing the basis of a socially unified society through a 'communal culture' is found in the writings of Jean Floud (1961, 1975) who is a member of the S.D.P.'s educational policy group.) Beyond the ideological parameters within which the S.D.P.'s educational policies are conceived, there are further factors which are likely to influence the formulation of policy. These include the educational interests and ambitions of the predominantly new middle class membership of the S.D.P., the need to negotiate with the Liberal Party a common programme and the role assigned to educational and training provision within the Party's economic programme and strategy for industrial modernization.

The predominantly libertarian and moral themes of the S.D.P.'s programme, which provide an important point of articulation with the ideological stance of progressive liberalism, are likely to outweight any decisive move to commit the S.D.P. to any radical programme of educational reform involving a substantial restructuring of either the form or content of state education. The terms within which educational policy issues have so far been conceived rest on a re-working of certain themes that were apparent in Crosland's work and Labour Party revisionism. This may be seen to involve an attempt to escape the ideological tension within the 'dual repertoire' of the Labour Party's approach to state education arising out of the co-existence of a socialist egalitarianism and a social democratic emphasis on equality of educational opportunity (Baron et al. 1981). It was the latter which was the dominant theme in Crosland's The Future of Socialism (1956) and associated with his arguments for greater equality of access to educational opportunities within a meritocratically ordered education system. Drawing on Runciman (1972) and Rawl's democratic conception of equality of opportunity, a more radical definition of equality of educational opportunity emerges in Crosland's later writings (1962, 1974). 'The strong definition of equal opportunity

is therefore that, subject to differences in heredi-
tary and infantile experience, every child should
have the same opportunity for acquiring measured
intelligence in so far as this can be controlled by
social action (Crosland, 1962). It is this analysis
which provided the grounds for policies of positive
discrimination, and the redistribution of educational and social resources, as the means of securing
greater equality of condition between social groups.

The terms in which educational policy issues
have so far been conceived within the S.D.P. rest in
part on a particular interpretation of Croslandite
social democracy. There is an emphasis placed on
the contribution of education to economic efficiency
and industrial modernization that is apparent in
Shirley Williams' proposals for the restructuring of
16-19 educational and training provision. Secondly
whilst Williams has called for the redistribution of
wealth, income and opportunity as a precondition of
social and political liberty, her defence of comprehensive schooling is presented largely in terms of
its contribution to social integration, improved
industrial relations and class conciliation. She
writes: 'the social case for comprehensive schools
has always been unanswerable. By educating children
of different backgrounds and of different abilities
together comprehensive schools should begin to break
down barriers and material ignorance and create the
context for a more democratic, open and unprejudiced
society' (Williams, 1981a). Paralleling the policy
of the Liberal Party, she has also called for wider
parental choice within the existing comprehensive
school system to enable parents to choose between de-
nominational and non-denominational schools, single-
sex and mixed schools, schools with different dis-
ciplinary procedures, and schools which offer expertise and facilities for minority subjects.

Whilst a case has been made out for a more
flexible system of comprehensive education and a
broader based liberal education that is less constrained than at present by the examination system,
I suspect that the S.D.P.'s educational programme
will display a strong continuity with liberal notions
of educational and social meritocracy, albeit underpinned by an emphasis on the role of education in
social and political reconstruction. Rejecting a
decisive push towards a more egalitarian society
there is instead a commitment to the values of individual liberty, social tolerance, fraternity and
equality of opportunity. As Crick has pointed out
'these values are not so much substantive (with a

content, pointing in some direction) as <u>procedural</u>
(how things should be done)' and by themselves
'procedural values do not point to social change'
(1982). If though there is any conception of society
that is subscribed to in S.D.P. texts it is a conception of a 'post-industrial society', an open, classless society, a notion which has been particularly
developed in the writings of Daniel Bell (1971,
1977). In a society that is largely comprised of a
broad stratum of middle class occupations held by
those in possession of theoretical knowledge and
technical expertise, the education system becomes
the crucial agency for promoting advances in theoretical and technical knowledge and as a 'gatekeeper'
of occupational and social placement. In a line of
analysis which parallels Dahrendorf's restatement of
the values of political liberalism and his attack on
egalitarian social policy, Bell has similarly defended selectivity in education and called for a 'just'
meritocracy as the means of cultivating achievement,
of expanding the productive wealth of society and
in establishing 'fair' criteria for the distribution
of opportunities and rewards.

> The idea of equality of opportunity is a just
> one and the problem is to realize it fairly.
> The focus, then, has to be on barriers to
> such equality. The redress of discrimination
> by representation introduces arbitrary,
> particularistic criteria which can only be
> destructive of universalism, the historic
> principle, won under great difficulty, of
> treating each person as a person in his own
> right. (Bell, 1977)

Such analyses, in so far as they inform an
understanding of the social structure of contemporary society found in S.D.P. texts, involve a clear
rejection of any class analysis or an adequate
recognition of the sources, depth and persistence
of class inequality. It is evident from much that
has so far been written on educational policy, that
the manifestations not only of class, but also
racial, gender and locational differences of opportunity and resource provision within the education
system have been inadequately understood. Under
the combined impact of cuts in public expenditure
and falling school rolls there is clear evidence of
both a deterioration of educational standards and a
growing disparity in the levels of educational
expenditure between local education authorities

(H.M.I. 1981, 1982). The gradual widening of social differences in educational opportunity and achievement have reversed many of the gains we appeared to be on the point of realizing in the early 1970s, when 'a sustained policy of expansion could at last attain, what for so long had escaped the intentions of reform' (Halsey, Heath and Ridge, 1980).

The policy suggestions that have been made so far with respect to private education, community and recurrent education and 16-19 educational provision illustrate clearly the characterization of the S.D.P.'s educational programme suggested in this paper. Rejecting Shirley Williams' proposals (1981a) for the eventual incorporation of private education within the maintained sector, the Party seems likely instead to review the charitable status and attendant tax advantages enjoyed by private schools and to explore plans for integrating private schools with state schools (J. Rae, 1981). Early discussions on private education have been marked by an absence of any recognition of the heightened significance of this privileged sector in the context of a highly competitive labour market and contracting higher education provision. Recent evidence (D.E.S., 1982) has indicated that the numbers of full-time students attending private schools increased by 5000 in 1981, despite a sharp rise in school fees. A significant part of this increase can no doubt be attributed to declining standards of provision in the state sector and the increasing emphasis placed on academic achievement by many private schools (Salter & Tapper, 1981; J. Rae, 1981).

Given the centrality of notions of decentralization and participatory forms of democratic control within the S.D.P.'s political programme, it is likely that the Party will be sympathetic to the development of community and recurrent education, and the implementation in some form of the Taylor Report's (1977) proposals on the management and government of maintained schools. Shirley Williams' work at the Policy Studies Institute and her comparative studies of different national training programmes have been influential in setting out the S.D.P.'s initial responses to 16-19 educational and training provision and measures to deal with youth unemployment. While her support for an integrated tertiary sector bears some resemblance to the Labour Party's policy proposals (1982) in this area, this is conceived as a long-term goal to be preceded by various short-term measures that build on existing practices and developments. In her Radford

Mather lecture, Williams advocated the development
of sixth form colleges and community schools:

> ...which can help bridge the divide between
> vocational and academic education. The sixth
> form college can offer a combined range of
> courses alongside the further education
> college, allowing students to take some
> courses in one institution and some in an-
> other...The sixth form college can also
> open its doors to adult students who would
> like to study a particular subject, since
> most student groups are small and teachers
> can easily manage a few additional students.
> (Williams, 1980)

Williams has also called for a substantial increase in training provision and a vocational school-
based foundation year for those pupils leaving
school at 16. She has also proposed various steps
which could be taken to maximize employment opportunities by substituting labour for capital where
this does not affect the costs of production (1981a,
1981b). The policy suggestions made with respect to
youth unemployment, post-16 vocational and skill
training and academic provision rest on a number of
assumptions. There is some optimism that from the
mid-1980s the problem of youth unemployment will be
less severe given the general decline in the secondary school population. Secondly a major emphasis is
placed on the inadequate and inappropriate skills of
young people as a major cause of youth unemployment.
Tackling the problems of shortages of labour skills,
the immobility and cost of labour are regarded as
crucial elements of the S.D.P.'s overall industrial
modernization programme and their strategy for
economic recovery. Implied here, but in the context
of a reassertion of human capital theory, is the now
familiar notion of a 'mis-match' between the level
and availability of skills within the population and
the skill requirements of industry.
It is hard to imagine that the predominantly
new middle class membership of the S.D.P. would concur with any fundamental restructuring of educational provision. Although the S.D.P. has a fragmented
electoral constituency, it is dominated by a new
middle class whose occupational and status position,
and relatively privileged economic situation, owes
much to their possession of symbolic capital, their
educational qualifications, professional and technical expertise. Prominent within this group are

those post-war generations who owed their social and
economic advance initially to the expansion of grammar school education (Halsey, Heath and Ridge, 1980),
and later their access to academic routes within a
largely comprehensive system, and their links with
an expanded system of higher education. Generally
this class, whilst favouring the development of
comprehensive education, reserved its judgement on
the capacity of this system to deliver the educational 'goods' they sought. Although for a time the new
middle class flirted with the philosophy and practice of 'progressive' primary education, they have
tended to be staunch defenders of a meritocratic
conception of comprehensive education, judging the
benefits that this bestowed on their children to be
justly deserved. This was consistent with their
perception of an open, classless society, and the
belief that 'they owe their position not to the
advantages of birth or wealth but rather personal
excellence' (Samuel, 1982). It is these generations,
now in or approaching mid-career, which have played
an important role in local campaigns against cuts
in educational expenditure and its consequent
effects on educational provision and standards.
Having an increasing insight into local educational
politics they seem destined to have a considerable
influence on the national and local educational
policies of the S.D.P., resisting any moves that
threaten to undermine private education, supporting
increased parental choice and representation on
school governing bodies and hostile to any fundamental restructuring of post-16 educational provision where this involves closure of educational
centres of excellence.

REFERENCES

Bacon, R. & Eltis, W. (1976) Britain's Economic
    Problem, Macmillan, London.
Baron, S., Finn, D., Grant, N., Green, M., Johnson,
    R. (1981) Unpopular Education, Hutchinson,
    London.
Bell, D. (1971) The Cultural Contradictions of
    Capitalism, Heinemann, London.
Bell, D. (1977) 'On Meritocracy & Equality' in J.
    Karabel & A.H. Halsey (eds) Power & Ideology
    in Education, Oxford University Press, New
    York.
Bogdonor, V. (1981) People and the Party System,
    Cambridge University Press, London.

Bradley, I. (1981) Breaking the Mould, Martin
    Robertson, Oxford.
Burgess, T. (1981a) 'Democratic Socialism & Educa-
    tion' in D. Lipsey & D. Leonard (eds.) The
    Socialist Agenda, Crosland's Legacy, Jonathan
    Cape, London.
Burgess, T. (1981b) Education, S.D.P. Conference
    Discussion Paper 6.
Crick, B. (1981) Letter to the Guardian.
Crick, B. (1982) 'The Many Faces of Socialism', New
    Socialist May/June.
Crosland, C.A.R. (1956) The Future of Socialism,
    Jonathan Cape, 1956, London.
Crosland, C.A.R. (1960) Can Labour Win? Fabian Tract
    324.
Crosland, C.A.R. (1962) The Conservative Enemy,
    Jonathan Cape, London.
Crosland, C.A.R. (1974) Socialism Now & Other Essays
    Jonathan Cape, London.
Dahrendorf, R. (1959) Class & Class Conflict in
    Industrial Societies, Routledge & Kegan Paul,
    London.
Dahrendorf, R. (1979) Life Chances, Widenfeld &
    Nicolson, London.
Dahrendorf, R. (1980a) After Social Democracy,
    Unservile State Papers No. 25, Liberal
    Publications Department, London.
Dahrendorf (1980b) 'The Collapse of Class Spawns a
    New Politics', Guardian September 15th.
Demaine, J. (1981) Contemporary Theories in the
    Sociology of Education, Macmillan, London.
D.E.S. (1982) Statistics of Education, Vol. 1,
    H.M.S.O. London.
Drucker, H. (1981) 'Social Democrats and their
    Members', New Society, Nov. 26th.
Floud, J. (1961) Sociology & Education in P. Halmos
    (ed.) The Sociological Review Monograph, No.
    4, University of Keele.
Floud, J. (1975) 'Making Adults More Equal: The
    Scope & Limitations of Public Educational
    Policy' in P. Cox et al. (eds.) Equalities and
    Inequalities in Education, Academic Press,
    London.
Hall, S. (1981) 'The 'Little Caesars' of Social
    Democracy', Marxism Today, April.
Halsey, A.H., Heath, A.F. & Ridge, J.M. (1980)
    Origins & Destinations: Family Class & Educa-
    tion in Modern Britain, Clarendon Press, Oxford.
Her Majesty's Inspectorate (1981) On the Effects of
    Local Authority Expenditure Policies on the
    Education Service in England, 1980, H.M.S.O.,

London.

Her Majesty's Inspectorate (1982) On the Effects of
    Local Authority Expenditure Policies on the
    Education Service in England, 1981, H.M.S.O.,
    London.

Howell, D. (1976) British Social Democracy, Croom
    Helm, London.

Husbands, C. (1982) 'The Politics of Confusion',
    Marxism Today, February.

Ingle, S. (1982) 'The Social Democrats and the
    Liberal Alliance: Can the Centre Hold?,
    Teaching Politics, Vol. 11, No. 1.

Jenkins, P. (1981) 'After the Puff of Euphoria, The
    Hard Questions Remain', Guardian, 5th October.

Jenkins, R. (1979) 'Unfreezing the Pattern of
    Politics in Britain', Extracts from Dimbleby
    Lecture, Guardian, November 23rd.

Jenkins, R. (1981) 'The S.D.P.'s Plans for Picking
    up the Pieces' Guardian October 5th.

Labour Party (1982) Discussion Document 16-19:
    Learning for Life, Labour Party.

Marquand, D. (1980) Taming Leviathian: Democracy &
    Decentralization (unpublished lecture).

Marquand, D. (1981) Russet-coated Captains: The
    Challenge of Social Democracy, Open Forum 5,
    S.D.P. Publications, London.

Meade, J. (1981) 'The Fixing of Money Rates of Pay',
    in D. Lipsey & D. Leonard (eds.) The Socialist
    Agenda, Jonathan Cape, London.

Meade, J.E. (1982) Stagflation: Vol. 1 Wage-fixing,
    Allen & Unwin, London.

Owen, D. (1981) Face the Future, Jonathan Cape,
    London.

Pimlott, B. (1977) Labour and the Left in the 1930s,
    Cambridge University Press, London.

Pimlott, B. (1981) 'When the Party's Over', New
    Socialist, September/October.

Purdy, D. (1981a) 'Government-Trade Union Relations'
    in Socialist Economic Review, Merlin Press,
    London.

Purdy, D. (1981b) 'The Social Contract & Socialist
    Policy' in M. Prior (ed.) The Popular and the
    Politics, Routledge & Kegan Paul, London.

Rae, J. (1981) The Public School Revolution, Faber,
    London.

Rawls, J. (1972) A Theory of Justice, Clarendon,
    Oxford.

Rodgers, W. (1982) The Politics of Change, Secker
    & Warburg, London.

Rose, N. (1980) 'Socialism & Social Policy: The
     Problems of Inequality', Politics & Power 2,
     Routledge & Kegan Paul, London.
Rustin, M. (1981) 'Different Conceptions of Party:
     Labour's Constitutional Debates', New Left
     Review, March/April.
Runciman, W.G. (1972) Relative Deprivation & Social
     Justice, Penguin, London.
Salter, B. & Tapper, T. (1981) Education, Politics
     & The State, Grant McIntyre, London.
Samuel, R. (1982) 'The S.D.P. and the New Political
     Class', New Society April 22nd.
S.D.P. Conference (1982) Discussion Paper 7,
     Economic Policy, S.D.P. Publications, London.
Taylor, T. et al. (1977) A New Partnership for Our
     Schools, Dept. of Education & Science & Welsh
     Office, H.M.S.O., London.
Ward, T. (1981) 'The Case for Import Control Strate-
     gy in the U.K.' in Socialist Economic Review,
     Merlin Press, London.
Weekend World (1981) Report of Opinion Research Ltd.
     Survey, November 29th.
Williams, S. (1980) Broad Path to the Future.
     Extract from Radford Mather Lecture, Times
     Educational Supplement, September 12th.
Williams, S. (1981) Politics is for People, Penguin,
     London.
Williams, S. (1981) The Broader Economic & Social
     Questions Relating to Youth Unemployment,
     Policy Studies, Vol. 1, Part 4.

I am grateful to John Ahier, John Beck and Jan Hardy
of Homerton College, Cambridge, and Gerald Grace of
the Department of Education, University of Cambridge
for their helpful comments on an earlier draft of
this paper.